THE
STARTUP
COMMUNITY
WAY

BRAD FELD AND IAN HATHAWAY

THE
STARTUP
COMMUNITY
WAY

EVOLVING AN

ENTREPRENEURIAL

ECOSYSTEM

Published by John Wiley & Sons, Inc., Hoboken, New Jersey.
Published simultaneously in Canada.

For general information on our other products and services or for technical support, please contact our Customer Care Department within the United States at (800) 762–2974, outside the United States at (317) 572–3993, or fax (317) 572–4002.

Wiley publishes in a variety of print and electronic formats and by print-on-demand. Some material included with standard print versions of this book may not be included in e-books or in print-on-demand. If this book refers to media such as a CD or DVD that is not included in the version you purchased, you may download this material at http://booksupport.wiley.com. For more information about Wiley products, visit www.wiley.com.

Library of Congress Cataloging-in-Publication Data:
Names: Feld, Brad, author. | Hathaway, Ian, author.
   Title: The startup community way : evolving an entrepreneurial ecosystem /
   Brad Feld and Ian Hathaway.
Description: Hoboken, New Jersey : John Wiley & Sons, Inc., [2020] |
   Series: Techstars | Includes index.
Identifiers: LCCN 2020013290 (print) | LCCN 2020013291 (ebook) | ISBN 9781119613602 (cloth) |
ISBN 9781119613640 (adobe pdf) | ISBN 9781119613626 (epub)
Subjects: LCSH: Entrepreneurship. | New business enterprises—Environmental
aspects. | Communities—Social aspects.
Classification: LCC HB615 .F4524 2020 (print) | LCC HB615 (ebook) | DDC
   338/.04—dc23
LC record available at https://lccn.loc.gov/2020013290LC
ebook record available at https://lccn.loc.gov/2020013291

Cover Design: Wiley

For Amy, who tirelessly supports me in all my endeavors.
For Suzy, co-founder of my favorite startup.

CONTENTS

FOREWORD

In 2020, startup communities, which once appeared on the landscape of business (as well as the literal landscape) like so many rare animals, are long past the point of being uncommon or even unusual. As you'll read in the many compelling stories of progress that follow, they're coming together everywhere now, both in this country and around the globe, filled with energy and potential and the desire to look ahead to the kind of future we all want for our society. This is a critically important development. Quite simply: We need entrepreneurs and their ideas to keep our society moving forward, not just economically but equitably. The nurturing of startups, which is amplified by magnitudes when they share in a community of organizations and people, is the best way to make sure we achieve that goal.

That startup communities exist in such abundance is thanks, in large part, to Brad Feld. Every startup is unique, unpredictable, and unstable, but that doesn't mean they can't be managed for success, provided it's the right kind of management. The same is true of every startup community. That's the subject of Brad's book, *Startup Communities: Building an Entrepreneurial Ecosystem in Your City*. It lays out clear practices and principles for managing the bottom-up (versus top-down) structure of startup communities, which, because they're built on networks of trust rather than layers of control, can't be maintained in the same way that public goods and economic development were in the past. Rather than a rigid, hierarchical set of rules and processes, they thrive on a responsive, flexible method of working that uses validated learning to make decisions with minimal error. Like entrepreneurs, startup community builders can't rely on hunches or assumptions; they need to get out there, gather data, and see what's happening for themselves. Only then can they bring together diverse, engaged organizations that draw on each other's energy and experience and are led by committed, long-term–oriented entrepreneurs. By detailing a system that was hiding in plain sight, like so many methods used by entrepreneurs, Brad made it available to anyone worldwide who wants to bring innovation and growth to their city or town.

All of which is why, now that we've reached the next phase of startup community development, there's no one better than Brad to address its central issue: what happens (or doesn't) when startup communities co-exist with other, more traditionally hierarchical institutions that, as much as they'd like to work with their innovative neighbors, can't break free of their old rules and management styles? And how can we ensure that all of these players work together with respect for each other's strengths, and with clarity, to maximize their positive effect on the world around us? Brad's answer, once again, is to clearly lay out the methods and tools that can affect this change. He and his co-author, Ian Hathaway, have combined deep experience with rigorous, intensive research and analysis to create a framework for this necessary path forward.

Every entrepreneur continues to iterate on their original product, and Brad is no exception. This book, *The Startup Community Way: Evolving an Entrepreneurial Ecosystem*, isn't just a follow up to *Startup Communities*; it's a refinement of those initial ideas—as well as an expansion of them. It encompasses the increasingly common and often complex relationships and interdependencies between startup communities and legacy institutions including universities and government (both local and federal) and corporations, culture, media, place, and finance. By situating startup communities within this larger system of networks, Brad and Ian shine light not only on the interconnectedness between them, but their connections to the larger community and society as a whole. *The Startup Community Way* zooms out to look at the big picture even as it provides a close, highly detailed look at each of the actors, factors, and conditions that can combine to create a successful entrepreneurial ecosystem. It also examines some of the mistakes that are routinely made, like trying to apply linear thinking to the distinctly dynamic, networked relationships in startup communities, and trying to control them rather than let them operate freely within thoughtful parameters. All of this is presented with the sole goal of helping to forge deeper connections between often disparate parts so that they can better work together toward a common purpose.

I feel a deep kinship with Brad, whose work echoes in many ways the development of my own thinking about entrepreneurship and its uses. I began with the methodology for building successful individual start-ups in *The Lean Startup* and moved on in *The Startup Way* to applying those same lessons at scale to bring entrepreneurial management to large organizations, corporations, government, and nonprofits. I share Brad's faith that the entrepreneurial mindset is crucial not just for improving our present day-to-day lives but also for ushering our world into the future as we apply it to all kinds of organizations, systems, and goals, including those involving policy.

One revision Brad has made since the publication of *Startup Communities* resonates with me in particular: Where he previously called for startup communities to operate on a simple 20-year timeline, he's changed that to a "20 years from today" timeline. The work of innovation is continuous, and thinking truly long-term is crucial in order to reap its true benefits. What I mean by long-term thinking is an ongoing, honest, and comprehensive consideration of what we want our companies to look like—and our country and our world—for upcoming generations. In order to have the future we strive for, one in which opportunity and assets are fairly distributed, thoughtful management and care for the planet and all of the people who live on it with us is central, and we need to look beyond the right now to the realization of all the promise of the work that's already been done. This book is a perfect entry point for doing just that.

Eric Ries

Author, *The Lean Startup*

April 2020

PREFACE

I n 2014, I* was in Downtown Las Vegas. This location is not the glitzy sunset strip where most people spend time when they are in Las Vegas, but the historic business district that was undergoing a massive renovation under the leadership of Tony Hsieh, the founder of Zappos. Dead buildings were coming back to life, and Las Vegas no longer ended at Fremont Street.

UP Global, a nonprofit dedicated to building startup communities that is now part of Techstars, was having its annual summit. I was on the board of UP Global at the time and over 500 entrepreneurs from 70 countries were in attendance. Organizers from all over the world of the three UP Global programs—Startup Weekend, Startup Week, and Startup Digest— were meeting each other and participating in sessions about how to run their programs, build their startup communities, and spread the ethos of startups and innovation.

The event was in full swing with energy and excitement around startups in the air. While English was the dominant spoken language, the body

---

*Writing a book together creates the challenge of using first person or third person when telling stories that refer to one or the other of us. We've chosen to use the first person to refer to Brad, given that many of the references are to him. We will refer to Ian consistently in the third person.

language, discussions, and personal styles of the attendees gave the event an unmistakable international feel. The gathering was a diverse collection of people of all ages from around the globe.

I participated in a few discussions on startup communities, signed a bunch of copies of my book, *Startup Communities*, and smiled for an endless stream of selfies taken with community organizers from all over the world. The weather was hot, and the emotions were warm.

At the final evening gala, the buzz of the event was building to a climax for many participants. I was worn out from the previous two days, and stood, observing quietly, in a far corner of the giant banquet hall. Suddenly, a person I did not know came up to me and shouted over the din, "Thank you for changing my life!" while simultaneously putting a baseball cap on my head.

I responded with, "What did I do?"

The young man said, "Look at the hat!"

I took the cap off and saw that it was from a Startup Weekend in the Middle East. I saw tears in the eyes of the person who was now several inches away. Arms opened, and a big hug followed.

A 20-something from the Middle East and a 40-something American Jew, hugging in Downtown Las Vegas, bonding over startups and startup communities. A life changed. Well, two lives changed.

In the fall of 2008, Ben Casnocha, a longtime friend of mine, wrote an article for *The American* called "Start-up Town" that began with the following teaser:[1]

In the past 15 years, Boulder has gone from a little hippie college town to a little hippie college town also boasting an impressive and growing congregation of Internet entrepreneurs, early-stage venture capitalists, and bloggers. How did Boulder pull this off? And what can other cities, policymakers, and entrepreneurs who want to boost their own start-up quotient—and overall competitiveness at a local level—learn from Boulder's success?

When I saw the article, it reaffirmed a hunch I had about what was happening in Boulder around startups and entrepreneurship. People started talking about entrepreneurship as a way out of the Financial Crisis of 2007–2008 and the Great Recession that followed. Places, including Silicon Valley, New York, and Boston, were being described as "entrepreneurial ecosystems." In his article, Ben mentioned, "Silicon Valley, New York, Boston, and Boulder." Yes, Boulder.

Boulder is very different from Silicon Valley, New York, and Boston. It's a small town of around 107,000 people, with about 315,000 in the metro area of Boulder County. While it is only a 30-minute drive from Denver, which has a population of 700,000 (and a metro-area population of 2.9 million), in 2008, the two cities couldn't have been further apart from each other when it came to identity. Two recurring jokes that I have heard regularly since moving to Boulder in 1995 are "Boulder is 25 square miles surrounded by reality" and "to get between Boulder and Denver on US-36 you have to pass through a guard gate and an airlock." From my perspective, the entire population of Boulder could probably fit on a single city block of Midtown Manhattan, if you turned the office buildings into condos.

Over the next few years, I spent much time learning about entrepreneurial ecosystems, reading everything I could on innovation clusters, national innovation systems, innovation networks, and startup incubators. As Techstars, which I co-founded in 2006, started to expand, first to Boston, then to Seattle, and on to New York, I began seeing similar patterns—both positive and negative—in the way startup culture developed. By 2011, I formed a view on a new construct I started calling a "startup community." In 2012, I wrote and published *Startup Communities: Building an Entrepreneurial Ecosystem in Your City*.

I built the book around a concept I called the Boulder Thesis, a set of four principles that defined how to create a lasting and durable startup community. Shortly after *Startup Communities* came out, the Kauffman Foundation did a short video called "StartupVille" that did a phenomenal job of stating the Boulder Thesis.[2] I did an extemporaneous, four-minute riff, Kauffman built a video around it, and "StartupVille" and my verbal description of the Boulder Thesis became the opening for many talks in the next few years on startup communities. Within a year, the phrase "startup communities" became the definitive phrase for the phenomenon while the premise that you could build a startup community in any city with at least 100,000 people became a mantra for entrepreneurs all over the world.

Ben wrote his article only 12 years ago, which isn't a very long time in StartupVille. If you have read *Startup Communities*, you know that the second principle of the Boulder Thesis is that "you have to have a long-term view—at least 20 years." Over time, I have adjusted that to be "you have to have a long-term view—at least 20 years from today," to emphasize the importance of both the startup community to a city and a long-term view for anyone involved in a startup community.

Several years ago, I became friends with Ian. We were first introduced in 2014 by our mutual friend, Richard Florida, and over the years, we communicated every so often to share ideas and chat about our respective work and writing. Among other things, I helped Ian develop content for a "Startup Cities" course he was teaching at New York University by offering my views on best practices for startup accelerators.[3]

In 2016, Ian was ready for a new challenge. At the time, his working life involved advising major tech and media companies by day, and spending his nights and weekends thinking about, writing about, and finding ways to work with startups and entrepreneurs. He reached out to me for advice about how he might better align his work around helping entrepreneurs. We began to explore ways we might collaborate directly and, after a few iterations, we ended up landing on co-authoring the book you are now reading.

By 2016, entrepreneurship was a worldwide phenomenon. The word *unicorn* no longer referred to a mythical beast, and the phrase "startup communities" was common. Ian came to Boulder to kickstart our work in the spring of 2017, and we started bouncing around ideas for this book.

In the United States, Donald Trump had just been elected president, and Britain had formally begun the process to leave the European Union. While that shouldn't have slowed us down, it caused us to take a step back and reflect on the dynamics of Western society. Ian had recently arrived in Boulder from London, where he had just witnessed Brexit firsthand as an American ex-pat. He arrived home to a very different type of political climate in the United States. There was something important, uncomfortable, and divisive going on. Against this backdrop we wanted the sequel to *Startup Communities* to be part of a broader solution, rather than a narrowly focused addition to fixing and evolving what I had written in *Startup Communities* in 2012.

Like many collaborations, it took some time for us to hit our stride. Ian did an enormous amount of research, consuming vast quantities of literature and studying a range of approaches to startup communities that had emerged in the previous five years. He talked to countless people building startup communities across the planet and he kept an open mind to everything he read and heard, including writing and ideas that criticized my approach of putting the entrepreneur at the center of things.[4]

Ian then sketched a first draft by mid-summer 2017, which, like all first drafts, we threw away. It was too conventional, and it didn't address a glaring problem. As Ian talked to more people, he realized there was an enormous divide between the approaches taken by entrepreneurs and others who were actively building startup communities and those taken by the range of actors who increasingly wanted to participate (e.g., universities, governments, corporations, and foundations).

While this disconnect was well-known, we decided that it was too easily explained away by saying that one group got it while the other didn't. This rationale creates antagonism, which causes a breakdown in meaningful collaboration—and that is why the problem persists. This simple explanation also turns out to be wrong. The real problem is one of structural limitations combined with deeply rooted human impulses that crave control and the avoidance of uncertainty. This hardwiring leads to predictable mistakes and missed opportunities in startup communities.

We decided our mission wasn't merely to expand and modernize *Startup Communities*, but instead to address the more fundamental issues around collaboration in a startup community. In addition to encouraging people to transcend the limitations posed by where they work, or those they impose on themselves internally, we wanted to help transform the way they think and behave.

We needed a framework to explain this. We knew that without meaningful evidence behind our ideas, they would easily be dismissed, and the gap between startup communities and the actors wanting to participate would persist. So, in the fall of 2017, Ian went on a quest to find a solution. It started with an unexpected journey—sparked by the discovery of an article on an obscure environmental sustainability website and a last-minute roadtrip to the Santa Fe Institute in New Mexico to speak with some insanely smart people—but he was on the right path.[5]

In January 2018, we got together and reviewed everything that we had gathered and written to date, along with a new outline Ian sketched out. He pitched me on the idea of making complex adaptive systems the centerpiece of our explanation of startup communities. I was familiar with complexity theory and the Santa Fe Institute and immediately loved the idea. We went deeper on the concepts surrounding complexity and started framing the contents of an entirely different book than the one we had originally set out to write.

At Techstars, our friend and colleague Chris Heivly, an entrepreneur, investor, and community-builder, was busy developing a new business line for entrepreneurial ecosystem development. He has personal experience as a leader in the Durham, North Carolina startup community, and is active in a number of other places. Ian and Chris had been having regular discussions for almost a year by this point, and I began to engage with Chris and others at Techstars on this topic more frequently. Chris's experience, coupled with the insights he was gathering on the ground in different cities, helped us bridge theory with practice.

Over 2018 and 2019, as we wrote, talked, and worked with colleagues at Techstars and elsewhere, we felt we had come up with something exciting to share that was worthy of being a sequel to the original concepts in *Startup Communities*.

CHAPTER ONE

INTRODUCTION

The last decade has been a transformational one for entrepreneurship throughout the world. The confluence of ubiquitous high-speed connectivity with inexpensive, powerful, and remote computing has dramatically lowered the cost of starting a digitally enabled business, allowing entrepreneurs to start new ventures in more places. In some parts of the world, capital available for startups is plentiful. In many others, it is still lacking. Consider Boston versus Orlando, or London compared to Caracas. Talent and technology are ubiquitous, but tangible opportunities are not.

The growth and geographic proliferation of innovation-driven startup activity is profound, empirically verifiable, and global in scope.[1] Today, we understand that communities of support and knowledge-sharing go hand in hand with other inputs and resources. The importance of collaboration and a long-term view has gained broad acceptance by entrepreneurs and startup community builders. These principles are at the forefront of the leadership behind many startup communities around the world.

Startup Communities: Building an Entrepreneurial Ecosystem in Your City, published in 2012, is a significant reason for this shift in thinking. Using the example of Boulder, Colorado, *Startup Communities* provided practical guidance for entrepreneurs and other stakeholders to improve the startup community in their city. Unlike most other works on the subject, *Startup Communities* stressed the behavioral, cultural, and practical factors that are central to a collaborative system of local entrepreneurship.

Although we've made progress in recent years, much more work is needed. A great deal of startup activity is still highly concentrated in large, global, elite cities. Governments and other actors such as large corporations and universities are not collaborating with each other or with entrepreneurs as well as they could. Too often, these actors try to control activity or impose their view from the top down, rather than supporting an environment that is led from the bottom up, principally by entrepreneurs. We continue to see a disconnect between an entrepreneurial mindset and that of many individuals and organizations who wish to engage with and support local startups. There are structural reasons for this, but we can overcome these obstacles with appropriate focus and sustained practice.

Our aim with this book is to get all relevant parties better aligned—from founders to governments to service providers to community builders to corporations and beyond. We hope this book will be transformational while building on top of the foundation created by *Startup Communities* and the work done by people in startup communities everywhere.

THE NEXT GENERATION

The Startup Community Way builds off of the success of *Startup Communities*, going more in-depth in some areas while correcting foundational mistakes in others. This book isn't an update or a second edition to *Startup Communities*. Instead, it is a sequel, picking up where *Startup Communities* leaves off. It benchmarks progress made, develops new areas of inquiry and exploration, makes adjustments, and takes the content in a new direction.

In *Startup Communities*, Boulder is the basis for a framework for building a startup community. Here, we broaden both the geography and the stage, shifting to a worldwide view around existing startup communities. We try to make the concepts more generalized, especially when addressing the question: *Now that we have a startup community, what should we do next?* We emphasize that no two startup communities are the same, have equivalent needs, or operate on a comparable time frame. For each example where something worked in one city, there's at least one other city where it didn't. That's the nature of these systems.

When I wrote *Startup Communities*, there was little substantive content on the topic of startup communities. The phrase was new and has become the canonical one for naming the phenomenon. In the past eight years, a great deal of exploration and progress has occurred around startup communities. However, we have observed that, as with many things, the advice and tactics around startup communities, especially as they evolve, has become overly complicated and inaccessible to many who just want practical guidance to get started. In conversations with many people over the last few years, we've heard many variations of this: "My startup community is following the *Startup Communities* Boulder Thesis, but we don't know what to do next."

In this book, we try to address this hurdle while creating a new conceptual framework for startup communities, differentiating them from (and integrating them with) entrepreneurial ecosystems, and providing substantive examples along the way.

OUR APPROACH

We have taken both a pragmatic and researched approach to cultivate the material presented in this book. As co-authors, we've forced each other out of our natural comfort zones. By coming at the problem with different perspectives, we have been able to challenge each other to see the entire picture, rather than get anchored on our frames of reference. While we each had more context than the people in the parable of "The Blind Men and the Elephant," by using different experiences, perspectives, and skills, we have been able to continuously challenge each other's thinking as we developed the ideas in the book.[2]

We collectively bring decades of experience to the practice and study of startups, startup communities, and their impact on local societies and economies. I have been a technology entrepreneur and venture capitalist for more than three decades. I've co-founded two venture capital firms, including the Foundry Group, the firm where I have been a partner since 2007. I also co-founded Techstars, the worldwide network that helps entrepreneurs succeed. Through that work, my writing, and my involvement in numerous entrepreneurial nonprofit endeavors, I have been involved in the cultivation of startup communities around the world.

Ian has a wealth of research and writing experience in the areas of entrepreneurship, innovation, cities, and economic growth for leading think-tanks, universities, and policy institutions. He also has a background in management consulting around analytics, strategy, innovation, and public policy. He began his entrepreneurship journey as a researcher, writer, and educator, but over time that has also evolved into the role of practitioner—first as a startup employee, then as a founder, and today as an advisor, mentor, and investor.

Our collective experience and knowledge are just a starting point as this book stands on the shoulders of many who came before us. Over many years, and intensively during the last few, we have reviewed thousands of pages of analysis and writing that covers a wide range of topics relevant to startup communities.[3] These sources span academic papers, business and policy research, practical and theoretical book content, case studies, and informal commentary on blogs and websites. For those who want to go deeper, these resources are carefully referenced throughout and detailed in the back of the book.

Together we have spoken with thousands of entrepreneurs and other startup community participants around the world. Their experiences and learnings informed our thinking immensely.

In this book, you will encounter four types of sidebars. The first is a short description of a principle of *The Startup Community Way*, which will appear at the beginning of a chapter. You'll find the second type sprinkled throughout the text. They contain examples written by entrepreneurs and startup community builders that are relevant to the immediately preceding text. Third, you'll encounter "Values and Virtues" sidebars, where we try to explain a specific set of behavioral characteristics that are crucial to the long-term health of a startup community. Finally, there are short essays we wrote that are relevant to that section but are distinct from the flow of the main text.

A DEEPER MOTIVATION

We both share a fundamental belief that every human being on the planet should be free to live wherever brings them the most joy. They should have opportunities to engage in meaningful work in those places. When such opportunities don't exist, they should have access to resources that allow them to create meaningful work for themselves. We believe they should be able to do this in a relatively stable, peaceful, and just society where basic human rights, the rule of law, and individual freedoms exist for everyone.

We have a long way to go in achieving that goal. Currently, around 10 percent of the world's population lives in extreme poverty, though that is a marked decline from 35 percent, which was the rate less than three decades ago.[4] More than half of humankind does not live in politically free societies.[5] Millions more are unemployed or underemployed—either in terms of hours or ability—and in many places, necessity rather than opportunity drives business ownership.[6] Millions of civilians see conflict daily. Most of the world faces some form of discrimination on a consistent basis. Many people have deeper holes to dig out of than others.

We believe entrepreneurship can transcend political, economic, and cultural boundaries. For us, this is especially important to address in our current geopolitical climate and in the face of the many societal challenges we face globally.

We don't think a person should have to move to Silicon Valley—or London or Shanghai or Boulder or Dubai or New York—to become a successful entrepreneur. Instead, we want people to be empowered to pursue entrepreneurial endeavors anywhere they choose to live. Doing so may come with inevitable tradeoffs, but people who start businesses in the places they want to live are more likely to succeed than those who do not.[7]

As I wrote in *Startup Communities*:

> I have a deeply held belief that you can create a long-term, vibrant, sustainable startup community in any city in the world, but it's hard and takes the right kind of philosophy, approach, leadership, and dedication over a long period of time. Hence, this book, whose goal is to help you understand how to do this and give you the tools to create an amazing startup community in your city.

Global entrepreneurial activity in the eight years since *Startup Communities* was published has strengthened our resolve. Talented, motivated individuals should be able to create and grow scalable businesses wherever they choose, and they can build communities of support and knowledge-sharing around those efforts. We believe that, through entrepreneurship, the world can become a better place.

Today, the proliferation of digital technologies, the availability of information on entrepreneurship, and the quest for sustained economic growth have put startups on the map for people, governments, corporations, and other stakeholders around the world. The momentum and excitement behind today's entrepreneurs feel unprecedented.

Along with the widely recognized growth opportunity presented by entrepreneurship in the digital age, the environment in which startups operate influences their success to a large degree. It is the nature of these external factors—and more critically their linkages with entrepreneurs and with each other—that explains why some places can consistently produce high-impact startups while others struggle.

In many cities, regions, and countries, little progress has been made in cultivating the communities of support and knowledge-sharing that entrepreneurs need to thrive. The gap between success and failure is not due to an absence of available knowledge about how to improve conditions for local entrepreneurs. Nor is it due to a lack of tangible examples upon which to draw. We have sufficient theory and data to guide us, and there are ample stories to motivate us. So, why is this so challenging?

THE BOULDER THESIS

While the attitudes, behaviors, practices, and values at the heart of vibrant startup communities are second nature to many entrepreneurs, they often are counterintuitive or misaligned with competing incentives, especially when the person represents an organization such as a large corporation, university, or government. These institutions, which are hierarchical organizations, operate in ways that are antithetical to startup communities, which, like entrepreneurial companies, thrive in a network model.

In *Startup Communities*, I introduced the idea of the Boulder Thesis as a basis for creating a startup community in any city. The four principles of the Boulder Thesis are:

1. Entrepreneurs must lead the startup community.
2. The leaders must have a long-term commitment.

3. The startup community must be inclusive of anyone who wants to participate in it.

4. The startup community must have continual activities that engage the entire entrepreneurial stack.

While simple yet powerful, there was an unintended negative side effect that created a gap between entrepreneurs and everyone else in the startup community. By labeling the entrepreneurs *leaders* and everyone else *feeders*, I segmented the people and behaviors of the startup community. While this approach is helpful for focusing on the unique role that entrepreneurs play, many people interpreted it to mean that leaders are more important to the startup community than feeders. This was not my intention. Both leaders and feeders are essential to the health and growth of a startup community.

STARTUP COMMUNITIES ARE COMPLEX ADAPTIVE SYSTEMS

As we started working on this book, we began with two simple questions: "What have we learned about the Boulder Thesis?" and "Is there a more robust framework for understanding how a startup community develops and evolves?"

We eventually concluded that startup communities are best understood and engaged with through the lens of complex adaptive systems, defined loosely as "the study of interactions."[8] We aren't the first people to connect these ideas. A smattering of this work has existed in the far reaches of academia, and even some popular works we admire are influenced by complexity.[9] We decided that our mission was to bring this concept mainstream by more deeply bridging the theoretical link with practice and by dedicating an entire book to making our case. We each went deep on complexity theory and developed a framework called the Startup Community Way, which builds on the Boulder Thesis while using the framework of complex adaptive systems to support it.

As we compiled a list of mistakes people make around startup communities, we found many similarities to the mistakes people make when interacting with complex adaptive systems. Some of these mistakes will be familiar to you if you are already well versed in *Startup Communities*, including:

- Applying linear systems thinking in a nonlinear world.
- Attempting to control a startup community.
- Addressing problems in isolation.
- Focusing on the parts of a startup community rather than the interactions between them.
- Believing that a startup community is formulaic or replicable.
- Measuring the wrong things, especially things that are easy to capture but are less important for driving performance.

While we will explore each of these mistakes, this book is not a manual describing how to build a startup community. Instead, we will provide you with guiding principles and insights to aid you in your own process of discovery. However, this is not merely a book of theory. *The Startup Community Way* contains practical insights that go far beyond startup community building, including managing a business, designing effective public policies, and being a better leader or mentor.

Insights from complexity science and startup communities help navigate complex systems of relationships where a group of people work together to solve thorny problems. Today's world has geometrically increasing inputs and a hyper-connectivity among them. Our ability to process this is often overwhelming. As humans, we have access to more information than ever before, but this comes with a drawback. When the wrong decision frameworks are applied, they can lead well-intentioned people and organizations to disastrous outcomes. Shifting from a linear system approach to a complex systems mindset is a powerful way to address these challenges.

WHERE WE WERE IN 2012

When I published *Startup Communities* in 2012, the transition from an industrial, hierarchical, top-down economy to a digital, networked, bottom-up one was already underway. Four significant events occurred around the same time that accelerated that process, profoundly changing the course of startups and entrepreneurs in the United States and around the world.

First, the world continued to slowly pull itself out of the deepest and longest recession since the Great Depression of 1929 to 1933. It became clear that the old model of production wasn't going to work for many companies and workers anymore. Jobs were scarce and unreliable. Many young, talented people began looking for new and better ways of contributing to society. During this period, as opportunities on Wall Street evaporated, topflight talent began shifting to Silicon Valley.[10]

Simultaneously, three digital technologies converged: ubiquitous high-speed Internet, smartphones, and cloud computing. Starting a digitally enabled company became much cheaper and easier to do in more places. All that was needed was an Internet connection, a laptop, and an imagination.

The third key factor, the full impact of which became clear only recently, was a low-interest-rate strategy adopted by central banks worldwide. It was intended to boost the economy as wary households and businesses rebounded from the recession. However, persistently low interest rates also pushed unprecedented amounts of financial capital into startups globally, as investors searched for riskier assets, such as venture capital, to generate higher returns.[11] This continues today.[12]

Finally, interest in entrepreneurship spread to a broader set of actors and places. In 2011, President Obama announced Startup America, a national initiative designed to cultivate startup community development throughout the country. Universities began prioritizing entrepreneurship programs. A variety of new venture capital funds, with many focused on very-early-stage investment, began raising and deploying capital, as did a growing number of corporate venture capital groups. A range of startup support mechanisms, including startup accelerators and incubators, grew rapidly in size and scope.[13] The media took a greater interest in startups. Entrepreneurship was once again accessible and set the stage for change.

As with other periods where change is rapid and pervasive, more people wanted to know how to apply the phenomenon of entrepreneurship. What felt different about this era, compared with the hysteria of the dot-com bubble, was a sense that people wanted to get things right. Instead of setting the singular goal of making money, they tried to understand how to effectively build a vibrant startup community in cities around the world.

Startup Communities provided a framework and practical guidance for startup community builders through the lens of my experience in Boulder, Colorado. In the mid-1990s, Boulder didn't have much in the way of a startup community. There was plenty of startup activity occurring in isolation, but there was very little bringing people together in a coordinated way. Slowly this began to change over time because of a small group of dedicated entrepreneurs who created an organic, bottom-up movement that built a startup community.

In Boulder, the culture of the community transcends startup activity and influences the entire city. This broader sense of purpose and responsibility translates to the local startup community. There was no plan, just a core group of founders looking out for each other, and a culture that encouraged this. Boulder, like many cities with successful startup communities, discovered that the key to jump-starting one is as simple as a small group of credible, dedicated entrepreneurs who lead by example.

Boulder has a lot going for it—a well-educated workforce, a leading research university, a flurry of high-tech companies and research labs, a plethora of amenities, and the strong sense of community I just described.[14] For that reason, using Boulder as a model for startup communities is criticized by some for being too idealistic. While understandable, this criticism misses the point. The lesson from Boulder is not that everything is perfect and that, if copied, a similar outcome can be achieved elsewhere. The true lesson is that Boulder's collaborative nature is what allows it to get the most out of the resources it already has in place. This increases the odds of success, which is the ultimate attractor of resources. A virtuous cycle then takes shape. Things weren't always that way and those of us involved in the Boulder startup community had to work hard at it. Rather than be concerned about imitating Boulder, instead draw the lesson that building a critical mass of people who are helpful and collaborative will improve the odds that entrepreneurs will succeed, no matter what other resources are available today.

WHERE WE ARE NOW IN 2020

Eight years later, the momentum building after the Great Recession culminated into an explosion of startup activity around the world.[15] The reset of the global economy, expanding technological opportunities, the extremely low cost of capital, and a massive increase in the number of people participating in startups accelerated into high gear.

The global startup community has grown in size, exists in more places, involves more people and organizations, and produces more events than at any point in history. It has an enthusiasm and optimism for entrepreneurship that is unmatched in many areas of society. This increase in startup activity is empirically verifiable. Research shows a substantial rise and a widening geographic dispersal of startup activity within the United States and around the world.[16] While growth in startups in America is setting annual records, startup growth in the rest of the world is growing faster.[17]

In spite of all of this excitement, there are several reasons for caution. While progress has been impressive, no one has addressed the question of what happens when inevitable setbacks occur. When some or all of the tailwinds that have been at our backs the last decade slow or take a turn, will enthusiasm evaporate with them? Entrepreneurs will always create new companies, but will actors in startup communities continue to bring resources and lasting commitments when the tailwinds become headwinds? In the final weeks before this book went to press, the winds of change came upon us as the COVID-19 coronavirus pandemic swept the globe, making it abundantly clear that such shifts can occur swiftly, decisively, and seemingly out of thin air.

Next, many of the metrics we just referenced are inputs to entrepreneurship and startup communities. An increase in inputs doesn't automatically equate to better outcomes. The payoffs to a startup community from increased participation and activities can be quite delayed—sometimes by a generation—which can lead to disappointment, doubt, and abandoned efforts in the near term. Cause and effect often can't be established in complex systems and compounds the psychological impact from long feedback cycles.

Finally, we often learn the wrong lessons and ignore the correct ones. We regularly see violations of each of the four principles of the Boulder Thesis in rapidly developing startup communities. Many of them are not entrepreneur-led and inclusivity remains elusive. While many people and organizations claim they are taking a long-term view, we are a decade into the current cycle, and there is already clamoring for better and faster results. Engagement across the entrepreneurial stack gets marginalized when participants start thinking that everything is working, and the entrepreneurial activities and events degenerate into generally useless awards, parties, conferences, and super-sized funding announcements.

USING COMPLEXITY THEORY TO EXPLAIN STARTUP COMMUNITIES

Over an extended period, a set of principles developed around managing systems. During the industrial revolution, they became formalized as a way to manage labor, improve efficiencies, and increase production. Hierarchical systems were built around these principles in the early 1900s by pioneers of thought and industry like Frederick Winslow Taylor and Henry Ford.[18] Contemporary theories of scientific management based on these principles took root through most of the industrialized world during the 20th century. But things changed with the emergence of the commercial Internet in the mid-1990s. Rapid innovation around communications technologies, including hardware, software, and networks, allowed new forms of business interaction to take place. In the past decade, there has been a torrid transformation from hierarchies to networks, and a rapid shift from a top-down business approach to a bottom-up one, with a corresponding change in principles similar to the Startup Community Way.

The Startup Community Way derives its intellectual backbone from complexity theory, which is an interdisciplinary science developed by physicists, evolutionary biologists, and social scientists to better explain the inherently complex nature of our world.[19] Complexity theory can simultaneously be illuminating and intellectually challenging as it explains the behavior of dynamic systems with many connected participants who are always acting and reacting to one another. It helps explain why things often don't go according to plan, why we make predictable mistakes, and how to overcome many inherent mental, social, and organizational limitations.

Startup communities are fundamentally complex adaptive systems. For the sake of brevity, we'll use the phrase "complex systems" to refer to "complex adaptive systems" throughout the book. The following are some characteristics of complex systems that apply directly to startup communities.

Complex systems cannot be controlled. We have deep human impulses to want to control things, but this is an illusion as we are in control of very little. In startup communities, any effort to control or engineer a desired outcome is futile. Our advice is much bigger than "don't try to control." Instead, we suggest that you "let go of the illusion that you are in control."

Complex systems cannot be fully understood. Systems with a high degree of complexity, like startup communities, are extremely uncertain. Predicting outcomes is a futile exercise. Humans have a deep-seated aversion to uncertainty, which causes us to make predictable errors. A better strategy for dealing with complex systems is to run small-scale experiments, learn from them, adapt as necessary, and repeat. Instead of trying to engineer the outcomes, focus on setting the right conditions so that the right outcomes can unfold naturally.

Complex systems must be viewed holistically. In startup communities, for every action there is a reaction, which can then set off a chain of further actions and reactions. These actions may be non-obvious or delayed. A reductionist or siloed approach provides minimal insight into what is happening, which can also create new problems while trying to solve existing ones.

The interactions are critical in complex systems. In complex systems, while the elements are essential, the interaction between them is what matters most. In startup communities, many people mistakenly focus on the individual elements rather than on connections and interactions between them. This occurs because the former are more tangible and easier to see or adjust, while the latter are more nuanced and require long time periods to evolve.

Run small-scale experimentation and learn from failure. Because of the uncertainty and nonlinearity in complex systems, participants in startup communities need to anticipate and be comfortable with failing. As failure is the most likely outcome for an experiment, we recommend taking an agile approach: try lots of small things, get feedback, adjust, and iterate.[20] Always keep the customer (in a startup community, that's the entrepreneur) in mind. Don't use a go-big-or-go-home strategy. Instead, start small so when things don't work, you don't have to go home.

Progress is uneven, slow, and surprising. Complex systems exhibit nonlinear behavior, phase transitions (large shifts that materialize quickly), and fat-tailed distributions, where extremely high-impact events are more common than a normal statistical distribution would predict. Seemingly small actions can produce massive changes that happen suddenly. There is little ability to link cause and effect, or to credibly predict the outcomes of various programs or policies.

Contagion is a force that can accelerate or constrain progress. The interconnectedness of complex systems means that ideas, behavior, and information can spread widely and rapidly, similar to a virus or a financial markets panic. It is essential to transfuse a startup community with healthy thoughts and practices that will help entrepreneurs succeed, illuminating what is helpful and dampening the influence of bad ideas, behaviors, and information.

Build on your strengths. History and local context are fundamental to complex systems. You can't recreate Silicon Valley, which is one reason why we often say, "Don't try to be Silicon Valley." Every startup community should focus on being the best version of itself, rather than replicating something else. Every city has its own origin story and historical evolution, as well as a unique set of cultural, intellectual, and natural resources. Instead of emulating another place, focus on improving your own.

Don't wait. You don't have to get the entire city on board, just a core group of credible leaders with a commitment to improving conditions. A critical mass can be as little as a half dozen entrepreneurs who are all committed to a 20-year journey together. Then, do stuff, get more people involved, be visible about what you are doing, and iterate. The contagion effects are impactful and can suddenly create a tipping point that changes the course of a startup community forever. When people see that the leaders aren't too busy to help entrepreneurs, they'll find time, too.

EVOLVING THE BOULDER THESIS TO THE STARTUP COMMUNITY WAY

By the end of this book, we hope to reinforce the value of the Boulder Thesis while building a stronger and more durable framework we call the Startup Community Way. Rather than a replacement, it's an evolution based on the experiences we, and many other entrepreneurs and community builders, have had in the decade since I started thinking and writing about startup communities. As with the Boulder Thesis, it's a set of straightforward principles that can have profound effects when you adopt them throughout your entire startup community over a long period of time. You will recognize all four principles of the Boulder Thesis, as this is a superset, rather than a replacement.

1. Entrepreneurs must lead the startup community.
2. The leaders must have a long-term commitment.
3. Startup communities are complex adaptive systems that emerge from the interaction of the participants.
4. Startup communities can be guided and influenced, but not controlled.
5. Each startup community is unique and cannot be replicated.
6. Startup communities are organized through networks of trust, not hierarchies.
7. The startup community must be inclusive of anyone who wants to participate.
8. Openness, support, and collaboration are critical behaviors in a startup community.
9. The startup community must have continual activities that meaningfully engage the entire entrepreneurial stack.
10. Startup communities must avoid the trap of letting demand for measurement drive flawed strategies.
11. Putting founders first, giving before you get, and having an intense love of place are essential values in a startup community.
12. Startup communities are propelled by entrepreneurial success and the recycling of those resources back into the next generation.
13. The best startup communities are interconnected with other startup communities.
14. The primary purpose of a startup community is to help entrepreneurs succeed.

We believe that entrepreneurship, and an entrepreneurial mindset, is valuable to our society. As startup communities have become pervasive around the planet, the lessons from the growth and development of startup communities apply to every type of organization. We believe that applying the Startup Community Way to governments, academia, large corporations, and nonprofit organizations can have powerful results. This is especially true when considering that hierarchical structures are often efforts to control complex systems. However, they are an outdated mode of management. The world has changed, and so must we.

PART I

INTRODUCTION TO STARTUP COMMUNITIES

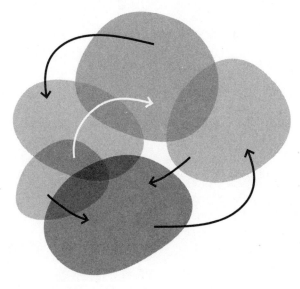

CHAPTER TWO

WHY STARTUP COMMUNITIES EXIST

T o set the stage for a more in-depth exploration of how a startup community works, given the premise that startup communities can, and should, exist almost everywhere in the world, we must first describe what entrepreneurs do and relate it to place. While a startup community is an abstract concept, it's important to remember that entrepreneurs and the participants in startup communities are all people.

WHAT ENTREPRENEURS DO

Entrepreneurship is a process applied by an individual or group of individuals, called entrepreneurs, to first explore and then exploit a commercial opportunity, generally by bringing new goods and services to the market, or substantially improving an existing product, service, or method of production.[1] This process typically occurs through a new company (a *startup*), and the entrepreneurs take considerable personal and financial risk.

Steve Blank, the grandfather of the Lean Startup movement, states that "a startup is a temporary organization formed to search for a repeatable and scalable business model."[2] This temporary phase tests and validates a business model before a shift in strategy to achieve high rates of growth and market share ("scaling-up"), or conversely, failing and ceasing operations.

Entrepreneurship is broader than starting and scaling companies. The approach, referred to as an "entrepreneurial mindset," can be applied to many different problems and types of organizations. Many firms achieve high growth later in their life cycle and for reasons that may differ from the original intent of the business founders.

Startup entrepreneurs differ from traditional small business owners through their ambition to create something new and substantially grow their business. Most small businesses expect to stay small.[3] Startup founders set out to do something fundamentally different, proliferate, and create significant economic value. In *Startup Opportunities: Know When to Quit Your Day Job*, my co-author Sean Wise and I wrote about this distinction.

> There is a big difference between the two types of entrepreneurial endeavors: (1) local businesses, also called SMEs (small- and medium-sized enterprises) or lifestyle businesses; and (2) high-growth companies, often referred to as startups or gazelles.
>
> Local businesses are what they sound like. These are the businesses that you find in your city whose customers are close to the business, such as the corner grocery, local bookstore, non-chain restaurant, or locally owned gas station. Occasionally these local businesses start to expand and turn into multi-geography businesses, resulting in a large enterprise, but many are local businesses for the duration of their existence.

In contrast, high-growth companies rarely have a local focus. While they are often started in one location, and, at inception, usually only have a few people involved, the founders of these companies aspire to grow quickly, independent of geographic boundaries. Their customers are all over the world, and regardless of whether the company ever expands geographically, the business is rarely constrained by geography.[4]

According to modern economic theory, knowledge—not raw materials, machines, or human muscle—is responsible for sustained economic prosperity.[5] Machines and labor have diminishing returns to scale while ideas and knowledge have increasing returns. Entrepreneurs are essential in converting knowledge into economic value, as they act on opportunities that others fail to see or are unable to execute on.[6] While ideas may be the wellspring of economic potential, entrepreneurs are the change-agents that bring that potential into reality, resulting in a wide variation in business performance and value creation. In the United States, and across multiple countries, around 10 percent of businesses generate more than half of annual revenue and employment growth.[7] Hence, a small number of entrepreneurs who build high-impact ventures drive the majority of economic growth. These businesses tend to be young and concentrated in knowledge-intensive industries and cities with highly educated workers.[8] They are innovation-driven companies, powered by brains, not brawn.

THE EXTERNAL ENVIRONMENT

Entrepreneurs combine good ideas with their determination to create jobs and economic prosperity. So, where are these ideas discovered?

In the industrial era, production typically involved the accumulation of resources, economies of scale, and vertical integration. Companies stayed relatively isolated behind concrete barriers, in nondescript office parks, or on elaborate corporate campuses. A significant source of ideas came from internal corporate research-and-development efforts or through tightly controlled supply chains.

In the information age, companies must accumulate ideas and talent while learning and adapting in the face of rapid technological change.[9] Ideas are not just produced in corporate labs and then integrated into a company's internal product cycle. Instead, they emerge in classrooms, university research facilities, competitors, and adjacent industries. They also come from knowledge and feedback from employees and users of products.

Consequently, entrepreneurs and the startups they create must have an external orientation because many of the best ideas, information, and resources exist outside of their companies and their direct control. As the depth of our collective knowledge widens, and the pace of technological advancement accelerates, no one person can know everything about anything. Because of this, the boundaries of a company in the information age must be "fuzzy."[10]

Entrepreneurs must acquire more than innovative ideas, technologies, or industry-specific information. They must also amass a team of skilled employees, customers, and suppliers, and support them with the startup funding and know-how that are specific to the venture-building process. The traditional market mechanism, where buyers and sellers exchange goods, services, or information at a specified price and set of terms, doesn't work well in this context. Instead, resource exchange often occurs informally at an arm's length, through relationships with other individuals and organizations.

As a result, startups are reliant on the external environment to secure resources that are central to their businesses. While not all critical factors exist outside of the control of a startup, many do.

While true to some degree for all businesses, this is especially important for startups. The market for intangible resources doesn't occur neatly in existing markets, and the method for acquiring these resources is relationship-based. Businesses have resource dependencies, where they rely on factors of production that are not wholly within their control—meaning that one legally independent organization is dependent to a degree on others.[11] The power Company B has over Company A is proportional to Company A's reliance on Company B's resources.

For startups, this presents two acute challenges. They are especially reliant on the external environment vis-a-vis most other businesses, and they are often deficient in critical resources. Their success depends on engaging with individuals and organizations that have the potential to exert tremendous leverage over them.

Evidence of a vibrant startup community occurs when people and companies who could take advantage of startups choose not to. Instead of harming startups, they consistently find ways to help them. The degree to which individuals want to exploit or forgo resource asymmetries helps determine the long-term viability of a startup community.

NETWORKS OVER HIERARCHIES

If much of the entrepreneurial process is acquiring any number of mission-critical resources, the network is the mechanism for delivering those factors of production. Both advanced and emerging economies have been undergoing a massive transformation in recent decades, from the centralized, command-and-control structures of the industrial era, to the decentralized, network-based organizations of the information age. These macro shifts are universal and inalienable, but organizational forms and human behavior have been slower to adapt.

Hierarchies are best suited for situations that require tight control of production, information, or resources, such as manufacturers or large bureaucracies that exist in universities, governments, and militaries. Hierarchies are robust and inflexible, requiring formal rules, standard operating procedures, and a chain of command. In contrast, networks are resilient and adaptable, requiring flexibility and horizontal flows of information. Healthy startup communities rely upon unencumbered information flows organized in network-based structures. Conversely, they suffocate under hierarchical control.

This thinking is influenced by the economic geographer AnnaLee Saxenian in her seminal work, *Regional Advantage: Culture and Competition in Silicon Valley and Route 128*. We believe Saxenian's book is probably the most important writing in the modern era on what makes a particular region consistently more innovative and entrepreneurial than another.

In her book, Saxenian compared two technology hubs—California's Silicon Valley and the Route 128 Corridor near Boston—that looked similar as late as the mid-1980s in terms of their ability to produce a high rate of information technology businesses. The Route 128 Corridor was arguably even better positioned as a technology hub coming out of World War II and stretching into the 1950s, 1960s, and 1970s. From there, however, the Route 128 region stalled while Silicon Valley pulled further ahead in the global technology race.

What happened in the 1980s and 1990s that caused Silicon Valley to accelerate its growth while Route 128's growth slowed?

A period of intense, rapid technological disruption and increased global competition left the more rigid hierarchical structure of Boston unable to adapt quickly, whereas the network-based structure shaped by Silicon Valley's open culture of "collaborative competition" made it better-positioned to recognize and capitalize on these changes.

As I summarized in *Startup Communities*:

Saxenian persuasively argues that a culture of openness and information exchange fueled Silicon Valley's ascent over Route 128. This argument is tied to network effects, which are better leveraged by a community with a culture of information sharing across companies and industries. Saxenian observed that the porous boundaries between Silicon Valley companies, such as Sun Microsystems and HP, stood in stark contrast to the closed-loop and autarkic companies of Route 128, such as DEC and Apollo. More broadly, Silicon Valley culture embraced a horizontal exchange of information across and between companies. Rapid technological disruption played perfectly to Silicon Valley's culture of open information exchange and labor mobility. As technology quickly changed, the Silicon Valley companies were better positioned to share information, adopt new trends, leverage innovation, and nimbly respond to new conditions. Meanwhile, vertical integration and closed systems disadvantaged many Route 128 companies during periods of technological upheaval.

Startup communities thrive in environments where information, talent, and capital flow freely and horizontally through networks. Since humans are involved, this network is a system of relationships. These factors are driven by cultural norms, which makes their cultivation inherently bottom-up, slow to evolve, motivated by action, and shaped by values.

NETWORKS OF TRUST

Social capital, or "networks of trust," are rooted in relationships based on a common set of norms and values that bind a group of individuals together and enable them to collaborate more effectively. Networks of trust are critical in complex systems that demand high performance under fast-paced, ambiguous, and evolving conditions. Successful outcomes in military special forces, modern aviation, championship sports, and hyper-growth startups all require teamwork that is grounded in trust and a shared sense of purpose.[12]

In startup communities, the network directs vital information and resources—such as ideas, talent, and funding—to company founders and employees. But it is social capital or the nature of these relationships that determines how well information and resources flow through the network.

Social capital and informal norms act as a type of lubricant for idea sharing, collaboration, and connecting people.[13] All businesses engage with external parties, such as customers and suppliers. But in complex environments, such as those faced by innovation-driven startups today, it is not always feasible to do so formally. Instead, startups must rely on informal agreements with one another and with the community as a whole. These are underwritten by trust, reciprocity, good-faith commitment, and stewardship.

Social capital represents the value to a startup community resulting from virtuous, high-trust relationships. For a given set of resources and entrepreneurial capabilities in a region, startup communities with more social capital will achieve better outcomes than those with less of it.

The importance of social capital to a well-functioning startup community increases and accelerates over time.[14] Startups rely on external networks that are constrained or enabled by the quality of those connections. A wealth of research ties economic growth to firms, communities, regions, and nations with strong social bonds based on trust, flexibility, and informal relations.[15] The network's value depends not only on the number of connections or network structure but on the nature of those connections and the importance of the information that travels between them.

The complex nature of today's innovations requires teams of people with diverse skills. As Victor Hwang and Greg Horowitt describe in their book, *The Rainforest: The Secret to Building the Next Silicon Valley*, we are in need of diverse teams more than ever, but we are unfortunately hardwired to distrust people who are different from us. The ability to consistently overcome this limitation of human nature separates vibrant innovation systems from the others.[16]

Values and Virtues: Be Transparent and Honest

Intentionally lying to or deceiving people with the intent of harm is destructive to a startup community. While that should be obvious, a lack of truthfulness—even done to protect other people or oneself—is harmful because it creates confusion, undermines trust, and ultimately leads to suboptimal outcomes. Honesty is a fundamental value of any healthy community.

The same goes for transparency. Make decisions affecting the startup community openly and with the input of all interested parties. Clearly explain the rationale for a course of action, including saying no to people, even if doing so is hard.

A chronic problem in startup communities is non-communication and passive avoidance, especially regarding disinterest in a person or a project. Ignoring messages or leaving things unresolved is the wrong approach as it undermines trust and destroys reputations. If you are not interested or can't engage in something or with someone, just say so, but do it with kindness.

Honesty and transparency are hallmarks of a healthy startup community. Express yourself honestly, directly, respectfully, and kindly while knowing that you could be wrong about the situation. Be constructive, especially in circumstances that are heated or emotional. Understand your surroundings and know that people give and receive feedback differently.

Adding kindness into the mix helps make progress in stressful situations. Critically, this is a two-way street as both parties in a conversation need to be willing to give and receive candid views. When conflicting opinions are framed and approached respectfully, the ensuing conversation can be embraced as a strength, not a weakness or something to be avoided. Conflict is a part of the evolution of a complex system, and progress emerges from the friction of two things rubbing against each other.

While candor and friction may lead to hurt feelings in the short term, in the long run, they lead to a more resilient and higher-performing system. Just as biological systems may experience short-term hardship to achieve long-term harmony, such as how wildfires preserve ecological balance, some short-term pain is a healthy and normal component of startup communities.

Hostile environments, or those that lack inclusivity, are the main culprits for why people choose not to share their unvarnished opinions. In a hostile environment, there is no trust to fall back on, and people assume the worst of each other. If people won't communicate honestly or resolutely, trust erodes, and the feedback loop that emerges is a negative one. When this becomes the norm, the environment stagnates or declines.

While it is everyone's job to ensure an environment where each person feels comfortable providing feedback candidly and openly, the leaders generally set the tone. One surefire way to build trust is to become vulnerable. Conveniently, this also bonds people together. In a startup community, how entrepreneurs interact with each other, especially in situations of disagreement and conflict, it is critical to how the startup community will evolve. While all systems will face conflict, misunderstanding, anger, disappointment, and failure, the behavior of the leaders over a long period, especially in response to these difficult situations, has a considerable impact on the long-term health and evolution of the startup community.

DENSITY AND AGGLOMERATION

The most valuable relationships for startups, especially early in a company's life, are local. While it is useful for entrepreneurs and other startup community participants to engage with people in other places, local relationships are the most valuable. For that reason, geography plays a central organizing factor in startup communities.

A dense co-location of many businesses and workers is valuable for most sectors of the economy because it lowers transaction costs and improves matching between companies, workers, suppliers, and customers. These "agglomeration effects" or "external economies" are benefits that exist outside a business at the local or regional level, and emerge when a network scales. They are particularly significant in industries where highly specialized inputs, including workers, are essential to production.[17]

Beyond lowering costs and improved matching, a third factor known as "knowledge spillovers," or the exchange of ideas, is vital to innovation and entrepreneurship.[18] In complex activities, like starting and scaling innovative businesses, idea exchange and learning from others are critical. Because complex activities are challenging to transfer verbally or in writing, learning is done best at an arm's length. These are also known as tacit knowledge transfers, or "learning by doing" and "learning by seeing."

On my *Feld Thoughts* blog, I've written about the phenomenon and the importance of density to entrepreneurial performance.[19] As one example, I describe that, when doing business in well-known startup hubs like San Francisco, New York, or Boston, I tend to remain in a relatively confined area. I call these areas "startup neighborhoods." For example, there are several startup neighborhoods in the Boston metro area, including at least three in Cambridge (Kendall Square, Central Square, and Harvard Square) and at least three in Boston proper (the Innovation District, Financial

District, and Leather District). Or consider New York City, where there are at least three startup neighborhoods below Midtown Manhattan alone: Flatiron and Union Square; the Meatpacking District and Chelsea; and the East Village, Soho, and Lower Manhattan.[20]

Instead of viewing these startup neighborhoods as competitive regions, it is more powerful to see them as part of a larger community with differences that flow across the boundaries. Often, people set artificial geographic boundaries, where the segmentation of communities between and within cities can create a zero-sum mentality. In this framing, one startup community has to be better than another. This attitude is at odds with how ideas, people, and resources wish to flow freely, in a way that transcends administrative or imagined boundaries.

Academic research confirms that measuring startup density at the level of cities or metropolitan areas is not fine-grained enough since there is a very high "decay rate" of knowledge sharing over distances. One study found that the benefits of knowledge sharing in the software industry when co-locating within one mile of similar companies are 10 times greater than the benefits of co-locating within two to five miles.[21] Another study estimates that the benefits of co-location among advertising agencies in Manhattan drained after just 750 meters (less than one-half mile)![22]

To quote Maryann Feldman, an expert on the geography of innovation:

> ...geography provides a platform to organize resources toward a specific purpose. While firms are one well-known way to organize resources, location provides a viable alternative—a platform to organize economic activity and human creativity. . . More than facilitating face-to-face interaction and the exchange of tacit knowledge, geography enhances the probability for serendipity—the chance for something unexpected to have a profound and transformative impact.[23]

Visionaries like Steve Jobs understood this, which is why he designed the Pixar campus in a way that would enable "spontaneous collisions" between colleagues from different departments—an idea that was pioneered by Bell Labs in the 1940s.[24] Google, Facebook, and other highly innovative companies have followed suit. They don't provide free food and table tennis without reason, and it's not just to give overworked engineers a fun way to let off steam. Instead, it's to get people who might not otherwise engage with one another to collide socially, open up, form relationships, share ideas, and find new ways to collaborate.

QUALITY OF PLACE

Quality of place is another role for geography in startup communities. Startup founders or early employees are highly skilled individuals who have options, and therefore, can choose where they want to live more freely than most others. They can live in many places, and the quality of the area they choose to live matters to them a lot.[25]

Economic development used to follow a smokestack-chasing approach—attract large, incumbent firms by offering preferential tax treatment and other subsidies. This zero-sum game pits regions against one another, with questionable overall results. Some of that legacy lives on today, as demonstrated by the Amazon HQ2 bidding process that captivated America in 2018 and 2019, or the fiasco in Wisconsin over its deal to bring the Taiwanese electronics manufacturer Foxconn to the state.[26] The usefulness of smokestack chasing has diminished in a knowledge-based economy because the inputs to production have changed, as both the Amazon and Foxconn cases reveal.[27]

Today's knowledge-economy workers, entrepreneurs, and startup employees want more than traditional attractors like affordable housing, access to transit, and high-quality schools. They also desire plentiful cultural, social, and natural amenities, and to be around other exciting and creative people. Unlike the post–World War II movement to suburban communities, these people and factors concentrate in and around cities.

Richard Florida, a world-renowned urbanist, built a reputation on a theory of the "creative class." We are both big believers of this theory and its relevance to startup communities. As I wrote in *Startup Communities*:

> Richard Florida describes the tie between innovation and creative-class individuals. The creative class is composed of individuals such as entrepreneurs, engineers, professors, and artists who create "meaningful new forms." Creative-class individuals, Florida argues, want to live in delightful places, enjoy culture with a tolerance for new ideas and weirdness, and—most of all—want to be around other creative class individuals. Network effects occur as a virtuous cycle exists where the existence of a creative class in an area attracts more creative-class individuals to the area, which in turn makes the area even more valuable and attractive. A location that hits critical mass enjoys a competitive geographic advantage over places that have yet to attract a significant number of creative-class individuals.

Empirical evidence supports this. Ian's research shows a relationship between high-growth entrepreneurship in American cities and the presence of workers in the creative class, even after accounting for workers with college degrees or in high-tech industries.[28] Academic studies in the United States and Europe have consistently found a positive relationship between measures of entrepreneurship and the creative economy.[29]

Surveys of founder sentiment suggest they value the quality of place. For example, a study of high-growth company founders by Endeavor, a group that promotes entrepreneurship worldwide, found that entrepreneurs make location decisions primarily on quality-of-life factors or because of personal connections—and they do so years before they start their companies.[30] Put differently, many of today's creative-class workers will be tomorrow's high-growth entrepreneurs.

Once entrepreneurs are rooted in a community, they tend to stay there. The same Endeavor survey shows that although high-growth entrepreneurs are highly mobile as young adults, once they start a company in a city, they are likely to stay there. Academic research further shows that entrepreneurs choose startup locations based in part on personal linkages and that those linkages can have a positive impact on startup performance.[31]

In his book, *The Innovation Blind Spot: Why We Back the Wrong Ideas—and What to Do About It*, investor and entrepreneur Ross Baird recalls a discussion about *topophilia* with John Hickenlooper, who was the Governor of Colorado at the time.[32] Hickenlooper loves to apply the term *topophilia* to describe why Colorado consistently ranks among the most entrepreneurial regions in the world, and why the leaders in the state invest so much back into their communities. He even used it as the centerpiece of his final State of the State speech before the state legislature.[33] Topophilia means "love of place," and for Governor Hickenlooper, this makes all the difference.

Before becoming governor, Hickenlooper was an entrepreneur, creating Wynkoop Brewing Company in 1988, one of the first brewpubs in the United States. He was governor from 2011 through 2019, a period of extraordinary growth and development in Colorado, both as a state and as an entrepreneurial ecosystem.

In 2018, Jared Polis was elected governor of Colorado and was sworn into office in January 2019, taking over for Hickenlooper. Before holding public office, Jared was also a successful entrepreneur. One of his undertakings was co-founding Techstars with me, David Cohen, and David Brown. Not surprisingly, a primary motivation for creating Techstars was to improve the startup community in Colorado, especially in Boulder, demonstrating topophilia in action.

Entrepreneurs want to build lasting things. This desire extends beyond their companies and is an amplifying motivating factor. As it turns out, they also want to do it in the places they love and where they and their families spend the most time.

Jerusalem's Lost Decade and the Bohemian Uprising that Revived Its Startup Community

Ben Wiener (Jerusalem, Israel)
Founder and Managing Partner, Jumpspeed Ventures

When I moved to Jerusalem from New York in 1998, there was meaningful startup activity in Israel's capital. While Tel Aviv was always going to be larger and more internationally recognized, there were numerous startups in Jerusalem and large venture funds to support them. In 2002, however, everything crashed, primarily due to the burst of the dot-com bubble and the onset of political instability. Jerusalem's startup activity was virtually dormant for over a decade.

In 2013, however, things began to change. For a variety of reasons discussed below, a new murmur of startup activity could be heard in Jerusalem once again. These tremors were probably first felt by Hanan Brand, a young Jerusalemite who was then serving as deal flow manager at Jerusalem Venture Partners (JVP). Hanan started to see a surprising number of funding submissions to JVP from local entrepreneurs, but many were too small or too early. Hanan started to privately run events in bars called "BiraTechs," where founders could meet and mingle. A Facebook group called "Jerusalem Startup Founders" was formed in parallel.

In mid-2013, there was only one accelerator program in Jerusalem, Siftech, formerly a student-run project started at Hebrew University to help students launch new companies. Siftech had run two cohorts, and not one company received funding. I attended one of Hanan's first BiraTech events, a "Startup Pitch Night." Over 40 entrepreneurs participated, but not one investor was present. Jerusalem was far off the radar screen. Returning home from that BiraTech event, I hatched the idea for my fund, Jumpspeed Ventures, which invests exclusively in Jerusalem-originated startups.

Several years later, the "Jerusalem Startup Founders" Facebook group went through a series of evolutions, turning into an organization called Capital J. It became an independent non-profit entity called MadeinJLM, with participation by the Hebrew University and an NGO, NewSpirit. Numerous funded startups have emerged from the Jerusalem ecosystem in the past six years, and there are literally hundreds of new attempted startups per year. Several other accelerators joined Siftech, including MassChallenge's Israel program, which accelerates over 50 startups from around the world per year in Jerusalem. Venture funding still pales in comparison to Tel Aviv but has risen dramatically within Jerusalem over time.

What were the contributing factors to this renaissance?

Most Jerusalem entrepreneurs tend to live in Jerusalem by choice, then start companies, rather than moving here to start them. Jerusalem attracts a diverse blend of residents, which gives rise to an entrepreneurial base made up of all types—Israeli-born, immigrant, men, women, religious, secular, Jewish, and Arab. A spirit of collaboration and helpfulness pervades the ecosystem.

Nicolas Colin of The Family has a fantastic three-part formula for self-sustaining technology ecosystems: (1) technological know-how, (2) capital, and (3) a spirit of rebellion. Jerusalem always had the technological know-how in its academic institutions and large companies. A new generation of primarily young entrepreneurs who were too naive and headstrong to know that Jerusalem was off the radar for Tel Aviv investors led the spirit of rebellion. Capital, which had been present in the late 1990s but vanished after the dot-com bubble burst, was needed. After some time and with some effort, capital started to slowly trickle back in.

When he was first elected mayor of Jerusalem in 2008, Nir Barkat (a former venture capitalist) made an immediate commitment to make Jerusalem the cultural capital of Israel. Richard Florida's thesis that a strong "creative class" is the harbinger of increased employment and technological innovation influenced Barkat. Whether intentional or unintentional, it's no coincidence that about five years after Barkat and the municipality started to invest heavily in the city's cultural events and activities, we saw a sudden upsurge in startup activity. You can't just throw money at a city and automatically create a community of startups. But, to an extent, funding can be a catalyst, particularly through indirect channels. A potentially non-obvious place to focus is funding the creative class. In fact, I was recently visited by a representative of a university in New Zealand, which had decided to allocate a few million dollars to "create" a startup community by seeding 200 new startups. I told her they'd likely lose the money and instead should invest in 200 rock bands. She was a bit taken aback until I explained the importance of Richard Florida's creative class and Nicolas Colin's spirit of rebellion to startup community building.

The best rebellions and renaissances occur because they have multiple concurrent origins, not just one single catalyst. That's certainly true of the Jerusalem entrepreneurial ecosystem. A confluence of negative factors around the Internet bubble bursting brought it down. Around 2013, positive factors combined to catalyze a resurgence in startup activity.

CHAPTER THREE

THE ACTORS

Startup Community Way Principle

The primary purpose of a startup community is to help entrepreneurs succeed. *Never forget what a startup community is all about. Without entrepreneurs, there is no startup community. If the entrepreneurs are not succeeding, the next generation will leave, and entrepreneurship will stall.*

N ow that we have broadly outlined how and why the external environment can either accelerate or constrain a startup's success, we will begin to explore in more detail the individual components that comprise a startup community. This chapter discusses one of the two key components within a startup community, its *actors*—the set of people and organizations involved. (In Chapter 4, we'll explore the other key component, a community's *factors*—the group of resources or local conditions that impact entrepreneurship.)

Who is doing what to whom, and in what way, matters. There are three types of actors: *leaders*, *feeders*, and *instigators*. Often, lines blur between the various actors and factors, and many individuals frequently transcend singular roles in a startup community.[1]

While the range of people, organizations, resources, and conditions involved in an entrepreneurial ecosystem are useful to understand, they are not the most critical construct. Instead, the interaction between each of the components is what matters. But first, we want to categorize the components. This exercise is especially helpful for newcomers.

LEADERS, FEEDERS, AND INSTIGATORS

A healthy startup community is a densely connected, open, trusting network where the most influential nodes of the network are entrepreneurs. This concept is one of the most controversial and misunderstood components of *Startup Communities*, where I used the terms *leaders* and *feeders* to describe the two categories of startup community participants. I wrote:

> Leaders of startup communities have to be entrepreneurs. Everyone else is a feeder into the startup community. Both leaders and feeders are important, but their roles are different... [feeders include] government, universities, investors, mentors, service providers, and large companies.

Some people misinterpreted this conceptualization. They felt that I was minimizing the role that non-entrepreneurs play in a startup community. Others found the term *feeder* to be diminishing. That was not my intent, and I will take this opportunity to clarify how I consider these two important groups.

Substitute different words for *leaders* and *feeders*; let's call them *apples* and *papayas*. Entrepreneurs are the apples. Everyone else is a papaya. They are each important, but they play different roles. The papayas are typically organizations or the people leading them. Most of them are hierarchical in nature. If you work for a papaya, even if your job is to engage the startup community, you are still judged by your employer based on how well you achieve the papaya's goals. Sometimes these goals will be consistent with those of the startup community, and other times they will not be.

Consequently, we make a strong assertion that the papayas can't play leadership roles in the startup community. However, individual members of the papayas—the *feeders*—can have influential leadership roles. We distinguish these people by calling them *instigators*, since they bring about new activity and initiate change.[2]

There are countless examples of instigators who have never been startup founders but work tirelessly to build startup communities. Often, they are central to the genesis of a startup community and sustain meaningful activity over time. This is critical since founders are often too busy building their companies to focus on the bigger picture. Sometimes this becomes a full-time job, through a nonprofit or other type of organization, but mostly they just love to participate and fill these gaps as a side hustle. These instigators are crucial to startup communities everywhere. Their contributions should be recognized and supported.

A startup community that lacks a core group of entrepreneurs who lead is not a sustainable one. While the instigators can and in fact typically do play leadership roles, entrepreneurs are role models for other entrepreneurs in a startup community, either as peers, mentors, or sources of inspiration. Not all of the entrepreneurs in a startup community need to be leaders, but you need a critical mass of them, which, fortunately, can be a relatively small number. Ultimately, it's vital to have entrepreneurs as leaders—they set the tone, are an essential source of knowledge, and help establish a culture of entrepreneurship in the startup community.

Existing entrepreneurs heavily influence new entrepreneurs, who derive a sense of what's possible from those who have come before them. Inexperienced founders look to more mature founders for inspiration, best practices, introductions, mental support, and advice about so many other subtle challenges. Non-entrepreneurs typically cannot serve this role in a complete way because they have never been on the journey.

In social networks, a relatively small number of people attract a disproportionate amount of direct or indirect connections (relationships). These network *nodes* (also called *hubs, super-connectors,* or *supernodes*) improve the cohesiveness of the network overall, compared with a network that has no or few supernodes. In this way, social networks, like startup communities, are represented by a power-law distribution, whereby a small number of people can have an outsized influence on the overall system.

Since I came up with the idea of entrepreneur-led startup communities, several research studies have established evidence in favor of the concept. For example, Endeavor built a series of entrepreneurial ecosystem network graphs in cities around the world. They found that communities with dense networks, where successful entrepreneurs (those who have scaled companies) are active leaders, have better outcomes than communities where the key leaders are not entrepreneurs.[3] A Kauffman Foundation study found that in Kansas City, entrepreneurs wanted most to connect with other entrepreneurs.[4]

In *Startup Communities*, I wrote about relying too much on government to either lead or provide resources for building a startup community. In spite of some successful efforts and the best of intentions, governments often lack the resources, expertise, mindset, and sense of urgency to mobilize resources that entrepreneurs need most.

The temptation to rely on government is understandable. After all, startup communities are a type of public good—something of value that exists to benefit everyone. In many domains, such as military, education, health care, and even vast swaths of innovation, the government provides public goods as one of its primary purposes. However, in the context of startup communities, governments can play only a supportive or indirect role. At the very least, entrepreneurs should not look to the government to solve their problems.

ACTORS

Actors, comprised of leaders, feeders, and instigators, are the people and organizations engaged in a startup community, defined by the role they perform. Individuals often occupy more than one role simultaneously and work with more than one organization. During one's career, a person will cross these boundaries many times. The following are short descriptions of each of the actors in a startup community, some of which are obvious and others that may be less well understood.

Entrepreneurs

A thriving startup community requires a sufficient number of entrepreneurs. These include experienced or serial entrepreneurs, novice or inexperienced entrepreneurs, and aspiring, nascent, or even dormant entrepreneurs. Also involved are social entrepreneurs, who are individuals applying scalable business models to solve social problems.

Entrepreneurs can be homegrown, can come from within the region or host country, or can come from another place. A startup community should be inclusive of any entrepreneur who wants to participate, regardless of their background, race, ethnicity, gender, where they are from, or their prior experience.

Startups and Scaleups

While entrepreneurship is broader than starting and scaling young companies, these two activities are the primary modes of entrepreneurship in a startup community. Entrepreneurs start companies that can create a new product, service, technology, method of production, or market approach.

At its formation, a startup consists of founders, a few employees, and perhaps some mentors or advisors—all working together to develop a new or improved product or service. Once the startup achieves customer traction—commonly referred to as product/market fit—the company moves into a new phase, where the focus shifts to scaling the company, expanding market share, and possibly moving into adjacent markets.

At each stage, the needs and challenges facing the company, its founders, and its employees differ. Personnel changes, often among the executive or founding teams, reflect changing demands. Successful startups evolve into growth-stage companies, or scaleups, which, while much more substantial than a startup, continue to be key actors in a startup community.

Startup Employees

Entrepreneurs can't build great companies alone. Skilled workers are particularly important in a modern, knowledge-intensive economy, where good ideas and brainpower are scarcer and more valuable than machinery and raw materials. Startups require talent and expertise of a technical, business, managerial, and temperamental nature. Employees can develop these skills in many different ways, including through traditional education, online learning, vocational or specialized training, or most importantly, through on-the-job training from other startups or corporations.

Mentors

Often these are experienced entrepreneurs or individuals with knowledge or expertise in an industry or discipline. Mentors should work on a volunteer basis and take a #GiveFirst approach, a concept I introduced in *Startup Communities* in the section "Give Before You Get." #GiveFirst means you are willing to put energy into a relationship or a system without defining the transactional parameters. However, it's not altruism—you expect to get something, but you don't know when, from whom, in what form, in what consideration, or over what time frame.

When their contribution is valuable, founders should reward mentors with equity in the company. When successful, the mentor relationship evolves, as mentors may transition from unpaid roles to paid advisors, investors, board members, or perhaps even employees. Note the distinction between a *mentor* and an *advisor*—the two are often talked about interchangeably, but they are very different. A mentor engages with a #GiveFirst approach, meaning they do not require a transactional relationship up front. In contrast, formal advisors are compensated with arrangements set in advance.

Values and Virtues: #GiveFirst

Originally, *Startup Communities* formulated the concept of "give before you get." Since 2012, this idea has evolved into a phrase called #GiveFirst, which is the mantra of Techstars and my fundamental philosophy of business.[5] As a refresher, the following is the section I wrote in *Startup Communities*.[6]

> One of my deeply held beliefs about the secret of success in life is to give before you get. In this approach, I am always willing to try to be helpful to anyone, without having a clear expectation of what is in it for me. If over time, the relationship is one way (e.g., I'm giving, but getting nothing), I'll often back off on my level of giving because this belief doesn't underlie a fundamentally selfless approach. However, by investing time and energy up front without an explicitly defined outcome, I have found that, over time, the rewards that come back to me exceed my wildest expectations.
>
> A group of us have worked very hard to incorporate this give-before-you-get philosophy into the Boulder startup community. You rarely hear the words, "What's in it for me?" around Boulder;

instead, it's "How can I be helpful?" Introductions flow freely, as do invitations. As I travel around the country, I hear people talking about how easy it is to engage with people in Boulder and how good karma flows freely, demonstrating give before you get hard at work.

An attribute of a great mentor is someone willing to contribute time and energy to a mentee without a clear expectation of what is coming back. David Cohen talks about this regularly, and he leads by example, not just with Techstars companies but also with many other companies in which he's not an investor. Techstars has specific programs like Techstars for a Day that is open to anyone who applies to Techstars, giving them a strong understanding of the mentor dynamics. And if you ask Techstars mentors why they participate, most of them say something like, "Someone once helped me when I was a young entrepreneur; I want to give back."

There are situations in which give before you get breaks down. When someone gets and never gives anything back, it becomes tedious, annoying, and uninteresting reasonably quickly. When a startup community embraces a give-before-you-get philosophy, people who only get but never give generate negative reputations and the startup community often rejects them, as a host organism rejects a parasite. So, make sure you are always giving at least as much as you are getting.

As the notion of give before you get has evolved into #GiveFirst, the definition has gotten tighter. #GiveFirst means you are willing to put energy into a relationship or a system without defining the transactional parameters. However, it's not altruism because you expect to get something. But you don't know when, from whom, in what form, in what consideration, or over what time frame.

It's easy to understand but goes against the grain of mainstream thinking about business relationships and networking. And, it's foundational to how startup communities work. Our friend and law professor Brad Bernthal has even written about this in formal academic journals under the legal terminology of "generalized exchange."[7]

If you can get all of the actors involved in the startup community engaged in a #GiveFirst approach, an enormous amount of energy goes into the startup community. This energy puts many things in motion without the friction of defining transactional relationships in advance. Suddenly, lots of stuff is happening, and immediate benefits start appearing all over the startup community. However, these benefits are unpredictable, and you can't anticipate the second-order impact. When we connected the idea of complex systems to startup communities, the importance of #GiveFirst came to light. The long-term implications of approaching business (and all aspects of life) came into sharp focus for us, as we realized this was a powerful way to engage with a complex system.

#GiveFirst doesn't start and stop with a startup community (and neither does complexity). As a philosophy, it's a simple way for entrepreneurs to think about giving back to their local communities as well as regions outside of the startup community.

If you embrace the idea of #GiveFirst, you can quickly have a positive impact on the health of your startup community. If everyone in your startup community embraces the philosophy, magic can happen.

Coaches

While a coach is a well-understood role in many domains, it wasn't popular in entrepreneurship until recently.[8] A coach can help a founder, a CEO, or a leadership team. The specific coaching approaches vary, but one of our favorite frameworks is the one popularized by Reboot, which focuses on practical skills, radical self-inquiry, and shared experiences as a means of developing enhanced leadership and greater resilience.[9] A great coach combines teaching practical skills while facilitating radical self-inquiry. That means helping the coached see her problems more clearly, be the source of her own solution, and encourage her to take action. The coach then builds a community that helps their clients to learn from the shared experiences of others, resulting in both enhanced leadership and greater individual resilience. Coaching differs from mentorship (learn from my experience) and advisory (learn from my expertise) in that coaches see the solution to problems as being within the coached. It differs from therapy in that the focus is not on healing the past (how did I get here?), but in moving forward (where do I want to go?).

Investors

Companies in startup mode often rely on funding to open their doors, develop their products, and scale operations. Funding may be in the form of equity, debt, grants, or some combination of these. Sources of startup funds may include venture capitalists, banks, angel investors, foundations, public markets, friends and family, corporations, crowdfunding (equity or peer lending), or government (subsidies, grants, funds-of-funds, direct investment, and development funds). Accelerators, incubators, studios, and an emerging class of "talent investors" (such as Entrepreneur First or Antler) provide funds in addition to other services like founder matching.

Service Providers

Like most businesses, startups rely on a range of service providers, such as lawyers, accountants, investment bankers, technical experts, computing services, and real estate lessors and co-working facilities. In healthy startup communities, service providers have an acute understanding of the unique nature of startups. They can make adjustments accordingly, such as accepting equity for service or similar arrangements that reflect the constraints and intangible assets of high-growth-potential business.

Startup advisors are a particular type of service provider. They are experts in one or more domains (technical, industry, venture, startups) who provide advice to early-stage companies for a short period (six months to a year) in exchange for shares in the company. In this way, they are part service-provider, part investor. Or, as Silicon Valley investor Jason Calacanis refers to them, "broke angel investors."[10]

Entrepreneurial Support Organizations

A wide range of for-profit and not-for-profit organizations exist specifically to support startups through mentorship, advisory, education, services, networking, connections, office space, and even funding. Some of these organizations may also engage in startup community-building efforts. These organizations include startup accelerators, incubators, and studios, co-working facilities, innovation hubs, hacker spaces, maker spaces, specialized vocational educators, and a range of industry, membership, entrepreneurship, networking, event, and facilitation organizations and associations. We distinguish these from traditional service providers because of their central focus on startups and because profit is often not their sole or even primary motive.

Universities

Universities are creators and disseminators of knowledge, technology, and science. They can have many spillover benefits to the local startup community, including as attractors of global talent (academics, researchers, administrators, and students). This leads to a well-educated workforce, a stable local economy, and entrepreneurial opportunities for commercializing technological innovations. In addition to spinning out technologies, universities are facilitators of entrepreneurship through education, training, funding, and other capacity-building activities.

Many universities are anchor institutions in their communities, serving as a significant local employer. They are also a potential source of customer revenue, a partner, and a convener. There are many individuals within the university in roles that can engage with the startup community, including students, professors, researchers, technology-transfer professionals, and entrepreneurship-program administrators.

Large Corporations

Large corporations play an important, and often underappreciated, role in startup communities. Large companies can spin off startups, or employees may leave to develop a complementary or competing product or service offering—critically, providing them with years of training and experience in business, industry, and craft. As with universities, large corporations can be talent magnets for the region, as well as creators, educators, and disseminators of knowledge through research and development, on-the-job training and experience, and via spinouts and partnerships. Perhaps most importantly, large corporations can be make-or-break partners for startups—as customers, suppliers, collaborators, and investors.

Media

The traditional news media, as well as more specialized business, industry, and entrepreneurship-specific media providers, serve a relevant function in information flow through national, regional, local, and international startup communities. Today, many of these organizations are primarily online and provide essential information about what is going on in the startup community through written articles, podcasts, and videos. Bloggers, or actors filling other roles who also blog (e.g., entrepreneurs, investors), can be among the most influential people in a startup community. Most healthy startup communities have some level of informal media in the form of blogging by influential actors.

Research and Advocacy Groups

Think-tanks, policy organizations, business groups, and a host of other research, advocacy, and membership groups can help by aggregating and disseminating information, promoting public policies, and providing additional support for startups in a variety of settings. The best organizations, such as the Center for American Entrepreneurship in Washington, D.C. or Engine in San Francisco, educate policymakers and the general public about the role of entrepreneurship in the economy and society.

Regional and Local Government

Regional and local governments play an influential role in startup communities. Regulation and tax policies can have a significant impact, as can developing an educated workforce. Regional and local policymakers are more likely to be more actively involved in coordinating and funding entrepreneurial activities, including underwriting incubators, facilitating connections and learning, supporting grassroots initiatives, and encouraging startups and company founders.

Local officials can also play an essential role in assessing the startup community through asset mapping or incorporating startups and entrepreneurs into a regional economic development agenda. Local officials have stronger ties to the startup community, which gives them a direct hand in enhancing or restricting those factors, enabling them to be conveners, connectors, and promoters in chief.

Values and Virtues: Stop Favoring Incumbents

Favoring incumbents over newcomers has been a hallmark of economic policy for as long as we can remember. In economic geography terms, this meant "smokestack chasing," which means lauding tax breaks and subsidies for large companies to move to a new city. This zero-sum strategy—let's call it "full-stack chasing" for the digital era—is typified in the United States by the Amazon HQ2 sweepstakes mania and the deal to bring the Taiwanese electronics manufacturer Foxconn to Wisconsin.[11]

Both of these instances involved enormous government subsidies to bring outside companies into a region, an ensuing public backlash, and, ultimately, foiled plans. In the case of Amazon, there was a high-profile split HQ2 between New York City and Washington, D.C., with an eventual abandonment of the former after public outcry. With Foxconn, nobody knows what's going to happen, but it appears the company will significantly scale back its investment in the state.[12] To its credit, Apple avoided the public relations fiasco altogether by quietly selecting Austin, Texas, as the location for its second headquarters.[13]

Aside from high-profile and company-specific initiatives, city and state economic development activity generally favors incumbent businesses, especially large ones looking to move a headquarters or create a major operations center in a new location. This activity hurts young startups, which are already at a relative disadvantage in terms of resources, customer traction, and financial capital. Cities should look to find ways to reduce barriers to entry, which are a drag on entrepreneurs, and reduce regulatory moats and other advantages that established firms have over young, high-growth startups.[14]

National Government

National governments can contribute to entrepreneurship, primarily through policies that "set the table." These make for a stable and competitive business climate.[15] They fund nascent technologies and scientific development, and provide activities and resources, ensuring a well-skilled workforce.

Political and macroeconomic policies set at a national level, such as those that pertain to security, the rule of law (property rights, contract enforcement, bankruptcy law), immigration, labor rights, science, innovation, technology, markets, infrastructure, taxation (including subsidies and incentives), regulation, education, inflation, and fiscal stability, can be positive or negative forces. Many policies have unintended consequences.

In addition to these broad-based public policies, national governments may engage directly in activities to stimulate entrepreneurship and innovation as part of broader growth objectives. These activities include funding for primary and secondary education and basic research and development, or the allocation of capital to stimulate the formation of early-stage, high-tech startups.

Like large corporations and universities, national governments may engage with startups as customers, suppliers, collaborators, or even investors.

Building a Different Kind of Startup Community Around Underestimated Founders

Arlan Hamilton (Los Angeles, California)
Founder and Managing Partner, Backstage Capital

Author, It's About Damn Time: How to Turn Being Underestimated into Your Greatest Advantage

In 2015, I started Backstage Capital, a fund that invests solely in underestimated founders. In our case, that means women, people of color, LGBT, and so on. After learning about and experiencing the discrepancies in the amount of funding that goes to anyone who isn't a straight, white male in Silicon Valley and many other markets, I wanted to do something about it. Now, obviously this doesn't mean that everyone who is a straight, white male gets funding. But when you compare the amount of money that goes into those groups versus women, people of color, LGBT, and other underrepresented groups, the discrepancies are staggering.

I've seen thousands of companies since starting Backstage. The community that emerged from this is wonderful. Backstage is a family, first and foremost. It is camaraderie, a loyalty. It is championing each other and of oneself. It is a brotherhood, a sisterhood, a family hood, and it is as diverse a group of founders as I've seen in one room.

How did we do it? We put the founder first. Backstage has two main products, capital and platform, which means funding supported by our resources, connections, and tools. Our customers are underrepresented, underestimated founders. And from day one, I listened to them.

I wouldn't have started Backstage if I didn't see the need for the fund. It's really important not to start something for the sake of it, or because you think it might be glamorous, or that it will put you in a position of leverage because people need you. These are really bad reasons to build any sort of community. Instead, the motivation should come from a place of passion and deep interest. Passion can only get you so far because it is movement. Passion helps you with execution in every way, but the intent is thoughtfulness. The intent is the steering wheel. Passion is the accelerator. So it's really important to understand yourself, understand why you're doing what you're doing, what you're setting out to do, why this thing, and why this time.

It's then critically important to execute on your conviction, trust yourself, and be dogged in your determination to get to the milestone that you've set. I don't call it the finish line, because it's never really done. You're never truly finished if you're doing something that's transformative.

Another thing we did was offer value without expectation of immediate return on investment. This #GiveFirst mindset is something that Brad has talked about for years. I can say from a personal standpoint that Brad practices what he preaches because I reached out to him in 2012 through some very, very amateur emails. They were too long. They were too wordy. They were too over the top. But he listened, and he responded, and he made connections and gave answers. He took me seriously.

The most important thing Brad did as part of my trajectory—even more than eventually investing capital in my fund—is that he took me seriously to begin with. What my emails lacked in elegance, they made up for in intent. Sure, I had passion. That passion was all over those emails, but the intent is what kept me on the right path and got me here today.

Finally, always remember that it takes a village. You are not going to be able to do something life-altering, industry-disrupting, or transformative alone. No one does. There's no such thing as a "self-made" anyone. I'm not self-made. I've been called that a lot, but it's not accurate. There were and are many, many people along the way. And that's true for each entrepreneur and each startup community.

CHAPTER FOUR

THE FACTORS

> **Startup Community Way Principle**
>
> *Startup communities are organized through networks of trust, not hierarchies.* Startup communities function through relationships where mutual trust and norms allow the exchange of ideas, talent, capital, and know-how to occur seamlessly. Hierarchies and top-down approaches destroy these dynamics and sap the energy that startup communities need to thrive.

Having discussed the types of people and organizations involved in a startup community, we now turn to the resources and conditions in a city that accelerate or constrain the ability of entrepreneurs to succeed. We call these *factors* and organize them using a framework we call the Seven Capitals.

While collectively, along with the actors, these parts of a startup community are of course important, it's critical to understand that the interaction between them is what matters most. Still, an understanding of the factors is valuable when engaging with a startup community.

THE SEVEN CAPITALS

Now that we've identified the *who* in startup communities let's shift gears and discuss the *what*, the critical resources and location-specific conditions that impact entrepreneurship in a place.

Let's start with a framework called the Seven Capitals. These are the core assets of a startup community that produce economic value. Like the traditional meaning of capital, they can be depleted and subsequently require replenishment through the investment of time, effort, or money. They are forward-looking in nature. Initial investments from the past produce current benefits, and to derive benefits in the future, they require further investment today.

A common refrain around startup communities is "we don't have enough capital." It usually refers to financial capital, and more specifically, to investment from angel investors and venture capitalists. Unfortunately, this is a narrow and self-limiting view since there are other assets, beyond just financial capital, that meaningfully impact a startup community. Many of these types of capital are abundant in young and developing startup communities, even if financial capital is scarce.

Categorizing these factors as types of capital is a useful framework because it provides a wider view of key resources in a startup community. It also describes their characteristics as valuable, degradable, and forward-looking. Finally, it turns around a tired complaint in startup communities.

1. **Intellectual capital:** ideas, information, technologies, stories, educational activities
2. **Human capital:** talent, knowledge, skills, experience, diversity
3. **Financial capital:** revenue, debt, equity, or grant financing
4. **Network capital:** connectedness, relationships, bondedness
5. **Cultural capital:** attitudes, mindset, behaviors, history, inclusiveness, love of place

6. **Physical capital:** density, quality of place, fluidity, infrastructure
7. **Institutional capital:** system of laws, functioning public sector, markets, stability

The Seven Capitals of Startup Communities and Entrepreneurial Ecosystems

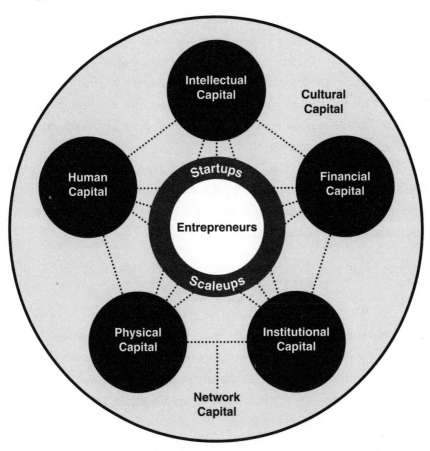

The first three of these, intellectual capital, human capital, and financial capital, provide essential inputs to building a startup community. They are aligned with the three most commonly referenced critical resources in startup communities: ideas, talent, and funding. Several of the others, such as network capital and cultural capital, are running in the background; they are harder to see yet provide critical infrastructure for the startup community to function properly.

For example, network capital ties everything and everyone in the startup community together and is used by entrepreneurs to locate and secure additional resources, such as talent, financing, and information. Cultural capital determines the nature of integration, the general lifestyle and business climate in a city, and the historical legacy of a place's way of being. Physical capital facilitates the exchange of resources through proximity and provides inhabitants with the necessary infrastructure and quality of life through physical and natural amenities. Institutional capital ensures that the general environment for entrepreneurs to operate in is stable and functioning properly.

Many of the Seven Capitals overlap and are interconnected through their underlying components. We refer to these resources and conditions as *factors*. As with all constructs around a startup community, the entrepreneurs are at the center of it.

FACTORS

In addition to being the resources used in startup communities, factors make up the general environment that entrepreneurs must operate within and the characteristics of a place that shape a startup community. As with actors, some factors are distinct while others are subtle. The following is a short description of each key factor.

Ideas and Skills

Without access to good ideas, technologies, and a suitable base of startup community actors (including workers and mentors), entrepreneurs have nothing new to create nor the means to achieve it. In the information and knowledge-based economy that we are currently living in, ideas, skills, and talent are at the core of value creation.

The development of ideas and skills comes from many places, with universities, corporations, and research labs (public and private) as the most prominent examples. Ultimately, primary and secondary education of children ensures a steady pipeline of people capable of generating new ideas. Easy paths to new people entering and engaging with the region are crucial. Many individuals will cycle in and out of a community over the course of their careers, so it's necessary for certain elements to be in place. These include a vibrant university system (for developing talent), a welcoming city (for retaining talent), and a permissive immigration policy (for attracting talent).

Knowledge specific to the entrepreneurship process—which goes beyond industries or technologies—is best gained through experience. While it can be studied and learned, it is most effective when passed down from the previous generation of successful entrepreneurs. This is achieved through employment in a startup, or obtained by working with many entrepreneurs and startups.

Cultural Norms

Local beliefs and norms feature prominently in startup communities. The history and nature of a place play a central role in the development of these cultural norms. Vibrant startup communities have a buzz around entrepreneurship. Founders are role models, leaders, or even local heroes. Many people—from students to employees to even children—look to entrepreneurship as a viable career path.

The foundational cultural norms in a startup community include a generally supportive view of entrepreneurs and entrepreneurship, an understanding of risk and reward, a tolerance of failure and ambiguity, and an embrace of new and different things, people, and ideas. Creativity, experimentation, ambition, wealth creation, entrepreneurship education, and the social status of self-made individuals are valued. Social interactions are honest, open, collaborative, and inclusive. Entrepreneurs are continually connecting among themselves and with other stakeholders in a supportive environment. Media and civic leaders highlight and promote the role of startups in the community.

Connectivity

A central feature of startup communities is the connectedness of people. This network capital—the connectedness of various actors and factors within a geographic area—is primarily local. But networks can also be non-local—including, for example, the people who grew up in a city but now live elsewhere, local university graduates employed outside the region, multinational corporations with a presence in the community, and professional ties that entrepreneurs have outside the area.

Some organizations exist in whole or in part to facilitate connections. These include professional associations, entrepreneurship clubs, meetup groups, and innovation centers. Experienced entrepreneurs and board directors, who are engaged with many startups simultaneously and take on an active role of stewardship or deal making, can be superconnectors. In the best startup communities, many participants play a connector role.

Entrepreneurship is a team sport—even at the founding stage. Being connected with others is vital. An estimated 95 percent of company founders involve others in the startup process substantively, and half of the new ventures are started by teams, with founders often drawing from their core networks to establish founding teams.[1] Entrepreneurs with more extensive connectivity with other entrepreneurs and the resources they need are more likely to succeed than those who are isolated.

Density

Density is the critical mass or co-location of actors existing and interacting in a relatively confined geographic area. By having density in a startup community, entrepreneurs increase the opportunity for meaningful connections, forge more significant relationships, and serendipitously interact with each other, building trust and increasing connectivity.

While a startup community can encompass an entire city, concentrated startup neighborhoods develop over time, especially in larger cities like Boston, New York, London, or the San Francisco Bay Area. In these cities, there are multiple, well-known areas where startups cluster. These neighborhoods should interconnect in the same way as city-based startup communities to build a startup community in a state or country.

Diversity

Startup communities require a workforce with a variety of talents, experiences, points of view, gender identities, races, and other characteristics. Complex problems—such as innovation and entrepreneurship in the information age—are best tackled with diversity and teams.

Other defining qualities of cities with vibrant startup communities include well-diversified economies with a healthy mix of creative and innovative industries, a community that welcomes and embraces outsiders to the region, a general embrace of diverse perspectives, backgrounds, and identities, and a culture of inclusiveness.

Fluidity

A steady flow of residents, workers, and businesses throughout a community contributes to the vitality of a region.[2] People from other cities, regions, or countries bring different perspectives and experiences. Labor markets allowing the free flow of workers between jobs ensure better matching between employees and employers. A dynamic business sector with many firms being born, failing, growing, and contracting, at all times, assures the reallocation of resources to higher uses, rewarding entrepreneurship.

A fluid startup community has the benefit of building greater connectedness, expanding the network, and increasing the likelihood of forming crucial relationships. Conversely, cities with stagnant populations, labor markets, and an abundance of stale incumbent businesses are less likely to develop robust startup communities.

Markets

Access to customers—especially those willing to engage early or with proof-of-concept products—is important for early-stage companies in gaining traction, developing products, and developing a stable financial footing. Initial customers and suppliers can lend expertise in product development and market fit, forge new partnerships, serve as references or credibility for future customers, and help with feedback and distribution. Local organizations, including institutions like government, universities, and large corporations, can play a significant role in this capacity.

Finance

Financial capital comes in many forms and runs the gamut from revenue from initial customers to traditional venture capital. At the early stages, the most common financing comes from personal savings or friends and family. Additional forms of equity and debt financing include angel, seed, and venture capital. Commercial loans or venture debt come from professional investors and banking institutions. Loans and grants may also come from the government or philanthropies. Newer forms of finance include crowdfunding, peer lending, and revenue-based financing.

Infrastructure

A sufficient level of infrastructure is needed for startups to thrive, including access to reliable and affordable telecommunications and Internet services, transportation and logistics, and utilities such as electricity, gas, and water. Other infrastructure, such as adequate commercial real estate, housing, and security, are also needed.

While these factors are generally less of a problem in more advanced economies or urban areas, we hear inspiring stories from entrepreneurs in places all around the world who are lacking many of these resources but find ways to overcome the constraints and build new companies.

Filling Gaps for Basic Infrastructure in Africa

Akintunde Oyebode (Lagos, Nigeria)
Executive Secretary and CEO, Lagos State Employment Trust Fund (LSETF)

In Lagos, Nigeria, the absence of critical infrastructure and declining government revenues means the state faces a long process of investing or stimulating private investments needed to boost infrastructure stock and grow its economy.

This must be done while facing a massive unemployment problem where, according to the National Bureau of Statistics, 32.7 percent of Nigeria's working population are either unemployed or underemployed. The sub-national situation is worsened by limited economic activity outside Lagos, which has led to the internal migration of approximately one million people annually from other Nigerian states.

The State Governor responded to this challenge by setting up an Employment Trust Fund with the purpose of providing financial support to businesses and young Lagos residents look to start and run businesses or acquire the skills to make themselves more employable. This institution manages a fund where the state government, private institutions, and international donor agencies can combine resources solely to help create jobs in Lagos State.

LSETF was set up to solve both short- and long-term challenges facing businesses and young Lagos residents while the state uses other means to solve the bigger infrastructure challenges being faced. Reliable energy, high-speed Internet, and office space are expensive and hard to come by in Nigeria, even in Lagos. Through the Lagos Innovates program, startup founders and operators of co-working spaces and innovation hubs are eligible for government-sponsored workspace vouchers, loans, and events sponsorship.

These actions provide needed support for our most promising companies of tomorrow, but also serve as an immediate response to the country's major socioeconomic problem—persistently high unemployment.

Formal Institutions

Sustained startup activity needs a business-friendly climate, well-understood legal and regulatory frameworks, and a general sense of political and macroeconomic stability. Countries and regions with strong economic growth, innovation, employment, income, and a business structure that enables new company formation and access to markets are generally conducive to high-growth startups. Political instability, corruption, anti-democratic rule, and other practices that don't encourage a safe and open society work against startup communities.

One of the most exciting developments in the last few years has been the rise of startup communities in spite of these significant headwinds. From Gaza to Egypt to North Korea, entrepreneurs are figuring it out. The Internet, the spread of startup communities' ideas, and inspirational stories of entrepreneurs overcoming significant obstacles play an influential role.

Quality of Place

Young and mid-career founders of high-growth companies tend to be geographically mobile. Beyond just work opportunities, they choose where to live based on the quality of life or personal ties. Once they start their companies, they tend to stay in these places. For founders and future founders with more than one option for where to live, quality of place can determine where they end up.

The general environment is also a tremendous factor in quality of place. A general sense of political and macroeconomic stability and a business-friendly climate are fundamental, if not significantly helpful for sustained startup activity. Some thriving startup communities are an exception to this. But, in general, areas where economic growth, innovation, employment, and income are strong are desirable. Political instability, corruption, anti-democratic rule, and other practices that don't encourage a safe and open society, work against startup communities.

Events and Activities

Catalytic events create opportunities for founders and others interested in engaging with local entrepreneurs to connect and build relationships in a meaningful format.[3] These events have to be more significant than annual entrepreneurial awards or networking cocktail parties. Examples that play an essential role include Startup Weekend, 1 Million Cups, hackathons, and conferences (with keynote speakers who are renowned successful entrepreneurs, particularly globally or nationally).

Storytelling

The cliché that *success begets success* is a powerful accelerant in startup communities. Storytelling is not merely marketing and PR, but entrepreneurs shouting from the rooftops about their startup community. This shouldn't be limited only to successful outcomes, as there is a preponderance of failure in the continuous evolution of a startup community. In fact, more is often learned from failures than from successes; lean-in to that discomfort. The storytelling should go far beyond cheerleading, with a focus on learning in the startup community.

The Value of Story in Startup Communities

Bobby Burch (Fort Collins, Colorado)
Co-Founder, Startland News

How can we connect and grow Kansas City's startup community?

That was the challenge from which *Startland News*—a nonprofit, digital publication focused on Kansas City's entrepreneurial ecosystem—was born in 2015.

Co-founder Adam Arredondo and I saw a disjointed community of exceptional entrepreneurs, makers, creatives, and supporters that lacked awareness of itself. Whether enabled through geography or socioeconomics, we knew Kansas City's detached startup community would never reach its full potential without a more united ecosystem.

Thus, the answer we found to our problem was through the power of a story.

By leveraging the power of a story, we'd connect members of the startup community, inform supporters, inspire new participants, and empower engagement. Through our storytelling, we aimed to create and cultivate a network of creative, collaborative people that we linked by their determination and curiosity.

But instead of a focus on startups' business plans, their technologies, or how-to resources for growth, we set out with an intentionally different mission. With an array of other organizations providing support for entrepreneurs to grow, we honed our storytelling efforts on the humanity of our community and what brings us together.

We set out to tell stories about people contributing to the ecosystem, highlighting their ambitions, fears, insights, successes, and failures. By unearthing and sharing these universal human experiences, we'd serve as a digital connector while also normalizing creativity, risk-taking, and collaboration. We wanted to show readers a bit of themselves in the founders they were reading about in hopes that they would not only develop the confidence to pursue their dreams but also become engaged with Kansas City's startup community.

Now, more than 2,500 Kansas City stories later, that mission endures, thanks in large part to the faith of our primary investors, Mike and Becky Wrenn, and key supporters like the Ewing Marion Kauffman Foundation.

We believe that founders, teachers, intrapreneurs, investors, policymakers, students, and curious citizens have so much to learn from one another. And fortunately, they've proven us right time and time again.

In the years following *Startland*'s launch, we've seen dozens of examples of the impact our stories have had on individuals, businesses, and the community. Here are a few.

Creating Connecting Opportunities

After *Startland* established itself as Kansas City's go-to source on startup community news, we were able to offer resources to our niche audience. One of the most popular tools to date has been our startup jobs board.

We created it to fuel startups with new talent and to bring more people into the area's startup community. It also helps organizations that exist specifically to support startups—such as mentor networks, investment firms, accelerators, and incubators— by allowing them to post open positions, explore up-and-coming firms, and see what area startups are growing.

To date, we've had more than 360 Kansas City–area startup positions listed on our jobs board. Tracking the placement of those openings is difficult, but we've been able to confirm 16 jobs filled thanks to *Startland*'s jobs board. We're expecting about 500 jobs by the end of 2019.

Validating for Startups

Startland News often provides startups with their first glimpse of fame. Our coverage has helped startups grow through a variety of avenues. An example is a Kansas City company that asked to remain nameless, whom we'll call GoTracktor.

Each year, *Startland News* generates a variety of lists that aim to highlight local businesses for their successes or great promise. In one such list, we featured GoTracktor because of its quality leadership, a new client, and its unique technology.

The list was widely disseminated across the United States, generating *Startland* thousands of visitors eager to learn about Kansas City's up-and-coming startups. We were pleased with our audience's reception, but even more thrilled to hear of the story's effect on GoTracktor.

A co-founder from the firm later told us that our feature on their company ended up on the screen of a Silicon Valley venture capitalist. The investor ended up hopping in to fund GoTracktor, helping to close out its seed round. This investor created valuable connections as the company expanded.

Increasing Media Competition on Startup Stories

Newsrooms often struggle to tell business stories creatively.

That's why over the years, I've been thrilled to see *Startland*'s storytelling help Kansas City TV and radio stations, as well as print and digital media groups, discover the fantastic stories in their backyard.

Traditional TV, radio, and print have subsequently featured more than 200 of *Startland*'s originally reported stories.

And that's because *Startland* serves as a validator for incumbent media. We help demonstrate that the founder, startup, or initiative is legitimate and that there's a good story to be shared. We make it easier for an assignment editor or producer to say *yes*.

A more competitive media landscape covering Kansas City entrepreneurship is a win-win-win.

More media competition is better for startups, which can multiply their exposure and thus fuel their business. It's advantageous to *Startland News* as it gains exposure and garners more prospective constituents. And, finally, it's a win for the Kansas

City community, which benefits from more informed and engaged citizens eager to get involved.

Storytelling is powerful!

It's been an honor to see Kansas City support Startland's efforts and to see its impact through the years. I've been consistently surprised by the incredible stories we're so fortunate to share.

Kansas City is but one example of a city that embraced entrepreneurial storytelling to inspire individuals and to empower a community. Most any community can tap into this value, but it requires dedication, trust, and patience.

Startups can rocket communities forward, and stories are the fuel.

CHAPTER FIVE

STARTUP COMMUNITIES VERSUS ENTREPRENEURIAL ECOSYSTEMS

Startup Community Way Principle

Putting founders first, giving before you get, and having an intense love of place are essential values in a startup community. The values of the people involved drive the startup community. To succeed, embrace a #GiveFirst mentality, prioritize the entrepreneurs above all else, and love where you are.

While communities and ecosystems are related, they are different things. To differentiate them, we call them "startup communities" and "entrepreneurial ecosystems."

Each are collections of actors and factors in a physical place that interact in a way that influences entrepreneurs and produces entrepreneurship. Each is intensely local in nature and critical to a vibrant economy.

However, a startup community is the beating heart of entrepreneurship in a city and sits at the core of an entrepreneurial ecosystem. The startup community has a collective identity, a shared sense of purpose, a common set of values, and a deep belief in putting founders first.

In contrast, an entrepreneurial ecosystem is a generalized structure that wraps around and depends on a startup community to give it life. Participants at the startup community layer are deeply connected and aligned with each other. Even though the actors at the entrepreneurial ecosystem layer are resourceful and impactful, they face incentive structures and organizational constraints that often don't align with the startup community.

Cultivation and support of leaders that emerge from the startup community are essential to consistently produce better entrepreneurs and startups. As entrepreneurs succeed, actors in the broader entrepreneurial ecosystem will engage more effectively with the startup community, and a virtuous cycle will develop that draws in more people, resources, and support. This is similar to the entrepreneurship concept of product/market fit, so we call it *community/ecosystem fit*.

In the short term, especially when entrepreneurial activity in a place is immature, the Startup Community Way is a useful model for getting going. However, once the flywheel begins to turn, the actors in the entrepreneurial ecosystem can engage in a way that positively reinforces both the startup community and the entrepreneurial ecosystem. As a result, we recommend prioritization of the startup community for most places, since it enables the entrepreneurial ecosystem to evolve more effectively.

ENTREPRENEURIAL ECOSYSTEMS

The foundation for entrepreneurial ecosystems can be traced back to the early-1980s when Johannes Pennings, a Columbia University management professor, referred to the impact of environmental factors on startup activity in places like Silicon Valley, Boston, and Austin. Pennings described how the entrepreneurial vibrancy of a region could be explained by factors "beyond the realm" of the entrepreneurs.[1] Over the next decade, others built on the notion of the local environment being important to entrepreneurship.[2]

In the early-1990s, scholars began likening external factors for businesses with ecological systems. The term "business ecosystem" was introduced and increasingly refined as the complex web of interdependent actors engaged in open and collaborative competition for innovation in the information age.[3] The ecosystem concept was later applied directly to entrepreneurship and was amplified in the past decade by academics like Daniel Isenberg of Babson College.[4] In 2012, I connected the ecosystem concept with the construct of a startup community. Since then, a flurry of activity, interest, and engagement has occurred across the range of ecosystem actors on a global scale.

The ecosystem metaphor—which references the interaction between living organisms and their physical, non-living environment—is helpful in the context of entrepreneurship. Like an ecological system, a system of entrepreneurship is adaptive, interconnected, and, importantly, highly localized. It is self-organizing, self-governing, and self-sustaining.

Like entrepreneurial ecosystems, startup communities are complex systems with many actors who interact in ways that impact the success of local entrepreneurs in a place. But, there are differences between the two.

ALIGNMENT OF ACTORS

Consider the following two definitions of *community*. One is from ecology (the domain of ecosystems), and the other is more informal.[5]

1. Community: (ecology) a group of interdependent organisms of different species growing or living together in a specified habitat.
2. Community: (familiar) a feeling of fellowship with others, as a result of sharing common attitudes, interests, and goals; a similarity or identity; joint ownership or liability.

In ecological nomenclature, a community is all the living things in the ecosystem. These plants, animals, and other organisms interact with each other and with their nonliving environment to form an ecosystem. In entrepreneurship, the actors and factors comprise the ecosystem.

The informal definition is quite different. When applied to startups, the definition identifies the set of actors with a deep commitment to helping entrepreneurs succeed. In this way, startup communities are deeper than ecosystems, having stronger connections and bonds between participants. At the same time, they are narrower, as fewer ecosystem participants engage in the community layer.

Merging the ecological and familiar definitions best defines a startup community, capturing orientation and purpose of the interactions of its actors:

A startup community is a group of people that—through their interactions, attitudes, interests, goals, sense of purpose, shared identity, fellowship, collective accountability, and stewardship of place—are fundamentally committed to helping entrepreneurs succeed.

Values and Virtues: Put Entrepreneurs at the Center of Things

Entrepreneurs must be the central focus of every startup community. All participants must place the needs of founders above all else, even their own agenda. After all, without entrepreneurs, there is no startup community! While this may sound self-evident, it is one of the most frequently violated principles in an entrepreneurial ecosystem.

Any participant in an entrepreneurial ecosystem, including governments, corporations, universities, or service providers, should precede every action with a straightforward question: "Does this help entrepreneurs?" If you don't know, ask the entrepreneurs. If you think you do, still ask the entrepreneurs since you might be wrong.[6]

A classic example of not taking this approach is launching projects aimed at catalyzing entrepreneurship, even major ones, without first seeking the input of entrepreneurs. An even more damaging move is when someone exploits the power asymmetry between themselves and a vulnerable startup. While we understand that everyone has a business to run and an agenda to pursue, exploitative behavior to gain a short-term advantage is destructive over the long-term.

Engaging entrepreneurs with the appropriate mindset can be as simple as showing up and listening to the founders in your startup community. Get a better sense of where their pain points are, figure out what you can do to be helpful, and involve others who can help. You don't have to be a miracle worker. Just listen and help. Furthermore, include entrepreneurs in all decision-making processes that affect them, as founders are often the best source of ideas for what other founders and the startup community need.

Eric Ries's Lean Startup methodology applies nicely here. Treat the founders as your customer and be obsessed with meeting their needs. Get out of the building, talk to them, and build hypotheses quickly. Experiment, gather feedback, measure, and adjust. Then, repeat. Eventually, you'll figure out what's useful and what's not.

DIFFERENT, BUT MUTUALLY REINFORCING, PURPOSE

All systems have three main ingredients: elements, connections, and a purpose.[7] While there can be many variations at the ecosystem layer, the ultimate purpose of an entrepreneurial ecosystem is to produce startups, generate jobs, and create economic value. Startup communities have a different purpose, which is simply to help entrepreneurs succeed.

While these purposes are both mutually reinforcing, they are not the same. The state of mind one uses when engaging with entrepreneurs is one difference. At the ecosystem layer, engagement is primarily economic and less driven by social norms. At the community layer, participants are more responsive to a drive for the common good.

The community layer consists of founders, startup employees, and organizations such as accelerators or incubators, who work with or inside of startups daily and exist exclusively to help build startups or support the entrepreneurs. However, it needn't stop there. Actors employed by organizations that don't exist primarily to serve entrepreneurs can also engage at the community layer, even if their institutions do not. Large companies, especially executives leading them, who understand that they can be impactful customers or partners of startups in their community if they engage with them in the right way, can have an outsized impact.

As an organization's central mission gets further away from helping entrepreneurs succeed, it will be more difficult for that organization to engage meaningfully at the community layer. Entities, including universities, governments, and large corporations that are critical to entrepreneurial ecosystems, have incentives and organizational structures with inherently different purposes. Consequently, they have a much broader agenda and set of constituencies that go far beyond merely helping entrepreneurs succeed.

SYSTEMS WITHIN SYSTEMS

Getting your arms around the breadth of actors and factors in an entrepreneurial ecosystem can be daunting. Some of them are far removed from direct engagement with startups and impact them passively or even unwittingly. Others are actively engaged through an economic incentive, but may not participate in community-building or align with a mindset of putting entrepreneurs at the center of things.[8] Finally, some exist principally to work directly with entrepreneurs, either as a core function of their official role or by incorporating community building into what they do.

While some of these actors and factors are directly or even exclusively involved in helping startups, many others are not. Getting these entities to work toward a common goal of helping entrepreneurs succeed is a challenge. This illustrates another difference between startup communities, which are a bottom-up phenomenon, and entrepreneurial ecosystems, which tend to function more as top-down systems.

Top-down efforts to be all-encompassing overwhelm practitioners who are searching for specific ideas about how to improve a system. Donella Meadows, a prominent systems theorist who you'll be hearing more from in this book, says:

> Once you start listing the elements of a system, there is almost no end to the process. You can divide elements into sub-elements and then sub-sub-elements. Pretty soon, you lose sight of the system. As the saying goes, you can't see the forest for the trees.[9]

We hear a common theme from entrepreneurs and startup community builders. While the fundamental idea behind ecosystems makes sense to them, they struggle to grasp where to start and how to prioritize their actions. Many well-intentioned entrepreneurial ecosystem models don't provide clear entry points for implementing meaningful change. In contrast, by focusing entirely on helping entrepreneurs succeed, startup communities and the Boulder Thesis create many immediate areas of focus.

It's important to note that startup communities are systems that exist within other systems. They are a subset of actors and factors inside of an entrepreneurial ecosystem, which is a subset of an innovation ecosystem, which is a subset of an economy, which is a subset of society. The further out you go from the startup community core, the more complexity you introduce. The more complexity there is, the harder it is to influence and shape the system.

Startup Communities Are Systems within Systems

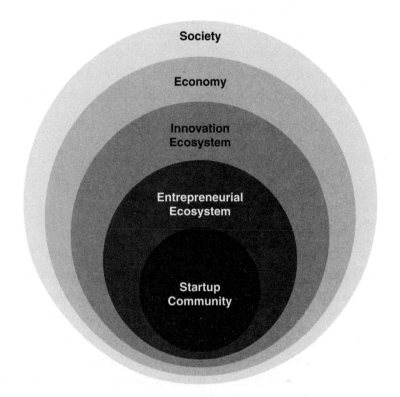

Organizing and motivating participants at the community layer, including those aligned with an entrepreneur-first focus, is difficult enough. Many are founders who have extremely busy roles within their own companies. Others may engage with founders as part of their jobs, be interested in entrepreneurship, or focus on the vitality of their city.

It is immeasurably harder to shape and motivate the layers of people who don't have the interests of entrepreneurs and startups as a focal point of what they're doing. Consequently, efforts to affect entrepreneurship at the ecosystem layer are much harder. Often, they appear in overly formulaic strategies or models. While they masquerade as a bottom-up activity, they are too often top-down initiatives.

While improving conditions at the ecosystem layer is worthwhile, its impact will be mostly limited until a sufficient level of startup activity has taken hold. The sequencing of events matters a lot. And, there is no simple roadmap; we must be entrepreneurial about building entrepreneurial ecosystems.

ENTREPRENEURIAL SUCCESS

While many things can improve an entrepreneurial ecosystem, the most important are entrepreneurial successes that occur when new companies get created, grow, and ultimately generate liquidity for founders, employees, and shareholders through a company sale, IPO, or ongoing distributions from a profitable business. The subsequent actions of founders, employees, and local shareholders, especially the early investors, are critical. Do they go into retirement, or do they recycle and reinvest their time, expertise, and wealth into the next generation of founders? And are they generous and well-intentioned about it?

Entrepreneurial success accelerates the development of a startup community because it creates a positive feedback loop as founders, employees, and investors gain practical know-how for building high-impact businesses along with the wealth that results from success. In addition to money and experience, success produces inspiration to the broader community and future generations of entrepreneurs through living examples of what is possible.

COMMUNITY/ ECOSYSTEM FIT

The concept of product/market fit is used in early-stage entrepreneurship. Product/market fit occurs when a company has established a reliable customer base and revenue stream. Entrepreneurs know when they have achieved it because customers aggressively try to get a piece of what the company is selling. Product/market fit is a difficult concept to pindown objectively; you just know it when you see it. Once entrepreneurs achieve product/market fit, they can begin to think about how to scale their companies.[10]

Community/ecosystem fit is similar. In many places, before it occurs, a large portion of actors are not engaged with the startup community. A common refrain is that there are not enough high-quality companies. There is endless discussion about what to do, but little action occurs. A more unfortunate version of that story is, "Why should I care? All of the startups here suck." Our response is, "What are you doing to change that?"

Once successes begin to materialize—especially one or more big achievements—the startup community shifts into a new phase and becomes a resource attractor for the entire ecosystem. These successes draw in more people as participants, supporters, or observers.

Over time, a state change occurs where the startup community and the entrepreneurial ecosystem connect effectively. Once community/ecosystem fit is established, entrepreneurs will immediately recognize it because it feels just like product/market fit. Suddenly, the number of people who want to be a part of whatever is going on increases rapidly, with seemingly little effort. When a large percentage of potential actors in the startup community and the entrepreneurial ecosystem become activated, you have achieved community/ecosystem fit.

How First Establishing a Startup Community Propelled Madison's Entrepreneurial Ecosystem

Scott Resnick (Madison, Wisconsin)
Chief Operating Officer, Hardin Design & Development
Entrepreneur in Residence, StartingBlock Madison

Rome was not built in a day. The same is true for StartingBlock, a 50,000-square-foot community-innovation center that opened in 2018. StartingBlock is the nexus for entrepreneurial programming, investment capital, and mentorship in Wisconsin. It is more than an incubator or office space for young startups; it is also a bright beacon for how far our startup community has come in the last decade.

By mobilizing a critical mass of committed, entrepreneurial leaders into a tightly knit startup community, we were able to create a more productive entrepreneurial ecosystem over time. Today, it is producing high-growth startups, attracting outside capital, anchoring homegrown talent, and reshaping our economy.

Madison's Transformation

Madison hasn't always been a place for entrepreneurs. A robust research university and thousands of government employees (Madison is the state capital) anchors our city. It has a historically anti-business climate. Our community lacked an urgency to embrace disruptive new technologies. Sure, Madison has had a respectable presence of biotechnology activity, but the fast-moving software startups powering today's digital economy routinely fled to big cities.

Today, Madison is an emerging entrepreneurial hub.[11] We are flourishing with technical talent, startup density, and supportive community culture. Young companies have experienced explosive growth in our city of about 250,000 people. Startups are now choosing to stay in Madison rather than leave for Silicon Valley.

How did we move the proverbial needle?

Madison has had entrepreneurial successes in the past, but efforts to build a sustainable community with repeated successes are relatively new. A group of local entrepreneurs formed Capital Entrepreneurs in 2009. The ongoing mission is to unite entrepreneurs and provide a forum for sharing stories, discussing common problems, and rallying around shared agendas. Membership is free. Seven company founders attended the first meeting. Their struggles became a powerful bond, and the group now has more than 300 members. It is the connective tissue behind new meetup groups and startup community initiatives.

Startup vernacular is now the language of Madison's established business and civic leaders. All of this happened because a core group of committed, entrepreneurial leaders had the vision to make change happen from the bottom-up. Nobody was in charge, there was no central plan, and we had no significant financial backers. Instead, we had the desire to make Madison the best place it could be for entrepreneurs.

Turning StartingBlock into a Reality

By late 2012, a group of entrepreneurs, including myself, developed a plan to buy a building that would rent space to startups and co-locate entrepreneurial resources. We'd be founder-friendly, and our focus would be on building community and enabling the type of soft collisions among entrepreneurs that would catalyze more significant growth in the ecosystem.

We wanted more than a building. We wanted to create a central hub for entrepreneurs to explore new ideas and grow as individuals. We viewed this new space as a long-term piece of infrastructure to serve the Madison community and take it to the next level. StartingBlock would be an economic engine for the city.

We were a bit early, and our vision was unrealistic. The project required a hefty $10 million capital campaign. Fundraising was a challenge. Madison lacked the business climate, scale, and successful entrepreneurs who had built similar centers in bigger cities. Naysayers stoked opposition. Folks said the project was too ambitious and bet on its failure. We had no blueprint to guide the project; we were learning at every turn.

The project's magnitude required that we'd bring additional partners to the table. Local influencers started taking notice, and the community buzz eventually became positive. Instead of selecting influential figureheads for our board of directors, we created a board of volunteer "doers" who met weekly.

Three factors contributed to the eventual success of the project. First, the Madison startup community was, by then, big and cohesive enough to represent a formidable constituency that was committed to the project's success. Second, two ecosystem partners—the City of Madison and our local utility, Madison Gas & Electric—stepped up in a big way by establishing a public-private partnership to provide financial resources. Third, business leaders embraced the idea of supporting next-generation companies. American Family Insurance made a significant contribution by allowing StartingBlock to locate inside its new building in downtown Madison. That put us downstairs from the internal business development teams, social impact institute, and venture fund of one of the most innovative companies in the Fortune 500.

Looking back, I can say that StartingBlock's opening was at least a six-year community undertaking, and our early metrics look good. Gener8tor, a nationally recognized multi-city accelerator; Doyenne, an organization that supports venture growth for women entrepreneurs; and more than a dozen startup companies have moved into the space. Rock River Capital's $23 million venture capital fund is a tenant. The space will undoubtedly evolve, but the core constituency has already energized the local startup community.

Lessons Learned

If your community is inspired to build an innovation hub, there are several lessons you can learn from our experience. First, know that it takes time. It took a full decade for Madison to build the necessary critical mass required to support StartingBlock. Even if your public and private sectors are eager to jump on board, you need to make sure you have the startups and community to justify the project. There are less expensive ways to spur collaboration in ecosystems where startup communities are nascent, and there is a lack of entrepreneurial density. Pay for pizza at meetups. Provide inexpensive office space. Sponsor startup events. Think about having a connection and support authority (like Capital Entrepreneurs) up and running for a while; get a track record of producing value before committing to a capital-intensive physical space.

Entrepreneurs should be at the heart of your project. StartingBlock is committed to a by-entrepreneurs-for-entrepreneurs mentality. Entrepreneurs must be in the same room, working through their challenges together. Our strategic priorities came from individuals with firsthand experience inside the startup community. They knew the highs and lows of leading a startup.

Public and private sector partners played a critical but supporting role. Countless well-intentioned communities make the mistake of trying to catalyze their startup community from the top down. No! Entrepreneurs must lead. Missing this critical piece almost always results in project failure.

The needs of the entrepreneurial community came first. Our goals were aligned to build a great community and pay it forward to the next wave of startups. We did not let private agendas derail the project.

We have an expansive view of startups that goes beyond measuring success by the amount of venture capital raised. That's a trap. Some companies either take a different route for financing or use an alternative growth model. Some of the most successful entrepreneurs never raised a dime of venture capital.

Finally, I cannot stress enough the importance of Capital Entrepreneurs in establishing the social fabric of the Madison startup community first—something a building could never do. The entire organization still runs on a yearly budget of a few thousand dollars and hundreds of volunteer hours to keep the wheels turning. The payoff in community benefit is incalculable. Mutual trust among community leaders steadily built up over the years of regular meetings, planning events, and sharing the passion for making Madison a great place for startups. The organization provides new entrepreneurs with consistent access and connections to seasoned entrepreneurs. That doesn't happen overnight.

I'm regularly asked, "How do you reconcile Capital Entrepreneurs, an organization with an entrepreneur-only ethos, with the institutional and private-sector partners who financially contributed to StartingBlock?" It is an ongoing balancing act. Early on, some notable entrepreneurs were leery of feeders, and their concerns were warranted. We had to reject some corporate partners who threatened the center's mission. Still today, we prioritize the needs of founders. We never wanted to become too corporate, a regular failing of entrepreneurial support organizations elsewhere. To our sponsors' credit, the entrepreneurs have been able to shine. Our partners were continually listening to our needs and opened their influence. Our government and corporate partners were never in front of the project. Instead, they used their resources to amplify our successes once we reached a necessary maturity level.

StartingBlock is the capstone to this phase of Madison's transformation—it is not what started it. Principles, instead of a blueprint, guide our organization. The result is a powerful tool to amplify startups in south-central Wisconsin. Our new job is to deploy that tool well. We'll keep you posted.

PART II

STARTUP COMMUNITIES AS COMPLEX SYSTEMS

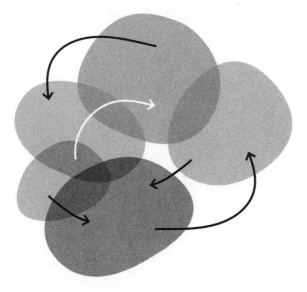

CHAPTER SIX

PUTTING THE SYSTEM BACK INTO ECOSYSTEM

Startup Community Way Principle

Openness, support, and collaboration are critical behaviors in a startup community. Collaboration is essential to a startup community. This requires an open mind, porous boundaries, acceptance of the uniqueness of others, and a sense of duty to support the startup community.

A startup community is best viewed and acted on through the lens of a system. While this may seem obvious, we frequently hear people refer to a "startup ecosystem" with one breath, and then with the next breath, suggest actions that are in direct conflict with how a system works. The *system* part of *ecosystem* is important, but it's treated too casually.

While the disconnect between systems language and systems practice is not intentional, a collective misunderstanding and lack of awareness about the systemic properties of startup communities inhibits progress and creates problems. Systems thinking is difficult in practice because it is often counterintuitive and runs against natural human desires to control things and avoid uncertainty.

Startup communities are complex adaptive systems—a particular type of system with nonlinear and dynamic properties that can easily confuse people. Over the next few chapters, we'll explain what that means, what the key characteristics of complex systems are, and how startup communities exhibit complex patterns. Most importantly, we will discuss the practical implications and strategies for effectively engaging with them.

INTRODUCTION TO SYSTEMS

A system is a group of entities that interact with each other to collectively produce something. Three elements—parts, interdependencies, and purpose—constitute the core of a system. You'll recognize them from the chapters in Part I, where we described each of these in a startup community: the parts (actors and factors), the interdependencies (networks of trust), and the purpose (communities versus ecosystems). Three additional system properties are particularly relevant here: boundaries, properties of scale, and dimensions of time.[1]

Systems boundaries can be open, closed, hard, or soft. In startup communities, we tend to stress boundaries based upon geography, typically at the level of a city or a metropolitan area or role (e.g., founders, non-founders). But boundaries exist around many other characteristics, such as industry, vertical, nationality, gender identity, or university affiliation.

Properties of scale refer to various subsystems and clusters that exist within larger systems. For startup communities, these may form around some of the boundary characteristics, while change at any scale can instigate broader changes across the whole system through mechanisms such as contagion (the spread of ideas, behaviors, norms) or attractors (actors clustering in one part of the system that get drawn to another cluster in another part of the system).

Finally, there is the dimension of time. Startup communities are dynamic systems that are continually evolving. Information flows and social cues prompt changes in behavior or thought patterns, which force further change in a perpetual loop of coevolution between the actors and the system as a whole. Substantial delays often occur between an action and when its effect manifests, which makes it extremely difficult to identify cause and effect. Time lags can present major challenges to the human mind.

THE WHOLE SYSTEM

The most effective way to engage with a highly interconnected system, such as a startup community, is with a holistic view. In startup communities, when solving a single problem in isolation, new problems are created. A reductionist or siloed approach provides minimal insight into what's really going on. Through this lens, good intentions can make things worse. A holistic approach, along with some humility, enables leaders to think deeply about which strategies and tactics will be the most beneficial.

The failure to take a holistic view is a fundamental challenge in startup communities. Often participants, especially feeders, undertake a narrow set of actions without fully considering the broader impact. Similarly, they fail to see how the activity around them is fundamentally affecting what they do and how they think.[2]

People focus on what's directly in front of them—their startup, organization, relationships, or agenda. While it is perfectly understandable why this occurs, it ends up causing them to miss the bigger picture. They don't look deeper to see what gave rise to the problem they're solving in the first place, why the same challenges tend to reappear, or how a proposed course of action will lead to other actions, reactions, or unintended consequences. The cliché "can't see the forest for the trees" applies.

People are busy and driven by accomplishing what they deem most important. Even the most generous people are inherently self-interested. A classic example of this is when entrepreneurial support organizations proliferate in a city, often with overlapping missions and funding sources.[3] Rather than finding ways to become more collaborative, they become competitive. As a group, efforts overlap or even cancel each other out, and the startup community benefits less than it otherwise could.

Humans are predisposed to reduce problems into discrete situations that can be solved analytically one at a time. We favor answers over questions, prefer confidence over doubts, and we tend to see the world narrowly through our own experience. We propose familiar solutions or ones that we have an existing capability to address. Another cliché, "When the only tool you have is a hammer, everything looks like a nail," applies here.

In the ancient parable of "The Blind Men and the Elephant," a group of blind men encounter an elephant for the first time. They each touch a different part of the animal. Based on their limited, individual understanding, they have little agreement about what constitutes an elephant. They miss the bigger picture. With a faulty mental model working in the back of their minds, they each engage with the elephant in very different ways—pursuing different agendas with varying goals in mind.

The Parable of The Blind Men and the Elephant

Many participants approach startup communities in the same way. Too often, they pursue limited agendas based on their frame of reference without considering the broader impact of their actions or the overall needs of the community. But individual actions don't exist in a vacuum. In complex systems, all of these things are happening simultaneously. They are jointly determined. The non-obvious solution is often a better one while the obvious solution can make the situation worse or create an entirely new problem.

Hierarchical organizations, such as universities, corporations, and governments, have a particularly hard time thinking holistically. People representing these institutions tend to see problems in startup communities through the lens of what their organization does, and, as a result, seek to impose solutions in a controlled manner. These organizations are typically structured by departments and product lines, which feeds the tendency to take a reductionist rather than an expansive view.

History is littered with failed attempts to control human systems. These setbacks lead to fatigue, which then causes us to abandon worthy pursuits. Against this backdrop, we take reductionist views of the system and only see the problems we understand. We fear the unknown and try to avoid it.

This approach doesn't work with a complex system. When viewing the problems as discrete and the solutions as cleanly solvable, the focus becomes much too narrow and turns into the challenge of seeing only the trees while missing the forest.

The collapse of the Internet bubble in 2001 surprised the majority of entrepreneurs and investors. By 2004, deep in what many were calling a "nuclear winter," articles were written about the end of entrepreneurship and Silicon Valley. Two decades later, it's evident that using the dot-com revolution to define entrepreneurship was the wrong approach. This reductionist perspective missed the foundational, holistic impact that the Internet was having on business and society. For entrepreneurs who had a holistic view, the period following the dot-com bust was one of economic stress combined with dramatic and continuous technological innovation. Try to imagine society today if Google had decided that this Internet thing was just not lucrative, or if Mark Zuckerberg had never bothered starting Facebook because entrepreneurship was dead.

A contemporary example of holistic thinking is found in the approach Mark Suster and his firm Upfront Ventures took in helping evolve the Los Angeles startup community. A decade ago, many perceived LA as a small, relatively unimportant startup community. Mark and his partners at GRP Partners rebranded the firm Upfront Ventures in 2013 and began a concerted effort to amplify, publicize, and evolve the LA startup community.

Mark was unapologetically bold about the awesomeness going on in LA. He started an annual Upfront Summit that was inclusive of all LA entrepreneurs, bringing venture capitalists and limited partners from around the country to LA for a two-day event showcasing everything going on in the region. By approaching the problem holistically, rather than attempting to solve one particular issue or to control things, Upfront dramatically accelerated the LA startup community while at the same time building an international brand for the firm.

Seeing the whole system and engaging startup communities with a whole-systems view is not easy. As we're about to describe, it's even more complicated than that. It's "complex."

Robert Noyce, Mao Zedong, and the Law of Unintended Consequences

In 1957, a group of eight Silicon Valley executives led by Robert Noyce resigned from famed Shockley Semiconductor to start a rival company, Fairchild Semiconductor. This sort of thing happens all the time in Silicon Valley today, but at that time, it wasn't common. This watershed moment sent reverberations throughout the region. The "Traitorous Eight," as they became known, changed the course of innovation forever by injecting the area with an entrepreneurial ethos that continues to this day and has made Silicon Valley the envy of the world.

Around the same time, nearly 6,000 miles (~10,000 kilometers) away, a very different type of revolution was taking place in Communist China. In 1958, Communist Party Chairman Mao Zedong launched the Great Leap Forward, a wide-sweeping series of economic and political reforms aimed at transitioning China from an agricultural economy to an industrialized one, and at consolidating power behind the communist regime.

One of the first initiatives was the Four Pests Campaign, an effort to eradicate insect, rodent, and avian populations thought to be threatening the health and well-being of the Chinese people. Birds, and in particular, the tree sparrow, were the most aggressively targeted because they fed on human grain and fruit supplies. The sparrow, it was feared, would cause starvation of the Chinese people.

The campaign worked—pushing the tree sparrow nearly to extinction in less than two years. The result? The disruption of a delicate ecological system that contributed to the Great Chinese Famine of 1959–1961, killing an estimated 15 to 30 million people.

What went wrong?

By eradicating the tree sparrow, the Chinese government exacerbated the very problem they were trying to solve.

It turns out that not only do tree sparrows eat grains targeted for human consumption, but they also feed on insects that have an even more detrimental impact on crops. With a critical predator out of the way, the insect population swelled, and grain supplies collapsed. This system feedback is how the eradication of the tree sparrow contributed to widespread famine. The policy was terminated in 1960 when it became clear what a disaster it had been.

So, how is the Great Chinese Famine and the essence of Silicon Valley's entrepreneurial spirit connected? Beyond their nearly simultaneous occurrence, they are both lessons in the law of unintended consequences, which are common in complex systems like startup communities.

The Chinese government took a heavy-handed, top-down approach to preserve food supplies and created a much bigger problem by not thinking systemically. They unleashed a destructive feedback loop that killed millions.

By contrast, the Traitorous Eight took the seemingly isolated and inconsequential decision of escaping a misguided (and reportedly tyrannical) William Shockley to create something better for themselves. And yet, what it helped spark was a new way of doing technology business in the modern era. It's hard to believe their immediate plan was to transform the regional business culture—one now emulated globally to promote innovation-driven entrepreneurship. But that's what happened, with or without their intentions.

The lesson for startup communities is that you might not know if a proposed course of action will produce famine or feast. Trial and error, informed intuition, plenty of humility, and a desire to learn from mistakes should determine the course of action. Take a measured approach first and see what works and what doesn't. Learn, adapt, and change course as needed. The biggest successes often come from small decisions driven by an idea to try doing something already being done, but better.

SIMPLE, COMPLICATED, AND COMPLEX ACTIVITIES

In an excellent guide to identifying and navigating complexity in the business world, *It's Not Complicated: The Art and Science of Complexity in Business*, management professor Rick Nason provides a useful framework for grasping the defining characteristics of complexity.[4] He asks three questions about any workplace task, to which we've added a fourth question, which he implies.

1. Is a successful outcome easily and objectively definable?
2. Are the resources and procedures for achieving a successful outcome well understood?
3. Are many steps involved, and does the process require coordination of efforts?
4. Is exactness in execution required, or are inputs and processes somewhat flexible?

You'll notice the words *complicated* and *complexity* in Nason's title. These words are often inappropriately interchanged, similar to how many conflate *communities* and *ecosystems*. While complicated and complex might be synonymous for most people, to a systems scientist, these are vastly different things. The best way to explain their differences is through a discussion of three types of activities: simple, complicated, and complex.

To illustrate the differences between simple, complicated, and complex, let's use three examples from Nason's book—making a pot of coffee, preparing financial statements, and executing a high-profile sales call. These are three everyday activities in business settings and should be familiar to everyone reading this book.

Brewing coffee is a simple activity. A successful outcome is well-defined since the result is either coffee or not; whether it tastes good is another matter. The process of making coffee requires just a few simple steps to follow, which one person with little to no experience can easily carry out with the right instructions. The set of procedures is robust, which means that portioning coffee grounds, water, and heat doesn't require exactitude—approximations will still more or less produce a pot of coffee.

Preparing financial statements is a complicated activity. Like the simple process of making coffee, the preparation of financial statements has a generally accepted definition of success: to comply with accounting regulations. For this activity, there is also a well-defined set of procedures to follow: the accounting rules and regulations.

There are two key differences that make preparing financial statements complicated instead of simple. The first is the number of steps required. Making coffee involves a handful of steps while preparing financial statements requires many. The second difference concerns the level of precision required when carrying out the tasks. When making coffee, approximations are okay, but when preparing financial statements, estimations may produce a result that is incorrect or exposes the company to legal liability.

Because of these differences, producing financial statements requires considerably more expertise, training, certification, the coordination of more tasks, and likely, a team of people. Pretty much anyone can make coffee, and it only requires one person to do it.

While there are differences, the two activities both have objectively achievable outcomes. The problems they present are solvable, there is a high degree of control over results, and a clear set of procedures to get there. Once the procedures have been mapped out, the outcomes are predictable and replicable, which are core features of linear processes.

A high-profile sales call shares none of these characteristics. In this situation, there is no objectively definable measure of success. A successful outcome varies depending on factors ranging from the participants, stage in the sales cycle, and expectations about sales goals, all the way down to more mundane ones such as what time of day the call occurred, or how much sleep the participants got the night before. A sales call with an influential customer doesn't involve a few simple steps or the mastery of a lengthy handbook. Instead, it requires an unknowable number of actions with the input of multiple team members. It's difficult or impossible to identify the decisive success factors in advance.

Consequently, the process isn't codifiable, and if it were, repeating it wouldn't produce the same result. The solution is typically non-obvious at the outset and only becomes apparent after the fact, if ever. Uncertainty is high, and a team of the best people won't guarantee a positive result, although they will increase the probability of it. A process of trial-and-error, and probably some luck and timing, is the only path forward.

These characteristics are what make a high-profile sales call a complex activity, which is an example of a nonlinear process. They are entirely different to deal with than simple and complicated activities. As Jonathan Fentzke, a scientist who runs the Techstars Allied Space Accelerator, once said to Ian, "The fundamental question about a system is whether it is linear. If it is, then it is easy to control. If it's nonlinear, it is teetering on the edge of disaster at all times."

These three examples of workplace activities are being carried out daily in businesses everywhere. The managers and professionals conducting these activities are likely doing so without much thought to the more in-depth requirements we outlined above. But a systems thinker sees these things differently. As Nason writes:

> There is nothing special about these tasks, and in fact they might be considered to be rather mundane. However, each of these tasks involves varying degrees of complication and complexity and requires differing levels of knowledge, skill, and expertise. A scientist thinks of each task as a type of system, while an engineer would likely draw a process flow map for each. A manager, however, goes about each of the tasks without consciously thinking about any of this. It is time for the manager to think a bit more consciously about the differences, as the scientist and the engineer do.[5]

Now replace the word "manager" with "entrepreneur" or "startup community builder." It's time for all of us to become systems thinkers.

MOVING FROM ACTIVITIES TO SYSTEMS

As with workplace activities, there are three types of systems: simple, complicated, and complex. (Chaotic systems are a fourth, but we'll leave those out since they have limited application here.) When we were explaining simple, complicated, and complex activities, we were actually describing three types of systems—each with parts, interdependencies, and a purpose.

Simple systems contain a limited number of elements and follow a straightforward script or set of actions. They require little to no expertise to understand, and they produce highly predictable outcomes. If people follow a straightforward set of instructions, they can reliably produce a desired outcome that can be repeated many times with a similar result. Examples of simple systems include baking a cake, unlocking a car door, and yes, brewing a pot of coffee.

Complicated systems involve more elements and subsystems, additional steps, a more considerable effort for planning and execution, a need for tighter control and integration, and stricter requirements for technical and managerial expertise. In spite of these challenges, complicated systems are predictable and result in controllable and replicable outcomes. Examples of complicated systems include landing a spacecraft on the moon, designing and assembling a car, and, yes, preparing financial statements.

Simple and complicated systems are examples of linear systems. Though complicated systems require more knowledge and expertise to manage, once a successful outcome and set of procedures have been determined, each is fairly controllable, predictable, and replicable. Changes to inputs or processes produce predictable outcomes, because cause and effect relationships are well-understood.

Complex systems are entirely different. They are all around us—traffic, families, the human body, cities, financial markets, and countless others. Complexity is everywhere, and yet we still have difficulty grasping the nature of complexity and adjusting our behavior and thought patterns to navigate it appropriately. Human intuition grapples with many complex situations, but we too often revert reflexively to our analytical brain, which isn't suited for handling complexity.[6]

Our failure to embrace the realities of complexity is driven in part by our innate desire to avoid uncertainty and to be in control. Humans want to understand and solve problems. Simple and complicated systems are well suited to these natural human impulses. Large organizations, such as universities, corporations, and governments, are designed with a complicated world in mind. Their top-down, hierarchical structure and management style is reflective of this. But most of our society is complex. So are startup communities.

A Comparison of Simple, Complicated, and Complex Systems

Simple	Complicated	Complex
Few elements; few if any layers and subsystems	More elements, layers, and subsystems	Many interconnected elements, layers, and subsystems
Little expertise required	More expertise required	Diversity of talents valued over expertise
Easily knowable and predictable	Challenging but still knowable and predictable	Not fully knowable, prediction is limited, and context is important
Easily controlled and replicated	Difficult but ultimately controllable	Cannot be controlled; only influenced and guided
A successful outcome is well-defined and replicable	A successful outcome is well-defined and replicable	A successful outcome is not clearly defined; replication is not applicable
Top-down with little need for precision	Top-down; precision is critical	Primarily bottom-up; precision is pointless

Simple	Complicated	Complex
Easily created	Can be engineered	Self-organized and emergent; cannot be engineered
Linear	Linear	Nonlinear
Mechanical	Mechanical	Evolutionary
Examples: Baking a cake Automobile key	*Examples*: Spaceship Automobile engine	*Examples*: Workplace culture Automobile traffic

If you have ever tried to shape company culture, you will intuitively understand a complex system. Corporations spend many resources creating policies on what company culture should be. They almost always take a top-down approach, and often enlist the help of high-priced consultants. These policies are then handed down by executives who expect employees to adhere to them. Many efforts to change company culture don't work because they apply a complicated system mindset onto what is an inherently complex system. Often, the values are the wrong ones, and the executives don't live by them. It's no surprise when the employees don't, either.

Instead, companies should focus on defining their cultural norms, not the culture itself. A more productive process involves soliciting input from employees at all levels and across all departments, convening multiple stakeholders, finding and supporting activities that are already working organically, and resisting the temptation to always do something new. Once the cultural norms surface, leaders in the company must be a living embodiment of them. Instead of providing a step-by-step manual for how to behave, companies should set some high-level values and be sure that every leader or manager exemplifies these cultural norms. Ultimately, as the venture capitalist Ben Horowitz explains, "What you do is who you are."[7]

Viewing startup communities as complex systems, rather than complicated ones, opens up a new approach for interacting, engaging with, and improving them. Analogies from other complex systems can help us understand and improve the practice of startup community building.

These analogies include why navigating traffic in London or Los Angeles can be so unpredictable, why gatherings of dysfunctional families can quickly spiral out of control, or why efforts to reduce crime by increasing policing are often ineffective, or more likely, counterproductive.

Throughout the next several chapters, we'll explore key concepts and implications of complexity in theory and practice. But before we begin, let's hear from law professor Brad Bernthal, who describes how the New Venture Challenge at the University of Colorado Boulder embraces a holistic view among the broader university and Boulder startup community.

How the New Venture Challenge Embraces the Startup Community Way

Brad Bernthal (Boulder, Colorado)
Associate Professor of Law, Colorado Law School
Director, Silicon Flatirons Center's Entrepreneurship Initiative, University of Colorado

There's the thing we think we're going to do, then there's the thing we do. One of life's joys is when the actual thing we do far exceeds what we thought we would do.

In 2008, I joined a grassroots, volunteer group of faculty, staff, and students that launched a fledgling New Venture Challenge (NVC) at the University of Colorado. A decade later, I found myself on stage before 600 people at the Boulder Theater for the NVC 10 Championships. The NVC 10 offered $125,000 in prizes and showcased an exceptional class of startups from all corners of the campus. The championships were so inspiring that—while I was on stage—community members yelled out from the audience to pledge $200,000 of support for NVC 11. I've never seen anything like it.

The NVC has become a bigger powerhouse than I ever imagined. We started with a way to help the next generation of entrepreneurs on campus. What resulted was an engine to engage the entire startup community of Colorado's Front Range (in this context, the axis of cities lining the eastern slope of the Rocky Mountains). Four perspectives explain the impact of the CU NVC on the campus as well as the broader Boulder startup community.

1. **The NVC complements other elements of the Boulder startup community.** As a pre-accelerator program, the NVC situates well among Boulder's many other startup offerings, including a bevy of accelerator programs that serve serious startups with full-time founders. The NVC provides a platform to help entrepreneurs that are beyond early ideation or the mere exposure to entrepreneurship but are not yet ready for the full entrepreneurial plunge of an accelerator. This pre-accelerator model works exceptionally well on a campus where faculty and staff have day jobs, and students have classes to attend.

2. **The NVC is inclusive.** The program kicks off each September at the outset of the academic year. Any startup can participate as long as at least one core company member is a current CU student, staff member, or faculty member. During the fall semester, the NVC helps entrepreneurs form teams, provides mentors, and directs startups to relevant campus resources and classes. During the spring semester, the NVC offers workshops to help participating startups test and develop startup ideas, provides experts to help teams improve their pitches, and culminates with the campus's NVC Championship competition in April. The NVC's top teams regularly go on to participate in Techstars Boulder, iCorps, and other high-profile startup programs.

3. **The NVC breaks down silos.** Our program serves as an entry point for the Boulder startup community to get involved in a campus-wide activity. University bureaucracies frustrate efforts to match community talent with areas of campus need. The NVC resolves many of these challenges between town and gown. A pool of 75 or so entrepreneurs, investors, and service providers volunteer as NVC mentors.

Furthermore, the nature of NVC participants—self-selected, highly motivated, creative, and hardworking—makes the NVC fertile recruiting ground for emerging companies looking to recruit motivated and creative students. Finally, the NVC Championships offer an end-of-year, community-facing party to celebrate campus entrepreneurship. The NVC showcases the campus's best entrepreneurs in a public forum and annually provides a highly visible and inspired answer to the question, "What is the university doing to promote entrepreneurship?"

4. **The NVC reflects the interdisciplinary nature of entrepreneurship and innovation,** highlighting entrepreneurship across the full campus. Instead of being housed within any one department or school, a diverse team of campus leaders—including the campus's Research and Innovation Office, the Leeds Business School, Engineering, Music, technology transfer, and Silicon Flatirons Center in the Law School—pitch in to run the NVC. This collaboration gives the NVC a presence within most buildings on campus. As a result, NVC participants come from a wide swath of departments and majors. These participants have a sense that teams work best when multiple skill sets and diverse

backgrounds are involved. Moreover, as mentors and others from the community help the NVC, they work with a platform that engages the full campus, not just a single group.

These four elements—(1) being complementary to rather than substituting for what's already working in the startup community, (2) being inclusive of everyone on campus, (3) breaking down the embedded silos within the university, and (4) respecting the interdisciplinary nature of entrepreneurship—have guided the success of the NVC program.

CHAPTER SEVEN

UNPREDICTABLE CREATIVITY

Startup Community Way Principle

Startup communities are complex adaptive systems that emerge from the interaction of the participants. Understanding and embracing complex systems and how they operate is essential to building a vibrant, long-term startup community. Principally among these is an understanding that value is created by the emergent processes that result from the repeated interactions of the many parts.

A startup community is a complex adaptive system of many interdependent actors (people and organizations) that are continuously acting and reacting with each other and with their environment (resources and conditions).[1] This perpetual loop of action and reaction means that a startup community is in a constant state of change, as the system and its constituent parts coevolve.

The interactions between the actors and factors define the startup community. But this interconnectedness introduces complexity because the actors have the freedom to pursue individual agendas, learn from the behaviors and ideas of others, and adapt their actions and thought patterns as a result. Since actors lack complete information and visibility into the whole startup community, imperfect decisions are pervasive. This gets multiplied as each ill-informed decision is passed along throughout the system, occurring continuously, while the actors and the system coevolve.

The lack of awareness about how complex systems function is a source of many errors in startup communities. Influencing a highly interconnected complex system requires a radically different approach from the typical top-down, isolated efforts that are pervasive in much of our professional, personal, and civic lives.

Insights from complexity theory, an interdisciplinary science developed to explain the dynamics of physical, biological, social, and information networks around us, can dramatically improve startup communities. The origins of complexity science begin with the work of mathematician Warren Weaver in the late-1940s.[2] The discipline was formalized and accelerated by a revolutionary group of physicists, evolutionary biologists, and social scientists through the creation of the Santa Fe Institute in the 1980s.[3]

A system exists where a set of individual entities connect in such a way that they create a collective pattern of behavior over time.[4] This coordinated behavior produces collective outcomes as a whole that wouldn't exist if the individual entities had functioned in isolation.[5]

A system becomes complex when there are many such entities, called agents or actors in our framework, with varying individual and collective motivations, and a seemingly infinite number of connections and subsystems. A complex system is adaptive when the agents learn, modify behavior, and react to the behavior of others. Such behavior is prevalent in all evolutionary human social systems, including startup communities.

Both the system and the actors are in a perpetual state of coevolution. You don't solve a complex system. It never finishes. It is permanently unfolding, the work is never complete, and there is no objective definition of success.

Cities, financial markets, rainforests, ant colonies, the human brain, the geopolitical order, and the Internet are complex systems. Each has many moving parts, an intricate web of interactions among them, and a constant state of evolution that occurs between the individual components and the system as a whole. But that's just the beginning.

EMERGENCE

The defining characteristic of a complex system is emergence, which has a double meaning here. Traditionally, *emergence*, rooted in the Latin term *emergere*, which means "rise out or up, bring forth, bring to light," refers to the process of coming into being or existence; to surface or appear.[6]

Emergence is also a process where the integration of individual system parts produces patterns and value in ways that can't be anticipated or fully understood, even with a perfect understanding of the different components.[7] Science author Steven Johnson describes emergence as "unpredictable creativity."[8]

Emergence conceptualizes the process of value creation and pattern formation in complex systems produced by the autonomous interactions of a system's parts. What emerges from this evolutionary process of actions and reactions is a semi-organized form with non-random and discernable patterns that are substantially different and more valuable than a summation of the parts. Unique properties, combinations, and outcomes occur that cannot be anticipated *ex-ante* (in advance) or replicated *ex-post* (after the fact). Emergence is a process of creation that is present in physical, biological, social, and information systems everywhere.[9]

Entrepreneurship itself is an emergent system, where companies create the conditions for experimentation and learning to occur, often symbiotically with customers. In 1978, Eric von Hippel (my PhD advisor at MIT) pioneered the notion of user-driven innovation.[10, 11] Back then, the conventional wisdom was that innovation only came from corporate, government, and university research-and-development labs. While some still believe this today, Eric's insight proved to be prescient in many areas, especially in the information age, as the widespread adoption of open-source software and Lean Startup methodologies have demonstrated.[12] Twitter is a tangible example since three of the platform's most popular features—the @ reply, the # hashtag indexing, and retweet sharing—were all generated bottom-up by users.[13]

In *Startup Communities*, I described the emergence of Boulder's startup community, which follows this pattern. No one designed it, nor was it created by the university or the top-down design of federal government labs in town. Instead, it emerged bottom-up from the entrepreneurs, who are the ultimate users of the Boulder startup community. It unfolded in a way that a central command couldn't design, plan, or execute.

Emergence has three hallmark characteristics: synergistic integration, nonlinear behavior, and self-organization. These and a fourth property of complex systems, dynamic evolution, are discussed in the next few sections.

SYNERGIES AND NONLINEARITY

The interaction of individual elements produces unique patterns and is the source of value in emergent systems. Through these interactions, the whole system becomes greater than and different from the sum of the parts. Complex systems don't just produce more of something; they create things that are inherently different from what could have occurred had the individual elements existed in isolation. These occurrences are known as *synergies*, a word that is derived from the Greek term *sunergos*, which means "working together."[14]

In a startup community, the interactions between participants produce synergies that have value and location-specific characteristics. Reducing startup communities to their constituent parts provides a minimal understanding of the system and presents an incorrect impression of what is really going on or where value comes from.

Synergistic integration also produces nonlinearities in a complex system. A nonlinear system is one where changes in output are not proportional to changes in input, which can result in a delightful concept called increasing returns, where things grow geometrically or exponentially.

In addition to being disproportionate, inputs and outputs are often not directly correlated in complex systems. Consequently, accurately linking cause and effect between actions and outcomes is difficult. As humans, we naturally want to embrace control and reject doubt, so we try to solve, understand, and predict things around us, even when doing so isn't reflective of reality. Nonlinearities confound us in the present moment but become more evident over time—something that has become abundantly clear as the pace and breadth of the COVID-19 coronavirus pandemic currently sweeping the globe has left many people flat-footed and slow to adapt.

An example from Boulder is the concentration of entrepreneurial activity in downtown starting around 2007. Up until that point, there were several areas located throughout Boulder County (including the neighboring towns of Superior, Louisville, and Broomfield), where traditional office parks, with fancy names like Interlocken Advanced Technology Environment, had been built. There was no physical center to the startup community, and the entrepreneurial density of the region was low.

Around 2007, several things happened. Foundry Group relocated to downtown Boulder. Techstars opened its first accelerator two blocks away. The St Julien, the first new hotel in Boulder in 100 years, had opened two years earlier a few doors down. Several startups, including Rally Software, moved downtown and grew briskly. The Global Financial Crisis of

2007–2008 resulted in landlords being more flexible, given their lack of traditional tenants, which allowed startups to start collecting in downtown Boulder. Several professors at CU Boulder, including Phil Weiser and Brad Bernthal, made a concerted effort to engage the Boulder startup community, regularly leaving campus to participate in activities and events in downtown, which was a mere five-minute drive from campus.

By 2010, entrepreneurial energy and activity packed the 5-by-10-block area of downtown Boulder. When you wandered around, you felt like you were on a university campus, continually running into other entrepreneurs on your journey from your office to lunch. The entrepreneurial density went through the roof.

For a small city like Boulder, this concentration of startups in a small downtown area was a nonlinearity in the development of the startup community. Exponential growth of startup activity happened, with the ratio of outputs to inputs far exceeding what it had in the past, often in unexpected, unpredictable, and exciting new ways. The whole was undoubtedly much greater than the sum of the parts, and with myriad things simultaneously occurring, it's impossible to untangle cause and effect—especially in advance of how things unfolded.

SELF-ORGANIZATION

Complex systems self-organize as broader patterns emerge from many interactions throughout the system. An ordered or semi-ordered form, as opposed to a disorganized or completely random form, appears organically from the bottom-up. There is no king, boss, or CEO of a complex system. Examples of such systems in nature include schools of fish, flocks of birds, and insect colonies, where organisms take biological and chemical cues to coordinate behavior in a collectively useful way, rather than carrying out explicit orders from a central authority.

Self-organization in the social sciences, as in startup communities, is often referred to as spontaneous order. Under such conditions, patterns emerge, but not in an intentional or planned way, organized in network structures that exhibit power-law distributions, whereby a small number of actors have an outsized influence on the overall system.[15] Organizations, on the other hand, tend to be structured into hierarchies. Complex systems cannot be structured or controlled hierarchically—they must be able to emerge in a spontaneous, self-organized way. Efforts to force creation within these systems fail because they don't allow for the natural process of self-organization, which signals what is useful and what is not, to take place.

Nonlinearities, feedback loops, and synergies drive self-organization.[16] Complex systems are continually evolving and, in spite of this instability, evolve toward one or more sticky states. These attractor dynamics explain why a change in complex systems—specifically a structural change—can require long time cycles.

Startup communities organize in the form of networks of human relationships, which are themselves organized into clusters and subgroups. This organization occurs along many dimensions, including in the roles individuals or other entities play, the activities they engage with, or their relative stature in the community. System structure will often coalesce around influential actors in a startup community. The formation of patterns in complex systems is not centrally planned, and attempts to control or coerce them only serve to undermine the system.

DYNAMISM

A dynamic system is one that changes. These changes produce additional changes, which themselves produce more change. Complex systems are in a state of constant transformation as the parts and the whole co-evolve. In addition to being nonlinear, the inputs and outputs change simultaneously.

Changes in inputs produce changes in outputs, but changes in outputs also produce changes in inputs, resulting in a feedback loop. Feedback loops are a constant force in startup communities and are a source of both complexity and value creation.

The adaptive nature of complex systems is a big part of what separates them from other systems. Take the example of setting a system-wide schedule for a major airline. There are thousands of aircraft, airports, flight paths, and flight crews to coordinate, generating hundreds of thousands of combinations. This problem is not conceptually difficult, but it is incredibly complicated because of the sheer number of possibilities.[17] Even so, solving its "combinatorial complexity" is possible through an engineering approach called linear programming.[18]

Setting airline schedules is a very complicated problem. It requires substantial algorithms, computing power, specialized software, and skilled people to put the whole thing together. It also requires accommodating the right margin of error that could result from equipment failure and weather disruptions. These are challenging problems, but they are still parts of an optimization problem nonetheless, and one that is ultimately solvable and repeatable.

Now imagine if the pilots all went rogue and decided they would depart whenever they felt like it, or more likely, they became more interested in departing when interest grew from other pilots. Then, let's say the pilots would follow whatever flight path they wanted to. Some pilots would say they would fly to one place, then go to another. Suppose the various airport authorities randomly reassigned arrivals, and several closed their airports entirely and went out for beers to celebrate the chaos. Algorithms, in this case, would be useless because the solution cannot be determined. There is no optimization problem to solve when the system lacks control. The behavior of the pilots has caused a complicated system to become a complex one (possibly even chaotic). You cannot unravel this "dynamic complexity" with engineering and models.[19] Applying systems thinking, which would look for high-leverage interventions to encourage greater cooperation, is the only approach that works.[20]

Feedback delays make complex systems even more challenging. Problems exist long before we become aware of them, and improvements occur well in advance of when we notice their impact. There are delays between when something is known and when we take a new course of action. Fortunately, the field of systems dynamics, created by Jay Forrester at MIT in the 1950s, helps us understand and navigate feedback loops and delays.[21]

The dimension of time is a major confounding factor in complex systems. Past and present conditions heavily influence current and future states—a phenomenon known as path dependency. Because of this, meaningful change can take a long time to occur. The stock of existing people, ideas, and behavior quickly absorbs the flow of new ones. When change occurs over long time periods, we struggle to process these dynamics.

Rich Jolly, a business professor and systems thinker, describes this with several examples:

> Humans have a lot of difficulty understanding processes that encompass very long time periods. For many years people did not understand that the Grand Canyon was etched by the flow of a river. This is primarily because people could not comprehend that such a massive structure could be formed over very long time periods by the flow of what seems, in scale to the structure, a very small amount of water. Similarly, it was not until the late 1800s that Darwin was finally able to understand biological evolution. Again, this is at least partly due to the long, in relation to a human life span, time periods involved.[22]

Our ancestors were programmed to think in the now—doing so helped keep them safe.[23] Why plan for tomorrow if something is trying to eat you today? Resisting long-term thinking is a biological response hardwired in our brains.[24] And as much as many startup communities are looking for quick fixes, it takes at least a generation for meaningful change to firmly take hold. Remember that Silicon Valley didn't unfold overnight—it is more than a century in the making.[25]

When I wrote *Startup Communities* in 2012, Boulder, and the Boulder Thesis, became a model for other startup communities around the world. However, since then, the Boulder startup community has continued to evolve at a rapid rate. Today, in 2020, many of the same participants are still visible, but some of the leaders from 2012 have faded from view. New leaders have emerged to take their places. Some of the activities and events that were predominant at the time still occur regularly, others have disappeared, and new ones have emerged.

Let's use two examples: CU Boulder and me. In 2012, I was very visible in Boulder. Once a month, I did what I called a random day, when I'd fill my day meeting with anyone for 15 minutes. I was a mentor for the Techstars Boulder program. I participated in Boulder Startup Week, was a regular speaker at Silicon Flatirons events, and showed up at least once a month at a different startup event. When new people came to Boulder, I tried to meet with all of them, and, if I couldn't, I made introductions to some other leaders in the Boulder startup community.

Today, my relationship with the Boulder startup community is different. I'm still visible, I periodically show up at events, and I continue to be extremely active online with anyone who wants to engage. However, my physical presence is substantially different because I'm in Boulder less than one-third of the time. I no longer do random days in person (I burned out on this after a decade and decided to take a break), and I spend my Techstars time across the global Techstars system, rather than just in Boulder.

However, the Boulder startup community is stronger than ever. A new generation of leaders emerged. The entrepreneurial density is significantly higher than it was in 2012. Connections between Boulder and Denver are remarkable, with the two cities emulating a construct similar to a binary star.[26] New entrepreneurs, companies, and activities are continually emerging. The shift in my behavior and presence hasn't inhibited the development of the Boulder startup community. In fact, I'd assert that since I let go, it has evolved more quickly and in more exciting ways.

The relationship between CU Boulder and the Boulder Startup Community has also evolved since 2012. At the time, the primary link between the two came from an unusual place in a university—the law school. Phil Weiser (now Attorney General of Colorado) and Brad Bernthal (still a professor at CU Boulder Law) played leadership roles, beginning a transformation of the relationship between CU Boulder and the Boulder startup community. They extended this leadership through CU Boulder as Brad Bernthal's sidebar on the New Venture Challenge hinted at, which engaged others from within CU Boulder to play leadership roles. Over time, the structural dynamics at CU Boulder began to change, and today the dynamics between CU Boulder and the Boulder startup community are stronger than they have ever been.

THE STUDY OF INTERACTIONS

Emergence, and its components, arise from interactions that are part of the magic of a complex system. Putting energy into the interactions between the parts of a system has more impact than putting energy into the parts themselves. These interactions give rise to emergence, which produces unexpected outcomes and requires unanticipated solutions to create these outcomes.[27] For this reason, investigating complex systems is aptly referred to as "the study of interactions."[28]

Since synergies are a primary source of value creation in a complex system, the interaction of the components in the system is the whole point. Many startup community efforts miss this. Instead of paying attention to the interactions, efforts focus on the individual parts. It feels like you are making progress since the number of inputs, like financial capital, university entrepreneurship programs, or startup accelerators, increases. Something measurable is happening, so that must be good.

This error in thinking is understandable because the parts are easier to see or change than the interactions. The parts are tangible. Meanwhile, human behavior, thought patterns, and social norms are intangible—and they are what drive the interactions. To envision this, think of the set of entrepreneurs, investors, talent, capital, workspaces, and other actors and factors as fixed in the short term. By focusing on better interactions between actors while working with the inputs already in place, you'll attract more resources over time and enter into a virtuous cycle where the size and vibrancy of the startup community can expand and evolve. This attracts more of the inputs and outputs you may be seeking.

Far too often, people point to a deficiency, perceived or real, of venture capital as the prime culprit for what is ailing the development of their startup community. While there will always be an imbalance between the supply of money and the demand for it, some capital formation initiatives can improve conditions on the margin.[29] Still, the underlying challenge persists, and complaining about it won't help. A more productive strategy for entrepreneurs is to concentrate on something they can control—building a great business around a problem they are obsessed with solving.

By complaining about capital, startup community participants are not grappling with the realities of complexity. Focusing obsessively on a lack of money reduces the constraints faced by the startup community to a single factor, when in fact many factors affect the startup community simultaneously. Even if there was only one factor holding back a startup community, obsession about capital assumes that this is the culprit, instead of many others. It further implies that the solution is external to the system, removing responsibility for current conditions on one's community. Finally, it ignores the practical reality that capital tends to follow investible companies, not the other way around.

Many startup communities around the world fall into the trap of "if only we had more capital, or investors, or entrepreneurs, or people interested in entrepreneurship, or . . ." Instead of playing this recording over and over, get everyone into a room and ask the question, "What are we going to do differently with the resources we currently have?"

The evolution of the Portland startup community exemplifies this. In the example below, Rick Turoczy explains how embracing constant experimentation, learning, and a willingness to follow the feedback allowed the characteristics of their startup community to emerge. Portland Incubator Experiment (PIE), an organization in Portland that Rick co-founded, can be thought of as a series of happy accidents that produced unpredictable creativity. It is the very essence of an emergent phenomenon.

Embracing Failure Enabled Our Startup Incubator to Better Serve Our Community Better

Rick Turoczy (Portland, Oregon)
Founder and General Manager, Portland Incubator Experiment (PIE)

When we were coming up with the name for the Portland Incubator Experiment (PIE)—an effort to support the startup community in Portland, Oregon—we were intentional about having the word *experiment* in our name. This wasn't because we were creative or seeking to be innovative and push the envelope. Instead, we felt that the word was more of an escape clause for us. It was a softer landing, an excuse for failure. We decided "Portland" was better than our first idea, the Digital Incubator Experiment, which ultimately formed an acronym that was a bit too morbid.

Admittedly, D-I-E does accurately and acutely describe the portending fate of the vast majority of startups, but we chose to focus on *Portland* instead. Fortunately, Dan Wieden, co-founder of Wieden+Kennedy—and ultimately the patron of our program—liked pie. Loved pie, actually.

Since we wanted Dan to love our experiment as much as he loved pie, the Portland Incubator Experiment, or PIE, was born.

We started with failures. And we anchored in experimentation. Here are some examples of what that experiment has taught us, so far:

- Failure is always an option. And a learning opportunity. Act accordingly.
- A startup accelerator is a byproduct of a community. Not vice versa.
- Don't focus on building the community. Focus on improving it.

Failure has been a recurring theme with PIE since the earliest days. To put it more pleasantly, PIE has been a journey through serendipity, an ongoing series of happy accidents. Each failure motivated us to try something new and continue moving forward, or backward, or in some direction.

We have consistently failed our way into opportunities that have enabled us to solve problems for the Portland startup community. By trying, failing, and retooling. Again and again. Still, to this day.

Some folks shy away from failure and see it as a negative. We, on the other hand, are perfectly willing to admit that PIE wouldn't be the program it is today without our embracing failure. And lots of it. Many of those failures predated the concept of PIE. We inherited those failures. Those failures laid the foundation. In reality, PIE started more than a decade earlier, when the PIE co-founders were working in, on, and around startups.

And failing.

There was the widespread failure of companies in the Portland startup community during the dot-com days in the early 2000s. This kept many of us working in startups and day jobs rather than spending the masses of wealth we were supposedly on a track to realize. The bubble bursting—and with it, our purported paper wealth—was a catastrophic failure that kept all of us engaged and working in the Portland startup community. We had no other choice.

In the mid-2000s, my startup failed, which brought with it my failure as a leader and as a co-founder. That failure was another learning process, albeit painful, which taught me, among other things, that I wasn't founder material. Now, I was entrepreneurial, a problem solver, and a firefighter. But I wasn't a founder because I didn't have the balance that a founder needs to have to be successful since I was far too one-sided.

Then, less than a decade later, another bubble burst— as the mortgage economy failed. That left many commercial spaces in Portland vacant. This economic crash enabled the opportunity for a group of entrepreneurs and early-stage startups to set up shop in an empty retail location in the base of the Wieden+Kennedy global headquarters in Portland to co-work even though they couldn't afford to pay rent. It was that concept and conversation around that coworking space that would become PIE.

But it wasn't just failure before the founding of PIE that informed the experiment. It is the ongoing series of failures that continue to inspire refinements in our model.

An example is Portland's failure to attract Techstars to our community, when they were actively searching for an outpost in the Pacific Northwest. The Seattle startup community wound up getting the Techstars program. And through the leadership of folks like Andy Sack and Chris DeVore, Techstars Seattle has become a fantastic program that supports many promising startups from Portland, as well. That failure inspired us to morph PIE from a curated coworking space fueled by peer mentorship into a Portland-flavored startup accelerator program, designed to facilitate both peer and expert mentorship for the founders in our community.

Motivated by significant interest from the market, we developed a startup accelerator consulting practice. But we were unable and partly unwilling to structure the program in a way that could be a scalable revenue-generating offering. That failure inspired us to open source our learnings as the PIE Cookbook. It made more sense to us, and more sense to the startup community, to make that knowledge available to everyone who was thinking about building a startup accelerator.

Recently, we realized that our existing startup accelerator model was failing to satisfy the changing needs of our community. Even though we had adopted programs and models that seemed to be working elsewhere, they didn't work the same way in Portland—or provide the same level of impact. Even though it was kind of working as a business, it was failing to deliver what our community needed, so we decided to continue to reorganize the experiment.

Throughout each of PIE's missteps and failures, there was community. It wasn't always tangible, and it wasn't necessarily self-aware. But the community provided the framework and foundation for things like PIE to occur. And it was that opportunity to engage and maintain that community that encouraged PIE to continue doing the work.

After working on this effort for more than a dozen years, I'm convinced that you don't actually build community or an ecosystem. And you don't manage it. You just discover it. You show up. You try to make folks more aware of it. You keep showing up. You give it a center of gravity. And then the job is to maintain it and improve it. All of the pieces already exist and they're already connected—sometimes more loosely than they should be.

Your job is to improve your community continually. To always be giving it a tune-up. To replace worn parts, tighten loose screws, and ensure it has fuel. And to keep it running at peak performance. I always remind myself not to get all heady and fool myself into thinking that I'm building something. I'm just the mechanic trying to improve performance, making sure nothing is leaking, and working to prevent the wheels from falling off. Think: *zen and the art of community maintenance*.

This doesn't just apply to the local community, mind you. Maintaining a community requires extensive networks, a multitude of viewpoints, and getting outside of your comfort zone.

You have to cheerlead. You have to create a bully pulpit. You have to use that megaphone to convince others that the community is in fact real. And you have to encourage anyone becoming aware to connect more deeply with the community.

PIE was initially a platform to promote startups throughout Portland, and we worked to ensure that we brought all of the right people to the table. As we developed gravity around that pursuit, we worked to become the front door for folks interested in startups in the city—the one-stop shop to get connected. Now, we use that position as a means of continually collecting information and resources to rethink what PIE needs to be doing for the community.

We made PIE a resource by the community, for the community, without expecting anything in return. We're not even close to done. But we'll keep experimenting toward becoming something precious and sustainable for the good of our community.

CHAPTER EIGHT

THE MYTH
OF QUANTITY

Startup Community Way Principle

Startup communities are propelled by entrepreneurial success and the recycling of those resources back into the next generation. Success produces wealth and intangibles that are critical to the process of entrepreneurship. Success also inspires entrepreneurship as a viable option. Recycling the resources, knowledge, and inspiration back into the startup community maintains its vibrancy and sustainability.

Perhaps one of the most significant errors that occurs in a startup community is the belief that doing more of something will result in a better outcome. In particular, people often equate increasing inputs, such as actors (e.g., investors, talent) and factors (e.g., financing, programs) with the increase of desired outputs (e.g., startups, entrepreneurs) and outcomes (e.g., exits, job creation).

Since startup communities are nonlinear and complex, thinking in quantities is a flawed strategy better suited to complicated systems. Nonlinear, network-based systems exhibit power-law dynamics, where a small number of actors and events drive overall value in the system. Quantity-based approaches operate on the assumption that averages, not outliers, drive system value. That is incorrect. Compounding this, inputs and outputs won't be directly correlated or proportional.

The myth of quantity is just that—a myth.

MORE OF EVERYTHING

We call the myth of quantity the *more-of-everything problem*, and it's one of the largest sources of frustration and discontent in a startup community today. The more-of-everything problem stems from placing too much faith and effort on blindly increasing system inputs with the mistaken belief that it will increase the right system outputs and outcomes.

More-of-everything thinking goes something like this: if we just get more of everything, then we can create a vibrant startup community. We need more capital, more innovation centers, more accelerators, more incubators, more university programs, more startup events. More, more, more. It follows linear systems thinking whereby an increase in critical inputs (resources like capital and talent) increases desired outputs (startups) and outcomes (value creation). The problem is, more of everything doesn't work.

There is a sizable body of research on what makes some regions consistently able to produce a steady stream of high-impact companies compared with other regions. Overall, what appears to matter most is a density of smart people of prime entrepreneurship age (mid-career) with an orientation toward entrepreneurship and the pursuit of enterprise in knowledge-intensive activities—plus a bunch of other stuff that we can't measure very well, such as network and culture.[1]

You may have noticed that many factors in the more-of-everything playbook are missing from that list—venture capital, research and patenting, university programs, accelerators and incubators, and government innovation programs.[2] It's also true that even among the leading startup hubs, the absolute number of startups and investors is not predictive of successful outcomes.[3] In study after study, these factors fail to register statistically meaningful relationships with high-impact entrepreneurship in a region, once one accounts for factors like a density of talent.[4]

Does this mean that these factors don't matter? No! Of course they matter. But they are not enough. These factors alone won't produce a steady stream of high-impact startups in a city. What differentiates entrepreneurial regions from others is how these factors integrate as a system—one that promotes collaboration, inclusivity, stewardship, and an entrepreneurial mindset, and exhibits many other social, cultural, and behavioral attributes conducive to the process of innovation and entrepreneurship.

Many people look to the example of Silicon Valley as something to be reengineered at home, failing to adopt the right lessons. The individuals responsible for the creation of Silicon Valley didn't set out to build the world's most innovative region—it emerged because of what and how they were doing things. What differentiated Silicon Valley from everywhere else at the time was a bottom-up culture of openness, collaboration, and a commitment to the region over individual people, companies, or institutions.[5]

What enabled Silicon Valley to become what it is today was its behavior, mindset, and seeding the environment for an innovative system to emerge—typically by accident and without a plan. Most everything else came later, over a long time, with no central plan to make it all happen.

The appeal of more of everything is understandable—the actions are controllable, tangible, and often immediate. More of everything feels good in the short term because you can see things happening in front of you. But over the long run, more of everything disappoints unless the participants in the startup community address underlying social, cultural, and behavioral obstacles. To borrow from Victor Hwang and Greg Horowitt in their book, *The Rainforest: The Secret to Building the Next Silicon Valley*: "Attempts to foster innovation that do not focus on changing human behavior are doomed to fail."[6]

Alternative names to the more-of-everything approach could be the resource-based approach to startup community development or the old-economy way of building a new economy. Regardless, the issue is the same: increasing critical inputs increases desired outputs, in a linear, controllable, and predictable way. More of everything is a factory-production approach applied to information-economy startups. While tempting, this thinking is unrealistic and counterproductive.

Before continuing down the more-of-everything path, consider an alternative. Sometimes the answer is more of something or even more of many things, but often, a more relevant question is how well you are doing something. Are you getting the most out of what you already have? What can improve interactions? To what extent are the existing pieces integrating productively?

In our experience, the answer to these questions comes not from adding, but from activating and transforming, with a particular focus on culture and mindset. Small changes in behavior—adopted widely and practiced consistently—can have a significant impact on outcomes down the road.

OUTLIERS, NOT AVERAGES

Implicit in the quantity-driven mindset is a belief—conscious or not—that value creation in a startup community follows a normal statistical distribution, whereby an understanding of the average outcome provides an understanding of the overall performance of an ecosystem. But this is entirely incorrect.

Given the nonlinear characteristic of complex systems, a central feature is the prevalence of rare, high-impact events over what a normal statistical distribution would predict. These are fat-tailed distributions, where a relatively small number of outliers drive total value in the system. Since the typical outcome for a startup is failure, a small number of big wins, instead of a large number of small successes, drive economic value for the entire startup community. Venture capitalists love to call this the power law, where the massive success of one company in a fund drowns out all of a fund's failures.

Ultimately, it's far more valuable to have a few high-impact companies and a few engaged, successful entrepreneurs than it is to have hundreds of new startups, co-working facilities, investor groups, or university entrepreneurship programs of average impact. Since value is not symmetrical in startup communities, the big wins matter more than the absolute number of inputs, people, and activities. There is a profound psychological impact by providing a tangible marker for founders to dream big and believe that they, too, can pull off what may appear to be impossible to others.

Since many failures offset by a few considerable successes are a regular and continuous part of a startup community, the cultural norms must reflect and support this. Pervasive failure reinforces the importance of successful entrepreneurs to exhibit leadership and give back to the next generation of startup founders.

Twenty-five years ago, there was a sense in Boulder that the entrepreneurial cycle had run its course. While there were dozens of entrepreneurs working hard at new businesses, there hadn't been any big exits in a long time. The community became segmented into two groups: the wave of wealthy entrepreneurs who had mostly retired or had since become disconnected from new entrepreneurial activity, and a younger set who were hustling but didn't have any local contemporaneous role models. There was a lot of action, but nothing seemed to be paying off.

However, within five years, a half-dozen of the companies were acquired for substantial amounts of money by four large public companies, each of which set up an operation based in Boulder following the acquisition. Two other companies went public, resulting in around a hundred newly minted millionaires. Within a few more years, while several of the founders checked out, the vast majority of them took some of their wealth and started investing in new startups, many of them started by some of their previous employees. Suddenly, there was a critical mass of activity that has now been building over the past 25 years, propelled by a relatively small number of high-profile successes.

ENTREPRENEURIAL RECYCLING

The presence of successful entrepreneurship—startups that achieve a large scale or a sizable exit—has a massive impact on a startup community. Even a few of these successful events can dramatically alter the course of a startup community forever. Entrepreneurial recycling is one reason these outlier events have an outsized impact on the startup community.

When a startup has a successful outcome, the wealth earned by company founders, early employees, and local investors can be recycled back into the next generation of startups. Additionally, the experience of the local talent base improves, since founders, managers, and employees have now gone through a successful startup and scale-up event. The labor market grows for technical, managerial, and professional roles. Attracting talent from outside the region becomes easier. The local service and creative sectors become more vibrant as the economy grows with more well-paying jobs to support them.

Highly visible success stories, ignored in many entrepreneurial eco-system frameworks, make the belief of success tangible even though entrepreneurial recycling is difficult to measure quantitatively. But success is crucial to the psychology of a startup community—particularly in places that have never experienced it, have an attitude of "it can't happen here," or generally have enormous structural barriers and limitations.

Chris Schroeder, an entrepreneur and investor, wrote about this in his 2013 book, *Startup Rising: The Entrepreneurial Revolution Remaking the Middle East*. Changing mindset is especially challenging in the Middle East, where nepotism and legacy pathways to success are deeply ingrained in the social psyche. There's even a term for it: *wasta*. In the book, Schroeder describes wasta as "a display of partiality toward a favored person or group without regard for their qualifications... [whereby] the net effect, culturally, has been an entropy of acceptance that there only could be one way of doing business."[7] In other words, only the well-connected can get ahead. Imagine the negative impact that has on ambition. Encouragingly, entrepreneurs in the Middle East are beginning to challenge that tradition.[8]

Entrepreneurship is a learning-by-doing process, and people who have been through it possess a set of experiential knowledge that cannot be adequately learned in a classroom or on the pages of a book. Tapping into the knowledge base of seasoned entrepreneurs is highly valuable to nascent and aspiring entrepreneurs. Academic research confirms the productivity advantage of serial entrepreneurs, as knowledge from one venture spills over to the next one.[9]

Entrepreneurial success must get recycled back into the next generation of startups. There are many channels for this, including from mentors, advisors, storytellers, board members, repeat entrepreneurs, and startup employees who continue to invest their capital, energy, knowledge, and time into new startups in their community.

Successful entrepreneurs, with the right approach, often make the best startup community leaders. In addition to being sources of wealth, knowledge, talent, and expertise, they are role models who embody what aspiring entrepreneurs can achieve. The question is whether—and how—they choose to engage.

Founders who have achieved success should be encouraged to continue to engage with the next generation of startups in their community. Don't take your capital, knowledge, and inspiration to the beach (at least not forever). Stay engaged. Help the next generation of entrepreneurs. Do this, especially if no one helped you. Work on leaving your community in a better place than it was when you were building your company. Try to ensure that the next generation of founders following in your footsteps have a smoother journey than you did.

LEADERS AS SUPERNODES

So far, we've emphasized outlier companies. But the people behind them are more critical. Companies are transient while people are lasting.

Entrepreneurial leaders are the key to bringing all of these pieces together. They set the tone. Startup community participants—especially other entrepreneurs—look to leaders for cues on behavior, activities, and attitudes. Without the right type of entrepreneurial leaders in place, a startup community cannot exist in any meaningful form.

Leaders are role models who demonstrate norms, behaviors, and attitudes of the startup community over the long-term. If you want a quick and easy way to determine the culture in a startup community, take a look at its leaders. That will tell you almost everything you need to know about the current state and norms of the startup community.

Maryann Feldman and Ted Zoller of the University of North Carolina offer convincing evidence in their study of dealmakers, which they define as highly connected individuals with deep entrepreneurial experience, fiduciary ties to startups, and valuable social capital. These dealmakers are the bridge-builders that make things happen, connect people, shape networks, facilitate the flow of resources, and form the backbone of startup communities. In their research, Feldman and Zoller found that the density of these dealmakers, and the connectedness between them, is more predictive of higher startup rates and a vibrant local startup community than are quantity-based measures of startups and investors.[10] In other words, the connectedness of key people supersedes the magnitude of inputs.

In follow-on work, Feldman, Zoller, and additional collaborators found that startups who became affiliated with a dealmaker, and therefore had access to the related network and social capital, subsequently had significant increases in business performance.[11] The authors attributed the performance improvement of the company to a causal relationship with a dealmaker.

This research demonstrates that the strength of local networks—and in particular the existence and connectedness of local leaders engaged with many startups—is more predictive of favorable startup outcomes than are aggregate measures of startups and investors.[12] The quality and cohesiveness of operators in the network are more critical to the success of the local startup community than having more entrepreneurs or more investors. A research consortium led by the Global Entrepreneurship Network came to a similar conclusion across several cities around the world.[13]

The quality of the network is more important than the size of it. While the phenomenon of online social networks (LinkedIn, Facebook, and Twitter) has generated and reinforced the idea that the number of connections (or followers) you have in your network is the primary determinant of your value to the network, this is simply not true. Instead, it's a simple formula:

Value = # of connections × value of information that
travels between connections

A person who has few connections, even if the information traveling between them is valuable, is not that impactful to a startup community. A person with many connections, but with little value of information traveling between them, is also not impactful to the startup community. In fact, they can actually be harmful. Someone with an average number of connections with an average value among them is likely more important to the startup community than either of the first two. And, a person with a large number of connections and a high value of information flowing between them is essential to a startup community.

We call these high-value participants in the startup community supernodes because their nodes on the network graph are much larger than the rest. These supernodes are critical to startup communities.

Endeavor has been researching networks in startup communities around the world for the better part of the last decade. They conclude that cities where the individuals of influence are successful entrepreneurs (experience bringing companies to scale) produce a higher rate of companies that reach high-growth and scale than do comparable cities without entrepreneurs in key influential roles.[14] Research from the World Bank produces similar conclusions.[15]

In their book, *The Rainforest: The Secret to Building the Next Silicon Valley*, Victor Hwang and Greg Horowitt refer to these individuals as keystones. In ecology, a keystone species is one that impacts many other organisms in the ecosystem. These keystone species are so essential to an ecosystem that their removal would fundamentally alter it.

As Hwang and Horowitt observe, in entrepreneurial ecosystems, keystone species play a vital role that cuts across multiple official job titles. These individuals are integrative, reaching across boundaries to connect people. They are influential and appeal to people's long-term interests and noneconomic motivations. Finally, they are impactful, making things happen. The authors stress the importance of keystones:

[Keystones] form a critical building block of the Rainforest. Without them, many Rainforests would probably struggle or even die... They are the people who are usually missing, or at least too scarce, in almost all regions that have failed at generating significant amounts of entrepreneurial innovation.

Similarly, in their 2009 book, *Start-up Nation: The Story of Israel's Economic Miracle*, Dan Senor and Saul Singer describe *bitzu'ism* as the beating heart of that country's entrepreneurial drive. In Hebrew, *bitzu'ist* loosely translates to someone who is an active pragmatist—someone who knows how to get things done.

Dealmaker, supernode, keystone, and *bitzu'ist* all refer to the same type of person—a leader in the startup community. Notice that we refer to "a person," not "the person," as healthy startup communities have multiple leaders, and, as the startup community grows, the number of leaders should evolve with it. Activated, engaged entrepreneurial leaders are critical to the long-term health, development, and success of a startup community.

How Entrepreneurial Recycling Accelerated the Startup Community in Indianapolis

Scott Dorsey (Indianapolis, Indiana)
Co-Founder, ExactTarget
Co-Founder and Managing Partner, High Alpha

Chris Baggott, Peter McCormick, and I started ExactTarget in December 2000 with a dream of moving marketers into the digital world. The odds were not in our favor. The Internet bubble had just burst, money wasn't flowing into startups, we were first-time tech entrepreneurs without technical skills, and we started the company in Indianapolis, Indiana. Good luck!

At the time, Indianapolis had experienced only modest success in tech. Software Artistry was our shining star. Having gone public in 1995, it grew to 300 employees, and ultimately sold to IBM for approximately $200 million in early 1998. Issues holding back Indy's tech sector ranged from two competing tech associations to a lack of connectivity with major tech hubs. We had an old airport with no nonstop flights to the West Coast. Our region wasn't even observing Daylight Savings Time, which meant we were always out of sync with the rest of the country.

Despite these many challenges, Indy turned out to be a substantial competitive advantage. The community was ready for progress. We moved downtown and built our identity around the heart of the city called Monument Circle. We leveraged the tremendous talent coming out of our state's universities—Indiana University, Purdue University, Notre Dame, Butler, and many others. Our government leaders supported us every step of the way by pushing for legislative change and offering economic development incentives to help us grow faster and create high-paying jobs. We drew the most from the resources we had and created others along the way.

ExactTarget overcame many challenges to achieve tremendous success, punctuated by an IPO and large-scale exit. We created more than 1,500 high-tech jobs in Indy and proved that scalable tech companies could be built anywhere. We showed that company building and community building could happen in parallel. Developing talent networks, working with university and government leaders, and showing what's possible, are ingredients to getting the entrepreneurial flywheel spinning in a startup community. Success builds on success. And most importantly, what follows a successful outcome is as critical to the long-term vibrancy of a startup community as the "big win" itself.

Building a Community While Building a Company

In ExactTarget's early days, raising capital was very difficult. Together, we invested $25,000 and raised an additional $200,000 from friends and family. The initial cap table was full of relatives and neighbors who had written $5,000 to $25,000 checks. We encouraged small checks to protect personal relationships in case the investment went to zero. It turns out that a $5,000 investment held until our acquisition by Salesforce yielded over $1 million!

Our first big funding break came when Bob Compton, an accomplished investor and entrepreneur, agreed to lead our $1 million angel round and become chairman. Bob had been chairman of Software Artistry, and he understood the importance of giving back to the next generation of founders (something that motivates us to this day). We were lucky to have his experience and wisdom on the team. Raising capital became much more manageable. Later, we raised our Series A from Insight Venture Partners and subsequent rounds from respected firms like Battery, TCV, and Scale. These coastal investors added tons of value to our company and our community, and they grew to love Indy and the Midwest.

Talent became the engine that propelled ExactTarget. We designed highly differentiated internship and new college graduate programs to bring the brightest young people into our business. Our executive team was assembled carefully over the years, with a robust emphasis on culture and Midwest values. Often, we would add an exec from another city. They would fall in love with Indy and ultimately move their family. We took pride in adding new jobs and fresh talent to our community.

The company culture was our secret weapon. Scaling from a few employees in Indy to over 2,000 team members around the world required a cultural framework that represented our core values, and created a collective identity and teamwork. Our brand color was orange. Partners, customers, and prospects always remarked that our people were so positive and had tremendous energy and passion for serving marketers. Our motto "Be Orange" was born and quickly became the common thread that linked our teams together, from Indy to offices in Seattle, San Francisco, London, Paris, Sydney, São Paulo, and others around the world.

Connections, our annual user conference, became integral to our culture. Bringing thousands of marketers to our hometown every year was strategic and a great source of pride. When conventional wisdom suggested that we move our conference to New York or Las Vegas, we resisted and found creative ways to make it work in Indy. Because of this, we could include all of our employees, which meant they could meet our customers and partners, have amazing speakers like Sir Richard Branson and Dr. Condoleezza Rice inspire them, and enjoy concerts from bands like Train and Imagine Dragons. Creating a positive economic development impact for our city was rewarding, given the support we had received. And when customers remarked that they were "proud to be Orange," we knew that we had delivered an experience consistent with our culture and community.

When you feel supported by your community, giving back is easy. Our employees drove a beautiful spirit of volunteerism. We were able to scale our impact when we started the ExactTarget

Foundation with pre-IPO stock from founders and early investors. We selected three pillars of giving, which matched our passions and company culture: education, entrepreneurship, and hunger. After the Salesforce acquisition, we rebranded the foundation to Nextech and decided to double down on computer science education. Through our partnership with Code.org, we have brought hundreds of Indiana schools into the digital age. We have inspired thousands of students to take computer science classes, learn to code, and consider tech as their career path. Indiana is now one of the leading states in computer science education.

Going public was never a goal. But over time, it became apparent that being a public company would enable us to elevate our brand with large-enterprise customers, better capitalize the business, and accelerate our growth. Our first attempt didn't work out so well. We filed to go public in December of 2007, right before the financial crisis! The market for IPOs dried up, and we had much of the burden of being a public company with none of the benefits. In early 2009, we pulled the IPO filing and raised outside capital. Our internal mantra was "better than an IPO," and it took every ounce of orange culture and leadership to keep our team focused and moving forward. To open the lines of communication, I started sending a company-wide email called "Scott's Friday Note" and never missed a Friday over the next five and a half years.

Fortunately, we did go public on the New York Stock Exchange on March 22, 2012. Ringing the opening bell and going live on CNBC with Jim Cramer were incredible experiences. Our offering was heavily oversubscribed. We priced at $19 per share and closed the first day of trading at over $25 per share, making our company worth more than $1 billion in enterprise value. It was one of the largest SaaS IPOs in history. We turned the NYSE orange. Every trader on the floor wore an orange jacket and we lined the floors with orange carpets. The best part of the experience was delivering for our employees, investors, and community who believed in us.

Life as a public company was going well. We exceeded Wall Street expectations for our first four quarters and continued to grow revenue over 40 percent year over year. Large cloud providers began to realize that IT dollars were shifting to marketing, and they needed a platform like ours to manage data at scale, power cross-channel marketing campaigns, and meet the needs of digital marketers. We had been partners with Salesforce for many years, integrating with their platform before the App Exchange even existed. Marc Benioff and their team made the first move and presented us with a compelling vision for working together. After months of negotiation, we agreed to be acquired for over $2.5 billion and announced the acquisition on June 4, 2013. It was a tremendous outcome for our shareholders, employees, customers, partners, and community.

Doubling Down on Indy: Building the Next Generation

Selling ExactTarget was certainly bittersweet. During the process, I hoped that we would end up with a progressive software leader that would continue to invest in our people, products, and community. Salesforce has delivered on all of that and more! They have added nearly 1,000 jobs in Indy, invested in the city via the Salesforce Foundation, and even helped to shape social issues and public policy within our state. Today, Indy is the second-largest Salesforce location in the world, only behind the San Francisco headquarters. And the tallest building in Indiana is now called the Salesforce Tower, forever branding our city as a tech community!

Indianapolis today looks very different from when we founded ExactTarget. We have a vibrant airport that has been voted the best airport in North America for the last eight years. We have multiple nonstop flights to San Francisco and other West Coast cities every day. We now observe Daylight Savings Time and feel synced with the rest of the country. Downtown Indy is booming with countless new locally owned restaurants opening every year and new housing construction on seemingly every corner. Millennials and empty nesters are moving downtown in significant numbers.

Our tech startup community is booming. Tech workers and entrepreneurs who have achieved any level of success are paying it forward by investing, mentoring, and starting new companies. Tech co-working spaces are ubiquitous. Steve Case and his Rise of the Rest team rolled through Indy and have already made several investments. The State of Indiana created a $250 million fund called Next Level Indiana to attract more venture capital to our state and help our startups become scale-ups. Our state's tech accelerator/association, called Techpoint, is growing quickly and adding value with high-scale talent-acquisition programs. And large tech companies based on the coasts are opening Indy offices at a brisk pace.

My next startup is High Alpha. Mike Fitzgerald, Eric Tobias, Kristian Anderson, and I created a venture studio to give back to the community and scale next-generation cloud companies. We are leveraging our experience to pioneer a new model of entrepreneurship that unites company creation (High Alpha Studio) with venture capital (High Alpha Capital). At the core, we are matchmakers, bringing together talented founders (many who are former ExactTarget colleagues), big ideas, and capital to build breakout SaaS companies. The High Alpha platform gives us a tremendous opportunity to coach and mentor the next generation of Indy tech founders. And if successful, it has the potential to make an even more substantial impact than ExactTarget.

So many of us from ExactTarget are investing our time, energy, experience, and capital to help build the companies of tomorrow. Those before us have set an excellent example, and we want to make a lasting impact that goes beyond one IPO or company exit. Breakout tech communities that grow and endure have founders building community while building their companies. And they are committed to leveraging their experience and resources to drive even more significant success in the future.

Every entrepreneur dreams of building something bigger than themselves. We were extraordinarily fortunate to be in the right place at the right time. We rode the wave of software as a service and digital marketing, and connected with a community where entrepreneurs, investors, universities, and government work together to create lasting progress. My wish is for you to do the same—but even bigger and better!

CHAPTER NINE

THE ILLUSION OF CONTROL

Startup Community Way Principle

Startup communities can be guided and influenced but not controlled. Instead of approaching a startup community from the top down, it should be seeded with the right conditions to emerge from the bottom up. Efforts to control people, activities, and information in startup communities are futile at best and destructive at worst.

C omplex systems are puzzling, but what makes them puzzling is also what makes them so valuable. Herein lies the challenge: our human minds desire the security of feeling all-knowing and all-controlling. We want to believe that we fully understand what's happening around us, that we can apply our skills to solve our challenges, and that we are in control of our destiny.

Compounding the innate human desire to be the master of our destiny is a system of hierarchical management deeply ingrained for generations.

Developed more than a century ago by efficiency consultant and industrialist Frederick Winslow Taylor, the field of scientific management promoted specialization, tight control of production, and top-down management.[1] Taylorism, as it became known, was popularized in the industrial age and increased after World War II. Its legacy continues to this day.

Taylorism is the essence of complicated thinking. So is the "Masters of the Universe" syndrome.[2] But, we live in an increasingly complex world, not a complicated one. Not only are these theories no longer sufficient, but they're also harmful. The illusion of control is just that—an illusion.

NOT CONTROLLABLE

The endless interlinkages, feedback loops, infinite possible outcomes, constant evolution, and decentralized network structure make controlling a complex system impossible. Instead, complex systems can only be guided and influenced. Entrepreneurs intuitively understand this, as the early life of a startup is a complex system.

If you have raised a child, you will intuitively understand a complex system. A parent should not try to control every facet of a child's life. That's impossible, and when attempted, it is counterproductive at best and destructive at worst. A better approach is for parents to guide children, when age appropriate, toward making better choices for themselves.

Economist David Colander and physicist Roland Kupers tackle the practical application of complex thinking to society and governance in their book, *Complexity and the Art of Public Policy: Solving Society's Problems from the Bottom Up*:

> One approach to parenting… is to set out a set of explicit rules for the child… If the rules are correct, and if the child follows them, then, assuming the parents knew what was best, the child's welfare will increase… That is the idealized "control approach" to parenting.

There are two problems with this—the first is that most parents are not sure which rules are the correct ones. If they pick the wrong ones, then the child's welfare won't be maximized. The second problem is that the child may not follow the rules...

...the true alternative to top-down control parenting is the parenting equivalent of the complexity approach we are advocating; a laissez-faire activist approach... [where] you have as few direct rigorously specified rules as possible. Instead, you have general guidelines, and you consciously attempt to influence the child's development so he or she becomes the best human being possible...

Instead of focusing policy on the rules, the focus of complexity parenting is more on creating voluntary guidelines and providing a positive role model.[3]

This dynamic is especially true when raising multiple children. Parenting each child the same way and expecting the same result would be futile because no two children are alike.

Since we can't control complex systems, they cannot be predicted, engineered, or replicated. Let's use Silicon Valley as an example. Silicon Valley was not born from the flawless execution of a carefully calibrated plan dictated by a central authority. Instead, it is the result of a deeply seeded environment that allowed for a virtuous system of entrepreneurship to emerge spontaneously over a very long period. Today, even Silicon Valley couldn't recreate itself.

For her book, *Regional Advantage: Culture and Competition in Silicon Valley and Route 128*, AnnaLee Saxenian contrasts two significant startup communities and how they evolved. In the 1990s, Silicon Valley's startup community flourished while the Massachusetts startup community (then centered around Route 128) stagnated. While there are many reasons for what happened, the cultural norms of the two regions stand out. Silicon Valley was a decentralized, fluid, bottom-up culture that built on the laid-back West Coast vibe. In contrast, Route 128 was a controlled, top-down culture that reflected a New England conservatism. Not surprisingly, both

Silicon Valley and Boston have evolved significantly since the mid-1990s, so it might be time for a new study.

As the Boulder startup community evolved between 2007 and 2012, there was no effort to control it. As explained by the Boulder Thesis, the opposite occurred, in direct opposition to efforts by both CU Boulder and the venture capitalists active in Boulder in the 1990s. At that time, both groups tried to act as gatekeepers. Instead of being inputs into a complex system that had increasing returns, gatekeeper actors stifled the growth and development of the startup community. Then, between 2007 and 2012, an organization called Silicon Flatirons, led by Phil Weiser and Brad Bernthal, had a tremendously positive influence on the Boulder startup community, as described in *Startup Communities*.

Values and Virtues: Don't Abuse Your Power

Feeders in startup communities often have dramatically more resources than startups. As gatekeepers of many of the vital resources that startups need to thrive, feeders can wield tremendous power over startups.

In healthy startup communities, feeders use their power for good with a view of helping entrepreneurs, even if this may be at odds with their short-term interests. Trust is essential to a startup community and is hard to build but easy to break. Ultimately, what is best for startups is best for the entire startup community.

NOT FULLY KNOWABLE

In complex systems, outcomes aren't knowable in advance, and predictions are frequently wrong. Knowledge at any point in time is limited, causing predictive frameworks based on top-down approaches to be ineffective or destructive. Predictions and forecasts are generally useless.

Envision a startup community in a city of 500,000 people. Three feeders—the university, a nonprofit focused on entrepreneurial development (with a co-working space as part of what it does), and city government—have teamed up to figure out what they need to do to improve their startup community. They hire a consultancy to publish a study and benchmark their startup community against other similar-sized, but more advanced ones. The study comes back with a plethora of data and analysis, some critical of the nonprofit trying to control the startup community. Additional feedback is that women and minorities are grossly underrepresented in the leadership of these three organizations relative to the general population and the nascent set of entrepreneurs in the city. The feeders, especially the nonprofit, are upset and try to get elements of the report rewritten to paint them in a more positive light.

Rather than using the data to inform and stimulate change, the feeder organizations are trying to reinforce their desired perspective. In this example, they withdraw and move into a defensive posture when criticized, regardless of how constructive that criticism is. Once they can't control things, especially the feedback and the message, they don't want to hear it. Think about how different things might be if instead of fighting the feedback, they tried to understand things better and improve their support of entrepreneurs.

In the face of uncertain outcomes, startup community building is a team sport best done by a group of people with diverse perspectives, talents, and backgrounds. Linear systems thinkers actively avoid diversity because it makes predictive models challenging to calibrate and maintain. In contrast, diversity is of central importance to complex systems as it builds resilience and produces different outputs and results.[4] Startup communities that include everyone at the table forge bonds, build trust, stimulate novel ideas, make better decisions, and generate more exciting outcomes.

Next, consider the age of participants in a startup community. Imagine a situation where everyone is over 50 and extrapolating from the previous 30 or more years of their professional experience. In contrast, now imagine a situation where everyone is younger than 25 and extrapolating from five years or less of professional experience. In a complex system, it's easy to understand that a full age spectrum will generate much more diverse inputs, which will result in much more interesting outputs.

Now, substitute gender, race, ethnicity, sexual preference, educational, work, or geographic background, or any number of other characteristics. In this context, diversity is survival, rather than merely fairness or worse yet some kind of signaling mechanism.

FEEDBACKS AND CONTAGION

Complex systems regularly expose actors to new ideas, information, and relationships. Feedback loops produce a chain of actions and reactions. These actions and reactions spur additional responses and adaptations. Complex systems are affected by reinforcing feedback loops, both from the bottom-up and the top-down.

The bottom-up factors determine the system, which impacts the individual actors and interactions, and occur over and over again. A classic example is the capital markets. The actions of individual traders determine the macro-dynamics (prices, volatility, and volume), and at the same time, the behavior of the markets influences traders. Similarly, when individual drivers determine traffic patterns in a city such as Rome, New York City, or Lagos, the behavior of each driver is jointly affected by traffic congestion in the respective city. Sometimes the linkage between cause and effect is evident, but most of the time it's not, even with the benefit of hindsight.

Contagion, where behaviors, ideas, and information can spread quickly and widely in highly interconnected systems, is a related idea. While harmful examples of contagion include financial crises and virus outbreaks, positive contagion is a driver of increasing returns and present in all networked systems, passing helpful ideas and behaviors on to others.

Contagion can be either helpful or harmful to a startup community. Healthy startup communities adopt and spread virtuous behaviors and ideas, especially ones that reinforce, amplify, or accelerate communities of support, knowledge-sharing, and collaboration. Correspondingly, healthy startup communities identify, call out, and shut down unethical or destructive behavior. The feedback loops reinforce good behavior while eliminating lousy behavior.

Note that we are talking about behavior instead of outcomes. A high-leverage strategy for improving a startup community is to carefully cultivate and then widely disseminate virtuous acts and ideas—to create a positive contagion.

An example from Boulder is the adoption of #GiveFirst by the entrepreneurs in the startup community that was amplified by the Techstars Boulder accelerator. The give-before-you-get attitude was infectious, as entrepreneurs regularly went out of their way to help other entrepreneurs. A mindset of open doors and asking "How can I help?" became the cultural norm of the startup community. When someone moved to Boulder, they were often amazed at how easy it was to get connected around and integrated into the startup community. They would quickly become part of the startup community and immediately start welcoming others when they showed up. And, when they talked to their friends from the cities they came from, they raved about the dynamics around give-before-you-get and Boulder.

GETTING UNSTUCK

The J curve of startup community transition demonstrates that communities can become locked into a state of low vibrancy, from which it is hard to break free.[5] This state is a low-performing one, and if it persists, the startup community will continue in a zombie-like condition. To get to a more vibrant and lasting state, underperforming startup communities have to go through a transition period where things become less stable. This transition is painful but necessary.

The J Curve of Startup Community Transition

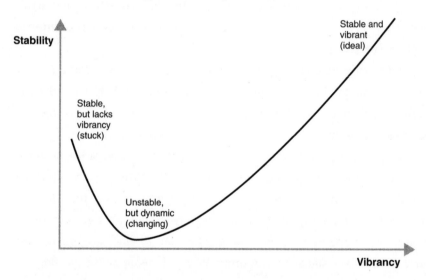

The startup community can introduce instability by trying new bold ideas. These are initiatives that may result in repeated or even spectacular failures, mix things up, and push the boundaries of people, forcing them to change. This transition will be uncomfortable for many, because it directly challenges powerful incumbents, entrenched interests, controlling power-brokers, and old yet comfortable ways of thinking and behaving.

In this way, startup communities should be made to be what Nassim Nicholas Taleb refers to as "antifragile."[6] Whereas a fragile system can be easily broken, damaged, or vulnerable to stressors, randomness, and failures, an antifragile system increases its capabilities and thrives in the presence of such shocks, disruptions, and disorder. Bureaucrats are fragile; entrepreneurs are antifragile. Wall Street, corporate employees, debt, academics, and Plato are fragile. Correspondingly, Silicon Valley, venture capital, artists, and Nietzsche are antifragile.[7] Leaders in healthy startup communities seek a degree of randomness and disruption, as this is where critical learning occurs. Through this, the antifragile system becomes stronger. Startup communities that are built against change are fragile. They are not built to last, becoming stale or stagnating, and eventually dying off.

The J Curve of startup community transition is an ongoing process, as a startup community unfolds over the lifecycle. The startup community

The J Curve of Startup Community Transition over the Lifecycle

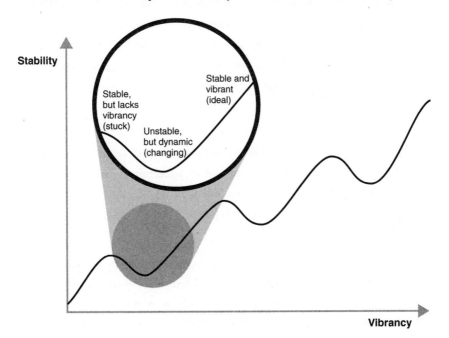

will continue to progress to more vibrant states (or less vibrant ones), with plenty of setbacks and periods of lock-in interspersed throughout.

Nobody knows which ideas will ultimately be the right ones. By taking an empathetic, open mind into a process of trial and error, you can try many things until you figure out what works and what doesn't. A radical embrace of inclusion helps because the best ideas often come from unexpected places. Many approaches will fail, but it only takes one good idea to alter a startup community's trajectory forever.

LETTING GO

When one actor dominates a startup community, the single-node problem occurs. This person serves as a gatekeeper to resources and relationships. It is challenging when the single node is a feeder, and it becomes particularly thorny when it is an organization designed to directly support startups, such as an accelerator, incubator, or co-working space.

Even when a single, dominant node has an unambiguously positive influence on the startup community—such as in the case of a serial entrepreneur who believes in #GiveFirst and places the needs of the founder community ahead of a personal agenda—this is not a sustainable long-term position. People die, they move on, and they burn out. The single node in this situation should look to cultivate the next generation of leaders in the startup community, letting go of that mantle over time—even suddenly, if necessary.

Accepting that you are not in control is one of the most powerful actions that a participant in a startup community can take. Management professor and systems thinker Rick Nason describes this elegantly:

> In essence, it is seductive to want to believe in a complicated world. Things that are complicated are well defined. They allow us to feel intelligent when we master them; they allow us to feel necessary; and perhaps most importantly, they allow us to feel that we are in control...

Related to our desire for order is the fact that complex problems tend to be messy. They do not have nice, neat solutions, as complicated problems do. In complicated thinking, the more elegant the solution, the better it is considered to be. We like things that can be tied up with a pretty bow...

There is a seductiveness to complicated systems. They make us feel intelligent and they make us feel needed and valuable. Complicated systems allow us the illusion that luck or serendipity played at best a limited role in our success and, thus, that whatever success we have is almost exclusively the result of our own skill and effort...

Probably the most significant incentive for engaging in complicated thinking is the fear of non-control and its effect on our egos and our sense of self-worth... The properties of complexity, such as emergence, develop in a leaderless fashion. Our egos find this difficult to take, and we risk succumbing to the imposter syndrome. Consciously or unconsciously assuming that the business world is complicated lets us avoid the problematic issues of self-awareness and self-confidence.[8]

Let go of the illusion that you are in control of things. Attempting to control a complex system is a futile attempt to impose a complicated view on it. It won't work.

A Guide to Student-Driven Entrepreneurship at the University of Utah

Troy D'Ambrosio (Salt Lake City, Utah)

Executive Director, Lassonde Entrepreneur Institute, University of Utah

When we started what is now the Lassonde Entrepreneur Institute at the University of Utah, we had a clear vision to welcome all students who wanted to take a risk and learn by doing. We felt the key to effectively doing this was to put students at the center of everything we do.

The key to our success is four simple words: "letting go of control."

Put students in charge of (almost) everything. We run our program with more than 150 student leaders who identify and create content, build programming, manage budgets, and allocate resources. Two of our most important programs are student-driven ideas: a prototyping fund (our Get Seeded grant program) and a large community space for student entrepreneurs (the Lassonde Studios). The result is an incredibly diverse community of student entrepreneurs representing almost every major on campus—ranging from undeclared freshman to PhD students. "Letting go of the reins and putting students in charge is the secret sauce that makes Lassonde work," says Taylor Randall, Dean of the David Eccles School of Business.

Listen to student entrepreneurs. Through our student leaders, we have a direct, constant, and unfiltered pipeline to hundreds of student companies. When one student helps another find resources, solve problems, and connect with experts, it creates a real-time feedback loop from active entrepreneurs. Students get tired of lectures and are good at finding and learning things online. Their favorite form of learning is kinetic—they want to do things and make things.

The concept of adding a residential component was the result of a meeting with hundreds of student entrepreneurs as we were developing the Lassonde Studios—which combines a 400-bed dorm for student entrepreneurs with 20,000 square feet (1,858 square meters) of innovation space.

These students identified the need to have a 24-hour-a-day space because: (1) when they have free time during late nights and weekends, campus spaces are typically closed; and (2) for some of them, their most creative time was during the wee hours of the morning. One student said, "This is not a job that I go to at 8 a.m. and then go home at 5 p.m. This is my passion that I think about 24 hours a day."

Meet the students where they are. As we got better at listening to students, we realized that student entrepreneurs come in many forms and range from those who have heard the word *entrepreneur* but could not define it, to students who have already fully formed businesses that generate revenue. To support this diverse group, we had to provide learning on demand. Today, one student will want to learn about web development, and next week she will want to learn about company formation. Another might need an introduction to design thinking or how to build a prototype. Because of this, we created a flexible, highly varied set of programs, content, and mentoring to meet the students where and when they need it. We now have more than 500 student startup teams working on businesses. Finally, to meet students that are unsure about being branded an entrepreneur, we have a 24-hour café where they can observe entrepreneurial behavior at a safe distance and decide if they want to be a part of it.

See one, do one, teach one. Borrowed from medical education, we found one of the best ways for students to hone their entrepreneurial skills is to help another student entrepreneur with one-to-one mentoring or other support.

Some of this is formal—we fund scholarships for students who want to be in a startup but do not yet have ideas of their own to work on, matching them up to help and be mentored by active student founders. There are also many opportunities for informal interactions and coaching through our founders' board.

Last but not least, get out of their way!

CHAPTER 10

THE ABSENCE OF A BLUEPRINT

Startup Community Way Principle

Each startup community is unique and cannot be replicated. Startup communities are shaped by a wide range of factors, individuals, and histories of each place. Instead of emulating others, startup communities should look to build upon their own unique strengths.

N o two startup communities are the same. The multitude of relevant actors and factors, which are often deeply ingrained in the local history and culture, along with the dynamic nature of complex systems, ensures this. Inherent differences mean inherent limitations to replication, but we humans don't like that, so we look for ways to abstract and generalize.

A human instinct is to compare things, particularly ourselves, to others, as this provides a mode for learning and feeds our competitive instincts. But comparison requires a certain level of generalization, which can lead to misguided understanding and strategies. The complexity of startup communities makes this problem especially acute, where abstraction can take away too much of the unique characteristics that make each startup community special. Comparison can inform, but more often, it distracts and leads astray.

The most obvious example is the endless comparison to Silicon Valley, but the problem goes much deeper than that. There is an urge (almost an obsession) to compare startup communities to one another by tabulating a set of standardized metrics that produce ecosystem rankings. These approaches suggest there exist formulae for indexing and a predictive capability of startup community performance, but that belief isn't grounded in reality. These models—even the best of them—attempt to apply a complicated mindset to a complex system. They frequently confuse correlation with causation and imply a level of understanding that simply doesn't exist.

While the individual factors can be relevant, they are insufficient because each startup community is affected by them in different ways, to varying degrees, and at different stages of their maturity. The interactions that drive system behavior are difficult to capture and assess. Several cross-geography studies find no statistically meaningful relationship between a wide array of standard resources and the desired systemic performance metrics such as startup rates, high-growth firms, venture capital, and the number of exits. These are, at best, outputs that have a limited role as inputs.[1]

While we encourage benchmarking and measurement, understand that local context matters a lot and the most critical factors aren't captured very well by standardized metrics. The most helpful comparisons are often within the same city at different points in time. Localized metrics should be highly customized. Since the essential data is often qualitative, it must be collected by interviewing or surveying individuals on the ground. This type of data is time-consuming and costly to get, which is why it is avoided or ignored.

Some of the most convincing research we've seen on the study of startup communities is in the form of case studies, informed by a few key principles, which take into account the local factors and emphasizing the network and the nature of those relationships in a local startup community. One of the best at this is Yasuyuki Motoyama of Ohio State University, along with his collaborators over the years. Motoyama recommends prioritizing what is most important (the support of entrepreneurs by mentors, individuals, and organizations) and focusing on the relationships between these entities—rather than trying to be comprehensive, which is impossible anyway.[2]

Values and Virtues: Don't Over-Engineer Your Engagement

Considering the problems with efforts to control complex systems, be mindful of over-engineering efforts to engage with a startup community. Each startup community is unique. What works in one place may not work in another. Adhere to a set of principles and values, rather than following a set script. Programs and initiatives in a startup community should reflect the central ethos of the place.

Try different things, see what works and what doesn't, make necessary adjustments, try again, and repeat that cycle. Embrace the fact that no one has all the answers and that there is no one single way to do things.

INITIAL CONDITIONS AND BASINS OF ATTRACTION

In complex systems, small changes in initial conditions can produce substantial and often unforeseen changes later on. A famous example of this is the butterfly effect, whereby a butterfly flaps its wings in Brazil, resulting in a tornado in Texas two weeks later. The idea was put forward by Edward Lorenz, an MIT mathematician studying weather patterns in the 1960s, who discovered that tiny numerical differences being input into his computer simulations produced wildly different outcomes as systems evolved.[3]

Thomas Schelling, an American Nobel Prize–winning economist, studied how small differences in racial segregation and individual density preferences could lead to outcomes that diverged massively from those preferences.[4] In their book on complexity and public policy, economist David Colander and physicist Roland Kupers said this about Schelling's insight:

> This is another important pattern from complexity: over time, micro causes can have large macro effects, whereas with a linear pattern in the back of their minds, people will look for a big cause for a big effect. The study of nonlinear systems leads to patterns in which cause and effect are not proportional to each other, and the history of the system is an essential determinant.[5]

It's hard to imagine what Silicon Valley would be like today had the "Traitorous Eight" never left Shockley Semiconductor to found Fairchild Semiconductor. Or what might have happened had Robert Noyce not been so supportive of spinouts started by former Fairchild employees.[6]

Consider if the American colonies had been established not on the East Coast but instead on the West Coast. Would a replica of Silicon Valley exist outside of Boston or New York today, as people pushed east instead of west to start a new lives on the other side of the country? Would the entire course of technological history be altered? Or, was there something special about the fruit orchards and sunshine near the San Francisco Bay? We'll never know.

What would Seattle be like today if Bill Gates and Paul Allen had loved Albuquerque, New Mexico so much that they decided to keep building Microsoft in the middle of the high desert? Would Microsoft have been as successful? Would Jeff Bezos have started Amazon in Seattle? Reportedly, Bezos founded Amazon in Seattle due in large part to the deep pool of software engineers attracted there by Microsoft.[7] Ironically, Gates and Allen founded Microsoft in 1975 in Albuquerque—the same place Jeff Bezos had been born in 1964. Was Albuquerque just unlucky?

Early on in the growth of Boulder, the federal government established several research laboratories in town. These laboratories had links to CU Boulder, where university research overlapped with the work done at the national labs. Several generations later, Boulder has the highest concentration of PhDs per capita in the nation, and the city has an influential culture around education and research.[8] It's no surprise that many "deep-tech" companies have set up offices in town and that large companies have established second offices for research and new product development.

The outcome of many systems is a single result or an equilibrium state. In complexity theory, a system has many possible states, also called "basins of attraction." Within a particular state, there is a significant amount of ongoing dynamism and evolution.

These basins of attraction exert a gravitational pull on elements of the system. While this causes the activity to converge toward a semi-stable place, it is difficult to predict which of the many potential states will become the dominant ones. Some may be healthy, and others won't. The basins themselves are not fixed and are continually evolving.

Because of these basins of attraction, complex systems exhibit strong inertia effects (also called *lock-in*), whereby healthy systems tend to stay that way. Similarly, unhealthy systems struggle to break free, which is why regional differences in startup activity tend to change slowly. Prosperous entrepreneurial regions stay successful while less successful entrepreneurial areas persistently lag.

These outcomes can change, although progress is slow and uneven, requiring persistence and patience to move to a better result. In *Startup Communities*, I talk about the need to take a long-term view. While I described it as at least 20 years, I subsequently modified this idea to have a 20-year view from your current point in time. Startup community building, done well, takes time before the big payoffs can be seen.

In Boulder, after a long period of successful entrepreneurial activity, things seemed to change in uncomfortable ways. New people were coming to town, the creation of startups continued, and many existing companies were growing. Still, a number of the early startup community builders began to complain that things felt different. Cliques, which had always existed, became more rigid, and factions began appearing. An entrepreneur who had moved away for a while commented that she felt disoriented when she returned. There was still a vibrant startup community, but it had a different vibe now. Its center of gravity had shifted so there were several.

THE NARRATIVE FALLACY

In his 2011 book, *Thinking, Fast and Slow*, psychologist, behavioral economist, and Nobel Laureate, Daniel Kahneman catalogs the myriad ways the human mind rejects the complexity around us in favor of a simplified version of the world.[9] We do this by applying mental shortcuts or rules of thumb, which are primarily shaped by our own experience. But these heuristics cause us to make mistakes—predictable mistakes that are nonetheless hard to avoid. Humans are not only irrational; we are, according to psychologist Dan Ariely, "predictably irrational."[10]

One of the predictable mistakes we are prone to make is assigning causality to situations where such relationships don't exist. This tendency is driven by an aversion to uncertainty, or what 18th-century philosopher David Hume described as a deep emotional need for coherence and meaning.[11] This pattern is so pervasive that Kahneman named it "what you see is all there is" (WYSIATI). It emanates from the reactive or sensory-driven part of our brains, which is instinctual and tends to dominate our decision-making, but isn't suited for careful thought and analysis.

We want to make sense of our world, even if we don't have all the facts. While this satisfies the deep emotional needs that Hume and Kahneman describe, we also do it because we want to be useful. We perceive utility in applying tools and methodologies to our work—we want to help. But to know what the right approach is (the "prediction"), we must first understand the underlying relationships (the "causality").[12]

However, in complex systems, causality and prediction are often impossible to know—especially in advance. Since we don't have all of the facts, we invent them and fill in the blanks with stories, which are often incorrect. By projecting our own experiences onto the world and drawing broad conclusions from them, we make predictable mistakes.

Nassim Nicholas Taleb also addresses this in his 2007 book, *The Black Swan: The Impact of the Highly Improbable*. Black-swan events are high-impact, low-frequency occurrences that few, if any, people foresee because they are complex and generally unprecedented. When attempting to explain these events, humans create stories about cause-and-effect that mislead themselves and others.[13] For Taleb, issues around these complex phenomena aren't only unclear in advance; they also aren't clearer after the fact. However, we regularly pretend they are well understood in retrospect, leading to interpretation mistakes. While black-swan events aren't random—there are underlying factors and relationships driving them—they are simply too complex for the human mind to understand and anticipate.

Silicon Valley is a type of black-swan event—high impact, low frequency, and entirely unpredictable in advance. There have also been countless failed attempts at recreating Silicon Valley, which means the story of how Silicon Valley came to be is just that—a story. It is what people tell themselves so they can bring coherence and order to the complex phenomena of entrepreneurial ecosystems. But too often, the wrong lessons are learned. There are certain principles to be learned from Silicon Valley, absolutely. In fact, this book draws from many of them. But there are no clear rules—only possibilities.

One of the many factors that gave rise to Silicon Valley early on was the unprecedented government spending on wartime research and development. The sheer size of the stimulus shaped entire industries, channeling vast sums of money—and therefore talent—into nascent electronics and communications companies. A superficial lesson learned from this experience might be: *A technology and startup hub can be created by injecting large quantities of government spending on R&D*. While that might be true somewhere, it's generally not. A more useful lesson from that story might be: *Entrepreneurs respond to demand for products and services. Where are the unmet, current needs for innovation?* A strategy that follows might be to look for ways to better connect would-be entrepreneurs with customers or to illuminate pathways into entrepreneurship for employees at large incumbents. What works may surprise you and would likely be different from what has worked elsewhere. To us, that seems more sensible than waiting around for the next World War, or some other existential crisis that motivates a mission-driven state.[14]

BUILDING ON STRENGTHS AND LEARNING FROM FAILURES

History and local context matter in complex systems. The startup community should focus on being the best version of itself, rather than competing with or replicating something else. This is vital to understand. This work is fundamentally about improvement and increasing the odds that something great will occur. Nothing is guaranteed. Successful outcomes end up looking different from what's expected and frequently emanate from unanticipated sources.

Each city on the planet was once itself a startup and today has a lengthy history and embedded culture that is the product of hundreds or thousands of years of human habitation. These complex physical, social, and economic structures are unique to each city, which should play to its strengths.

The wrong question is: How do we be more like Silicon Valley?

The right questions are: Where are we now, and how do we get where we need to go? What seems to be working already, and what's not working? How do we better support efforts that are working and wind-down those that are not? What are startups in need of today, and how can I help them?

Because of the inherent uncertainty and nonlinearity in the outcomes of complex systems, participants in startup communities need to be comfortable with failure, which is a normal and healthy part of the process of entrepreneurship. If you are not failing frequently, then you are not taking enough risks. If you are not taking enough risks, then you won't advance anything meaningfully over time. Being comfortable with and destigmatizing failure is compelling. Failures, or let's call them learning opportunities, are to be welcomed, not avoided or shamefully hidden away.

Endless experimentation that illuminates improvements through trial and error is much more useful than major interventions that aren't informed by signals. Lasting improvements result from the ongoing repetition of small and seemingly inconsequential behaviors. This fact makes it easier to take risks with smaller-scale programs and policies since the cost of failure is much lower. An inherent part of the journey is failure, adjusting experiments, and trying again. This is where learning occurs, feedback can be absorbed, and a new strategy can be developed and launched.

A culture of persistent risk aversion is a foundational obstacle to startup community development. It shows up as a concern about investing time in something that doesn't end up having an impact, and the fear of rejection by other people in the startup community. If you are afraid to take chances, fail, and change course, you'll limit your development along with that of the startup community.

This risk aversion also manifests itself by avoiding people because of their past failures. A great deal of learning occurs in failed ventures, and, instead of falling into the fear trap, embrace people who have experienced failure and encourage them to take new risks unless they've done something fundamentally illegal or immoral.

Aversion to failure also shows up as dishonesty. People lie about failure and sometimes will take extraordinary lengths to conceal it. But doing this simply delays the inevitable and will most likely make things much worse. Avoid this dangerous and ultimately futile path.

Finally, remember that startup community building is not a zero-sum game, where there are winners and losers. In a startup community, the pursuit of narrow self-interest undermines the entire system. It also works against the perpetrators over the long term, as they will become increasingly isolated from other participants in the startup community. Instead, embrace the notion of increasing-returns systems where everyone gains more by being a positive contributor to the collective. Adopt a mindset of abundance, rather than scarcity.

CULTIVATING TOPOPHILIA

Startup community participants must have topophilia, or a love of place for where they live, manifested as a deeply held desire to improve their community. While people who spearhead startup community–building efforts are likely to have a deep commitment to their city, it's worth remembering that many who share a similar topophilia may not be active in community-building efforts. Appeal to that sensibility as a means of converting those on the sidelines to engaging with startup community-building efforts.

John Hickenlooper, a successful entrepreneur who was the governor of Colorado from 2011 to 2019, made topophilia the central theme of his final State of the State speech before the Colorado legislature. He said:

> We're here, as public servants, to make this place we love, stay a place we love; a place we can be proud of. That's called topophilia—it's our love of place, and reflects our love of Colorado. . .
>
> Popular culture has tried to sell us a tall tale that Colorado's history is only about rugged individualism and conflict. But cooperation has always been the defining part of our DNA. . .
>
> Sometimes in this building, we stray from this Colorado way. . . But I believe love of place is a key ingredient of most economic development. And people aren't eager to make the investments that all prosperity demands if they don't trust the people who lead them, and trust that those leaders will work together.[15]

A reverse-causality problem occurs when startup community participants equate an abundance of resources present in established, thriving entrepreneurial ecosystems with the factors and initial conditions required at the outset. Governments or other feeders that look to the model of Silicon Valley or another thriving entrepreneurial ecosystem take an inventory of the current circumstances and attempt to adopt those same factors in their city.

But this gets things backwards, or at least, out of sync. They confuse what occurs in sustainable, mature startup communities with the initial conditions that helped get them there. The development of many of the resources and support mechanisms in startup communities occurs as entrepreneurship becomes more prominent. Entrepreneurs build a community as they develop their companies, producing a virtuous cycle that makes local entrepreneurship more likely.[16]

As regional entrepreneurship scholar Maryann Feldman notes:

An important concern is how environments lacking an entrepreneurial tradition change and became munificent [bountiful]. Conventional wisdom about the factors that promote entrepreneurship is drawn from analysis of munificent environments. Rather than viewed as causal factors, strong local networks, active research universities and abundant venture capital may be attributes of successful entrepreneurship in established clusters. The genesis or initial formation of firms, the building of institutions and social relationships appears to be a distinct phenomenon. . . . many of the conditions the literature indicates should be in place to promote entrepreneurship appear to lag rather than lead its development and thus question our understanding of the dynamics of regional change and the implied policy prescriptions.[17]

How Local Government Can Best Engage with and Help the Startup Community

Rebecca Lovell (Seattle, Washington)
Executive Director, Create 33
(Former) Acting Director, Office of Economic Development, City of Seattle

One of the things that government officials should keep in mind when engaging with the startup community in their city is this: Stick with what you know best. I would know since I spent over four years doing this on behalf of the City of Seattle. Startup communities are uniquely local, and governments at the local level can play a helpful (or harmful) feeder role.

Whether you're in government and are "here to help," or are a resident with ideas about what your city can do for startups, you will likely find the answer by asking three questions: What is needed? What is missing? What can the government do?

Whatever your vantage point, you must first assess the local landscape.

If you're a government official, the next step is to take a long look in the mirror. You may have a (perhaps well-deserved) reputation for being overly top-down and prescriptive. What you need is a paradigm shift. For entrepreneurship, try a bottom-up, capacity-building orientation first, and always hire entrepreneurs with the lived experience of the founder's journey. Career bureaucrats are limited in their ability to help in this context.

When the City of Seattle hired me as their first "Startup Advocate," I spent the first three months listening to entrepreneurs by offering 1:1 support and identifying patterns and trends. This process of listening and collecting data informed the initial programming priorities, which we regularly refresh through constant community engagement. And although a few good ideas may come out of City Hall, when it comes to supporting startups, it's essential to get out of the building and engage with your local startup community!

What Can and Should Be Done?

I'll start with two areas we have chosen not to play in Seattle, but could be worth exploring in your community:

> *Financial capital*: In Seattle, we are fortunate to have a critical mass of committed, early-stage investors who prioritize local founders. With these assets in place, we did not prioritize setting up a city startup fund. (We also happen to have a state constitution prohibiting this.) But even so, it's important to remember that governments typically make for lousy venture capitalists.

Physical space: Whether it's by providing cheap rent to startups or facilitating collaboration, workspace and serendipitous collisions can reduce barriers to entry for entrepreneurs, and this may be an asset that governments can provide. In Seattle, it's not. We target every bit of land we own for affordable housing, and the private sector has answered market demand with 40 co-working spaces and counting.

What Is Missing?

Another set of areas where we did play a role is what I describe as frequently outside the traditional part of many governments, but where the government can step in to fill gaps and have a significant impact.

Connecting: From cataloging resources via our Startup Seattle website, to providing direct support to startups (in co-working spaces around town, not in City Hall), Seattle's current Startup Advocate (David Harris, an entrepreneur) is an expert in triage. He either answers entrepreneurs' questions, expedites a solution to a problem, or connects them to someone who can help, which works in our community because we have a critical mass of founders who are willing and able to help other founders. For communities that haven't achieved this critical mass, even a small group of committed leaders can begin to spark change. In Seattle, we have an undercurrent of collegiality that fuels the innovation engine—it is easy to get a cup of coffee with just about anyone. But we have room to improve—for barriered populations, that engine may be difficult to access. As such, we focus on underrepresented communities facing institutional barriers, including access to both financial and social capital. We try to reduce those barriers for communities of color, women, and immigrants, not just because it's the right thing to do, but because it's the smart thing to do (diverse communities perform better).

Develop talent: Even in a city with a high concentration of engineers, it's difficult for startups to compete for technical skill, a recurring theme in most every 1:1 meeting or community event, year after year. As our four-year universities and community colleges can't keep up with demand, we have worked to support (and funnel federal and state funding into) accelerated training programs. As computational thinking has become a life skill, early exposure and education can be a boon to innovation. Public school districts across the country have implemented such programs as Code.org, which pays teachers a stipend to receive training on delivering computer science curriculum in schools. Local governments can play an influencing role in such implementation, as well as paving the way for skills centers and STEM schools.

Convening: Though not a superpower per se, it's remarkable who elected officials can bring to a table—including competitors who normally wouldn't speak, let alone collaborate. While the government uses this convening power to explore solutions to civic issues, listening sessions can yield real results for startups. In 2012, then Seattle Mayor Michael McGinn convened a group of startup leaders that ultimately led to the City's launch of the Startup Seattle program. In current Mayor Jenny Durkan's first months in office, she convened a similar group to vet policy proposals and explore new ideas for her administration. However, startup communities can grow weary of such convenings should they not see evidence of turning talk into action. So, governments need to do more than just facilitate discussions—they need to be agents of change.

What Is Government Good At?

Finally, here are two critical areas more in the traditional mold of local government where leaders in Seattle are only just beginning to engage. Don't overlook these!

Policy development: It's no secret that the government holds the keys to public policy. But elected officials would benefit by acknowledging what they can control (versus where they can wield influence), and by engaging with community voices in policy formulation. While any number of city processes and regulations may dampen innovation, governments can offer incentives, such as extending tax exemptions to new businesses or by taxing net revenue instead of topline income. Non-compete agreements are generally the purview of U.S. states. California has long enjoyed a competitive advantage because it doesn't enforce such restrictions on talent mobility. At the national level in the United States, the carrots and sticks are too numerous to list. Still, from capital formation policies to immigration policy and the (languishing) Startup Visa, much work can be done to support startups!

Megaphone: The most surprising insight I gleaned from Seattle Mayor Durkan's startup convening was how strongly participants urged her to use an asset that costs nothing but can be priceless in its impact—her voice. We may have historically suffered from a Seattle-nice, self-deprecating mentality. We will likely never beat our chests and declare we are the "Silicon Valley that never sleeps" (like former New York Mayor Michael Bloomberg). But passionately and authentically amplifying the incredible stories of local startups is an asset that every mayor has at her disposal.

With that, I'm hoping that a brief overview of what we are doing, not doing, and could be doing can provide helpful insight on how to engage your local government in support of startup communities everywhere.

CHAPTER ELEVEN

THE MEASUREMENT TRAP

Startup Community Way Principle

Startup communities must avoid the trap of letting demand for measurement drive flawed strategies. The most tangible and therefore easiest factors to measure in a startup community also have the least amount of impact on its performance over the long term. Given limited resources and understanding, many organizations, particularly feeders, let the desire to measure things steer strategies in the wrong direction.

Legendary management thinker Peter Drucker is credited with coining the phrase "If you can't measure it, you can't manage it." Today's contemporary version, "What gets measured gets managed" is one of the most commonly referenced quotes in the business world. But there are two problems. First, Drucker never said it.[1] Second, and more important, it's conceptually misaligned with his more nuanced views on effective management.

While Drucker was a strong advocate for "the measurement of results," he also knew a more important task for business leaders is to establish something less tangible.

> It is the relationship with people, the development of mutual confidence, the identification of people, the creation of a community. . .
> It cannot be measured or easily defined. But it is not only a key function. It is one only you can perform.[2]

While relationships can be measured to a degree, not everything that can be measured matters and not everything that matters can be measured. This is a vital lesson for participants in startup communities and entrepreneurial ecosystems to absorb.

THE FUNDAMENTAL MEASUREMENT PROBLEM

Effective measurement of startup communities and entrepreneurial ecosystems is still in its infancy, but demand for metrics is growing, as the scope of participants widens and the amount of committed resources expands. However, the measurement of complex systems is inherently difficult. Consequently, the void gets filled with quick fixes and substandard approaches that emphasize many of the least important factors. This leads to confusion about what matters most and results in misguided strategies that ultimately fail. Using data to dictate which strategies get implemented, the proverbial tail is wagging the dog.

This problem occurs because people, especially in feeders, need to demonstrate the direct impact of programs or activities to justify their continued investment and support. Since the easiest things to measure are tangible, quantity based, or input oriented, this motivates the design of programs around those types of factors. Unfortunately, these are often the wrong factors to be applying pressure to because they have the least amount of impact on the long-term performance of a startup community.

This gets compounded by the fact that many of the metrics being emphasized take a long time to materialize and are simultaneously affected by many other factors. And yet, the impact of a course of action is expected to occur quickly and be directly attributed. These expectations are misguided.

In complex systems, the interactions matter more than the magnitude of people or resources, and the value of these interactions takes time to materialize. The intervention points with highest leverage are those dealing with the system structure, such as behaviors or relationships, and the underlying attitudes and values of the people involved. But the qualitative, localized, and personal nature of these factors makes measuring them challenging to capture, requiring a lot of bespoke on-the-ground work that imposes significant time and cost burden. Furthermore, data collection is best done at the individual level, continuously, and over a long period of time. The longitudinal data is much more important than cross-sectional data at one moment in time.

Unless the proverbial rich aunt or uncle (or successful entrepreneur) is going to underwrite the master dataset of startup communities around the world, we're stuck in a difficult situation where there is pressure to collect data and measure impact quickly, but without adequate resources or understanding in place to do it well. This presents a trap—quick fixes are implemented, suboptimal strategies are adopted, and poor outcomes result.

To reorient the misattributed Drucker quote: "What can easily be measured gets prioritized." Or, as columnist Simon Caulkin once quipped: "What gets measured gets managed—even when it's pointless to measure and manage it, and even if it harms the purpose of the organization to do so."[3] In startup communities, this translates into strategizing around things that can easily be seen and parameters that can easily be adjusted, even if doing so has a limited or even negative impact.

In spite of these challenges, a lot of smart people have been hard at work over the past decade to advance the field of entrepreneurial ecosystem measurement. Collectively, it is informative, and when used skillfully, can be beneficial. However, there is no ideal approach and there are no short-cuts. Each approach has benefits and limitations. Ultimately, the name of the game is pragmatism and humility. To do this work effectively, you have to take a broad approach and put in the hard work, knowing that it will be imperfect.

ACTOR AND FACTOR MODELS: A CATEGORICAL APPROACH

The most prominent entrepreneurial ecosystem frameworks are actor and factor models. These are lists of the relevant people and organi-zations, most often organized by role or function, along with the resources and conditions involved. These models developed in the last decade as the phenomenon of entrepreneurial ecosystems began to take shape, and they were the first models to go along with the popular movement.[4]

When applied practically, ecosystem mapping is the process of devel-oping categorical models in a particular place. It is an audit of the "who and what" occurring in an entrepreneurial ecosystem, where individu-als and organizations are cataloged and given a role or function. Often, people transcend or overlap multiple roles. This is a useful exercise for understanding the people and activities in a city and establishing a baseline model of a startup community at a moment in time.

An excellent example of this work is being developed by researcher and community builder Chad Renando in Australia.[5] Among other things, he is mapping the ecosystem in that country from the bottom-up in impressive detail and is building a set of useful tools to go along with it.[6]

Another example is the way I categorized leaders and feeders in *Startup Communities* (instigators were added in this book). Today, we have compressed this into two categories. The first is the actors, which includes the leaders, feeders, and instigators. The second category is the factors, which includes the Seven Capitals. We distilled the critical essence of the details into a simplified and memorable construct by consolidating these many elements into a few categories. Following is a simple graphic that illustrates this visually.

Actors and Factors in an Entrepreneurial Ecosystem

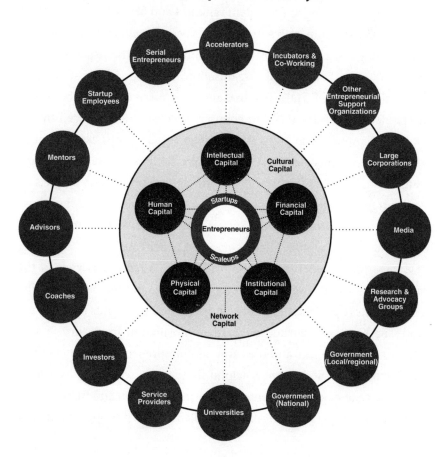

STANDARDIZED METRICS MODELS: A COMPARATIVE APPROACH

Another entrepreneurial ecosystem model that takes a comparative approach occurs when researchers apply existing data sources to quantify the actors and factors—directly or by proxy—and, in some cases, create metrics where existing data sources don't exist. Using standardized metrics allows comparison across different entrepreneurial ecosystems in a systematic way, often resulting in ecosystem rankings and benchmarking tools.

A number of comparative models have been developed over the years at the country and city levels by organizations such as the Aspen Institute, World Economic Forum, and Organisation for Economic Co-operation and Development (OECD).[7] Two that are widely used today are the Global Entrepreneurship Index (GEI), a country-level ranking produced by the Global Entrepreneurship Network, and Startup Genome's assessment of high-tech entrepreneurial ecosystems in global cities and regions.[8] Some organizations, such as Techstars, have developed proprietary models to assess entrepreneurial ecosystems in cities around the world. All of these models input data from existing sources, such as the World Bank, Global Entrepreneurship Monitor, PitchBook, and Crunchbase.

Comparative models are useful for forming a high-level view of the relative strengths and weaknesses of a geography and for benchmarking specific inputs (e.g., the amount of venture capital) or outputs (e.g., startup rates.) The best ones include qualitative information from surveys that capture information like attitudes around entrepreneurship and community. Comparative models are a helpful first step in wrapping your head around the state of play in an entrepreneurial ecosystem and finding clues about where to apply pressure, resolve challenges, or spur opportunities.

However, these models can easily deceive. The breadth of variables is too often equated with comprehensiveness and accuracy. Input variables are frequently proxies—even crude ones—of what we actually want to measure. Tradeoffs are needed for standardizing variables across multiple geographies; depth, usefulness, and consistency are inherent challenges. There is nothing unusual or wrong about producing models with such limitations in the economic and social sciences, but it's important for users to know what the limits are. Comparative models aren't a cure-all, even if they seem to be.

Comparative models can become problematic when they are built into ecosystem rankings. These schemes, in which one entrepreneurial ecosystem is said to be better than others, are oversimplifications of reality. Rankings are indexed and formulaic in nature, and are built around the assumptions of uniformity, linearity, and predictability. None of these are applicable to complex systems. Rankings also tend to lead directly to a problem discussed earlier: they may encourage strategies around things that can easily be seen and parameters that can easily be adjusted.

When misapplied, comparative models result in a false sense of predictability that is unwarranted and amplifies the narrative fallacy (simplifying things we don't fully understand). By design, comparative models typically don't capture the most important factors—the interactions and underlying mental models of the actors involved—because gathering credible data at the required detail across many geographies is too difficult. While we understand the appeal and even the fun in competing against other ecosystems, we urge you to resist taking this approach too seriously. Use these models to inform, not to prescribe. View them as one piece of a much larger puzzle. Learn from the individual metrics contained in them without having to resort to indexing or competitions.

Practical methodological quibbles aside, on a conceptual level, we urge you to avoid the trap of being overly comparative. Instead, recognize that the most important comparisons are within the same ecosystem at different points in time.

NETWORK MODELS: A RELATIONAL APPROACH

Understanding the network that ties actors together in an entrepreneurial ecosystem is critically important. Two well-documented approaches provide excellent examples of how to analyze these networks. First is the dealmakers approach, posited by academics Maryann Feldman and Ted Zoller.[9] The other is a series of network graphs produced by researchers at Endeavor and the World Bank.[10] These models show that ecosystems that regularly produce high-impact companies have a higher proportion of successful entrepreneurs in influential positions compared with cities where non-entrepreneurial actors are more dominant or where the startup community is disengaged. Collaboration between influential actors is also an important characteristic of the successful entrepreneurial ecosystems.

Network analysis demonstrates established relationships in a startup community, at both an individual level and the systems level, on dimensions such as mentorship, investment, or prior employment. It also shows who is influential in the network and whom they are connected to. The most critical factors to startup community performance are connectivity and network structure, along with the underlying values, attitudes, and worldviews of the individuals themselves. Network analysis can reflect this, which makes it an extremely valuable modeling approach.

The following graph from Endeavor shows the prevalence of tech startup founders in New York City, highlighting those that were previously employees at other tech startups in the city.[11]

Unfortunately, network models are difficult to produce, which is why they are severely underutilized. You can't easily download a master dataset of connections in a startup community. Instead you have to map them out one by one from the bottom-up. This takes time, resources, and expertise. It also requires credibility and trustworthiness because data collection

Network Map of Former Employment between Tech Entrepreneurs in New York City

CONNECTIONS:

→ EXPERIENCE: Former employment of founders at other tech companies in New York City

YEAR FOUNDED:
BEFORE 1999
1999-2003
2004-2008
2009-2013

ACTORS:

● ENTREPRENEURIAL COMPANIES

The size of the circle reflects the number of connections originating from the founders of each company. Founders are represented by their most prominent company or organization.

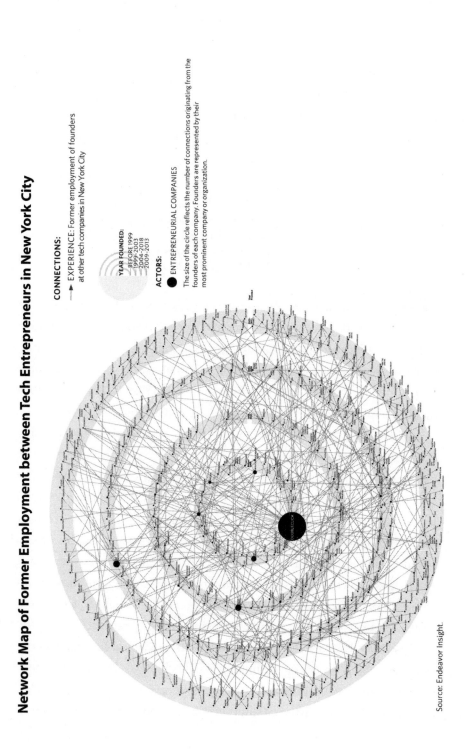

Source: Endeavor Insight.

occurs via the interviewing of many actors about formal and informal relationships relating to their business. Interviewers must weigh subjective and potentially sensitive information, such as who has invested in a company or where a person sees problematic behavior in the startup community.

DYNAMIC MODELS: AN EVOLUTIONARY APPROACH

Complex systems are dynamic, evolving over time and existing along a continuum of stages of development and maturity. Some, such as Silicon Valley, are advanced and self-sustaining. Others, such as Seattle, Austin, and Singapore, are emerging and represent the next generation of global entrepreneurial ecosystems. Others still are in earlier stages of development or perhaps even in dormancy. Some are in decline.

Taking an evolutionary view toward startup communities can be valuable in practice.[12] Understanding initial conditions and path dependencies causes participants to think about how deeply ingrained factors impact them. The search for phase transitions and basins of attraction can illuminate potential inflection points that prompt actions to advance the system into the next stage. Too often, people incorrectly equate the factors existing in a more advanced entrepreneurial ecosystem with what's needed for a less-developed entrepreneurial ecosystem to become more advanced. It is important to recognize that what gets things started is different from what accelerates and sustains things.[13] The system and the factors driving it coevolve.

There are five stages of maturity for an entrepreneurial ecosystem—nascent, developing, emerging, sustaining, and declining.[14] The last of these—declining—is often overlooked. For example, there are striking parallels between the leading startup communities today, and Cleveland and Detroit

Lifecycle Model of a Startup Community or Entrepreneurial Ecosystem

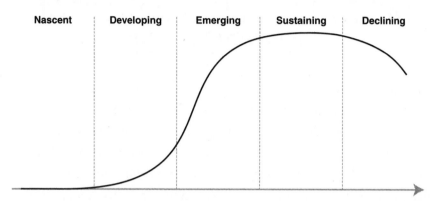

as frontier hubs at the turn of the 20th century, including for early forms of entrepreneurship, angel investing, and business incubation.[15] Boston, the leading American innovation hub coming out of World War II, experienced a deep decline in the 1980s. In contrast, Silicon Valley's ability to continually reinvent itself in the face of technological change is part of its resilience.[16]

While dynamic models provide a useful thought exercise, there are challenges with applying them. Let's say we create broad benchmarks along each of the Seven Capitals—intellectual, human, financial, institutional, physical, network, and cultural. What are the objectively defined thresholds or inflection points for each stage on each dimension? Defining this can introduce subjectivity and doing this type of work inherently requires comparisons between entrepreneurial ecosystems.

Nonetheless, taking into account the dimension of time when conducting an assessment of a startup community is a useful exercise. It causes the participants to think about how these factors might evolve and what success looks like at different points in time. We can still learn from the historical evolution of other ecosystems at more advanced stages. And, most importantly, accounting for time can remind us that the work is forever ongoing—startup communities are never complete.

CULTURAL-SOCIAL MODELS: A BEHAVIORAL APPROACH

Startup Communities and the Boulder Thesis are different from the aforementioned models. First, they identify practical steps for improving a startup community from the perspective of entrepreneurs. Unlike a top-down approach that is implied by many categorical and comparative models, bottom-up change is central to *Startup Communities*. The behavioral approach acts as a qualitative guide for actively improving a startup community, even if just incrementally.

A second distinction is that *Startup Communities* focuses on the cultural norms and practices that help make a vibrant startup community possible. *Startup Communities* is primarily concerned with the nature of human connections, behaviors, attitudes, and values that contribute to a healthy startup community. In that regard, *Startup Communities* is fundamentally about improving human relationships.

Another cultural-social model is also the most similar to *Startup Communities*. Victor Hwang and Greg Horowitt, two experienced entrepreneurs and ecosystem builders, published *The Rainforest: The Secret to Building the Next Silicon Valley*. As with *Startup Communities*, *The Rainforest* is a model for practical change that stresses a human-centric focus for improving relationships between diverse individuals, allowing them to better collaborate and help entrepreneurs succeed.

Both models point to an underutilized but powerful means of measurement—the survey of individuals to assess behaviors, attitudes, and views on various cultural and social norms in a startup community. The sentiment and actions of these individuals can be tracked over time, assessing how they are responding to various initiatives. Tracking how people change behaviors and thought patterns over time, particularly when benchmarked against a specific initiative (e.g., a new coffee meetup, a new startup accelerator, etc.) or event (e.g., a large exit of a local company, a high-profile failure, etc.), is one potential path to tying cause and effect together in a complex system.

Don't forget that an essential part of a startup community is finding ways to get people to be more collaborative and supportive around entrepreneurship. Surveys, if done well, can help build evidence around those key behavioral and attitudinal outcomes.

LOGIC MODELS: A CAUSAL APPROACH

Causal models are generally theoretical ones and often the basis for academic papers. Some limited research has been conducted in this domain and has generated several useful ideas.[17]

Consider an entrepreneurial ecosystem as a value chain where the front end is what goes into it (actors and factors) and the back end is what comes out of it (startups). To create a value chain model, you identify the internal processes and informal governance structures that are a part of converting the inputs into outputs. Rather than focus on the before and after states, concentrate on the processes. Then, specify what you want to change in the system and why, hypothesize what might cause change to occur, and track progress, assess impact, and make adjustments. While abstract, it's important to understand that your approach should be highly dependent on local conditions and remain flexible under a high degree of uncertainty.

While cause–effect relationships cannot be credibly established at a system-wide level in the context of complexity, causal thinking can be a useful exercise. First, it prioritizes what drives value creation but can't easily be seen. By mapping the impacts a course of action is expected to produce, we are forced to think harder about underlying relationships and feedback loops. This leads to explicitly stating the "so what?" and the "then what?" for an approach.[18] Too often, we operate with assumptions and goals operating subconsciously in our minds. Stating these explicitly often reveals that different stakeholders are operating with a different framework in mind—even those working together toward the same goals.

A logic model is one way to implement this approach. A logic model is a chain of if-then statements about how change is expected to occur. There are four components:[19]

1. *Inputs*: The actors (people, organizations) and factors (resources, conditions).
2. *Activities and outputs*: What we do, how these things are combined, and where we intervene. These can be natural (emergent processes) or interventionist (programs).
3. *Outcomes*: The expected, follow-on results of these activities and outputs. They are of a short-, medium-, and long-term nature.
4. *Goals, rationales, and assumptions*: What we are trying to achieve, what we believe about how change occurs, and the conditions we believe are necessary for success.

Inputs are treated as fixed. Activities and outputs can be measured and attributed to a source. Complexity makes outcomes difficult or impossible to measure and attribute, which gets even more challenging the further out in time one moves from the direct action or output.

Feeders, particularly governments, put significant pressure on directly tying outputs to long-term outcomes like jobs created. But, in practice this is next to impossible to do in a complex system and will result in suboptimal strategies that prioritize compliance with metric demands rather than doing what's most effective. Instead, use an "if this, then that" approach, which does a much better job of modeling how change actually occurs. It may require a few extra hoops to jump through, but it's more honest about the realities.

Example of a Logic Model of Value Creation in an Entrepreneurial Ecosystem

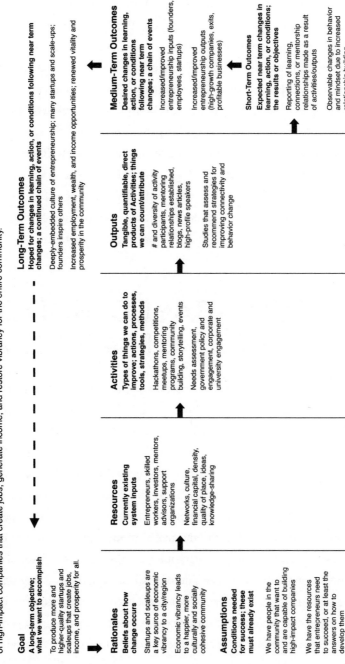

Problem Statement A particular challenge we want to solve for the population of interest

The local economy is not delivering enough quality opportunities for workers and households. We lack the types of high-impact companies that create jobs, generate income, and restore vibrancy for the entire community.

Goal
A long-term objective; what we want to accomplish

To produce more and higher-quality startups and scaleups that create jobs, income, and prosperity for all.

Rationales
Beliefs about how change occurs

Startups and scaleups are a key source of economic vibrancy to a city/region

Economic vibrancy leads to a happier, more culturally and socially cohesive community

Assumptions
Conditions needed for success; these must already exist

We have people in the community that want to and are capable of building high-impact companies

We have the resources that entrepreneurs need to succeed, or at least the answers on how to develop them

Resources
Currently existing system inputs

Entrepreneurs, skilled workers, investors, mentors, advisors, support organizations

Networks, culture, financial capital, density, quality of place, ideas, knowledge-sharing

Activities
Types of things we can do to improve; actions, processes, tools, strategies, methods

Hackathons, competitions, meetups, mentoring programs, community building, storytelling, events

Needs assessment, government policy and engagement, corporate and university engagement

Outputs
Tangible, quantifiable, direct products of Activities; things we can count/attribute

and diversity of activity participants, mentoring relationships established, blogs, news articles, high-profile speakers

Studies that assess and recommend strategies for improving connectivity and behavior change

Long-Term Outcomes
Hoped for changes in learning, action, or conditions following near term changes; a continued chain of events

Deeply-embedded culture of entrepreneurship; many startups and scale-ups; founders inspire others

Increased employment, wealth, and income opportunities; renewed vitality and prosperity in the community

Medium-Term Outcomes
Desired changes in learning, action, or conditions following near term changes; a chain of events

Increased/improved entrepreneurship inputs (founders, employees, startups)

Increased/improved entrepreneurship outputs (high-growth companies, exits, profitable businesses)

Short-Term Outcomes
Expected near term changes in learning, action, or conditions; the results or objectives

Reporting of learning, connections, or mentorship relationships made as a result of activities/outputs

Observable changes in behavior and mindset due to increased relationship building

By using a causal approach, also known as a *theory of change* exercise, you can bridge the divide over expectations about what programs should deliver in a startup community and on what time scale. In addition to the growth and development of a startup community, governments want job creation, corporate sponsors want high-impact acquisition targets, and universities want future donors. It is understandable why these goals are selected but expecting a singular program to directly achieve such lofty, long-term outcomes is unrealistic. By sketching out a theory of change, we can define a more realistic set of expectations about what can and should be measured, and what the initial indicators of longer-term success might look like. Moreover, this exercise allows multiple stakeholders to surface and align assumptions, rationales, goals, and expectations.

AGENT-BASED MODELS: A SIMULATION APPROACH

Agent-based models are a common approach used to analyze complex adaptive systems.[20] In these models, "agents" act based on a series of "rules." In the case of human actors, the rules constitute things like behaviors, ideas, principles, or resource endowments. The rules determine how agents independently act or how they respond to the actions of others and the environment around them. Agent-based models simulate how the many individual actions aggregate to shape system structure and produce emergent patterns.

This approach is commonly used to model tipping points or contagion in areas such as traffic congestion, viruses, or financial crises.[21] Recall our description of how Nobel laureate Thomas Schelling famously demonstrated that small differences in preferences for racial homogeneity and density could lead to sorting outcomes that diverged widely from those preferences over time.[22]

Research applying agent-based models to entrepreneurial ecosystems remains sparse, though a few examples do exist. In this work, researchers have modeled activities like the diffusion of startup formation or knowl-edge in an entrepreneurial ecosystem.[23] In addition to the rules, the various types of actors in entrepreneurial ecosystems, their search space (for resources and information), their objectives, and their connectivity to other actors, all work together to determine the characteristics of the emergent system.[24]

Perhaps too abstract for some practitioners, this is an area that, we believe, is ripe for testing many of the ideas presented in this book. For example, what is the saturation rate required for a #GiveFirst mentality to be widely adopted in a startup community? What is the magic threshold number for such a cascading contagion to occur? How might that unfold over time? Or, what is the critical mass of supportive community members required to counteract a resource-rich but ultimately harmful organization (e.g., an extractive angel investor group or an ill-equipped government-sponsored business incubator)?

Answers to these questions could be valuable to startup community participants not only in theory but in practice. They could serve as perfor-mance guideposts, be used to set meaningful goals, or help to illuminate how the performance of an ecosystem can improve over time just from tweaking a few behaviors to be more collaborative and helpful to entrepreneurs. Like the other approaches discussed in this chapter, agent-based simulations are not without important limits, such as difficulty capturing nonlinear behav-ior or the full complexity of interactions inherent in all models.

APPLYING THE DIFFERENT MODELS

While each model described above has shortcomings, taken together they are helpful for understanding, describing, and measuring an entrepre-neurial ecosystem. Following is a summary of each model along with its strengths and weaknesses.

Overview of Existing Ecosystem Models

Model	Description	Strengths	Weaknesses
Actor and Factor Models (Categorical)	Identification of roles and functions; when applied, can be an audit of the people, organizations, resources, and conditions in an ecosystem.	Can provide a clear accounting of what's happening in an ecosystem—the who and what involved; easy to understand.	Descriptive, often doesn't provide information on the qualities or quantities of the actors and factors, nor the relationships between them.
Standardized Metrics Models (Comparative)	Applies standardized metrics to actors and factors, inputs and outputs, which can then be used to benchmark one ecosystem to another in a systematic way.	Typically utilizes readily available data; allows for relatively uniform comparison across ecosystems to identify strengths/ weaknesses, and some performance measures; easy to understand.	Formulaic; often misused as rankings, which can erroneously shape strategies around surface-level parameters rather than the underlying connections, behaviors, and attitudes that drive an ecosystem.
Network Models (Relational)	Maps relationships in an ecosystem, often by role, function, and direction; illustrates the structure of the network (who the influential actors are, and how they are connected with each other).	Establishes relationships in an ecosystem; visualizes system structure; measures connectivity and density (which are critical factors for system performance).	Resource intensive; doesn't scale across cities easily; has to be built from the bottom-up in each location; can be too abstract for some.
Dynamic Models (Evolutionary)	Addresses the issue of change and evolution in an ecosystem, and the role of maturity or stage of development.	Signifies that needs change depending on stage of development; helps identify what those needs are; can identify inflection points in an ecosystem's evolution.	Abstract and subjective; difficult to objectively define threshold cutoffs between the various stages or apply data or other information to set those parameters.

Cultural-Social Models (Behavioral)	Focused on improving human relationships that promote collaboration, trust, and support between diverse individuals.	High leverage, action oriented; direct measurement of behaviors and thought patterns; can evaluate interventions, track changes over time.	Cost and time intensive, requires some expertise in survey/social science methods; generally not comparative to other places; slow to develop.
Logic Models (Causal)	Based on "theories of change," these models force one to explicitly state how value is created and what the expected impacts are for a course of action.	Maps expected impacts from a course of action at various stages; useful for program evaluation and planning; action-oriented; can align expectations about what is achievable over what timelines; surfaces goals and assumptions of the stakeholders.	Theoretical; cause and effect are difficult or impossible to establish in complex systems; might be too abstract and less systemic than some would prefer.
Agent-Based Models (Simulation)	Simulations of how complex factors such as behaviors, ideas, objectives, and connectivity of individual actors aggregate to shape and influence the system over multiple time periods.	Focuses on the core functionality of ecosystems as emergent phenomena—the interaction of actors; illustrates how patterns may evolve over time, identifying leverage or inflection points for systemwide shifts.	May be too abstract; highly sensitive to assumptions and input parameters, which are hard to know; adjustments needed for modeling may oversimplify complexity and emergent behavior.

Rather than choose one model, take a pragmatic and comprehensive approach. For example, conduct an audit of the actors and their roles or functions; gather readily available data on standardized measures to look for areas of strength, weakness, or macro performance; map and analyze the existence and nature of relationships in the network; collect qualitative information such as attitudes, behavior, and culture, and track how these things are changing over time among the same individuals; evaluate programs by establishing a theory of change and collecting information to assess progress; simulate how and when systemwide changes might occur from the spread of a few ideas or behaviors; and integrate these insights into a holistic view of the health of a startup community.

To conclude, here are a few easy principles to remember to avoid the measurement trap.

Be wide-ranging and pragmatic. There is no one path. Each model has strengths and weaknesses. Take a wide-reaching approach to assessing your entrepreneurial ecosystem in a holistic way by implementing all of these methods, or perhaps incorporating some of your own. Be honest and candid about the limitations of each, and be realistic about how the most important factors will be the hardest to capture and will take time to evolve.

Resist the temptation to be overly comparative. If you accept that you are working with a complex system, you should also resist being overly concerned with comparing one system to another. Benchmarking is helpful, but don't fall into the rankings trap. While it might feel good (or bad) in the short term, complex systems can't be gamified. Remember that the most important comparisons are within the same place or person at different points in time.

Focus on the connections, not the parts. Insight results from measuring and tracking relationships in the system rather than the parts of the system. If you want to change a complex system, you change the interactions, not the parts. Included in this is understanding not only the linkages and their nature, but the overall structure of the network—who's most influential matters.

Track everything, especially the changes, over time. Understanding what happens over time, especially changes in behavior or attitude of individual actors, is more important than measuring any specific category of things in a cross-sectional (fixed point in time) way.

What I've Learned from Measuring Entrepreneurship Communities for a Decade

Rhett Morris (New York, New York)
Partner, Common Good Labs

Over the last 10 years, I've led projects measuring entrepreneurship communities with partners including the Bill & Melinda Gates Foundation, Techstars, and the national government of Colombia. These projects spanned dozens of cities, such as New York, Detroit, Miami, Taipei, Bangalore, Mexico City, Istanbul, and Nairobi.

It is clear that entrepreneurship measurement has changed significantly in the last several years. While some lagging organizations are still just counting things that are easy to count, leading institutions are now developing sophisticated measurement systems using tools from network analysis and other disciplines. Based on my experience, the best organizations design entrepreneurship community measurement strategies that follow these four steps.

1. **Define and Align.** Why are you supporting your local entrepreneurship community? Do you want to create new jobs, increase economic growth, promote inclusion of underrepresented groups, work to do all of these things, or accomplish something else? The first step of effective measurement is to clearly define the goals of your work.

Once this is defined, it's time to align. No single measurement system is perfect for every entrepreneurship community. The tools and methodology you use should be the ones that are best aligned to provide actionable feedback on two things:

1. How much progress is the community making toward the goals you've defined?
2. What can be done to improve the ability of the community to reach these goals in the future?

This doesn't mean you need to design it all from scratch. A recent partner in the United States was interested in measuring the values of local entrepreneurship community members. Rather than create an entirely new methodology, we identified questions from the World Values Survey that addressed the issues they wanted to track. This gave them confidence that the project could effectively assess what they wanted to measure, since other researchers had already invested time to make sure these questions were effective. It also enabled us to benchmark data from one community with data on the values of other communities across the country.

2. **Share and Discuss.** Entrepreneurship communities are built on trust. If you are working to measure your local ecosystem, it is important to be a good community member and share what you learned. (Demonstrating transparency can also make it easier to collect measurement data in the future.)

Communities require more than just sharing information. Leading organizations should also bring together local decision makers (e.g., key founders, leaders of support organizations, investors, leaders of local foundations, government officials, etc.) to discuss how to apply the findings from measurements in order to make things better for entrepreneurs. Additional discussions and presentations for other community members should also be encouraged.

As this book clearly explains, entrepreneurship communities are complex systems. In these sorts of environments, data should be used to inform decision making, rather than to "drive" it. An effective measurement system will provide many things, but it isn't complete on its own. The perspectives and experiences of community leaders should be combined with the findings of local measurement initiatives to interpret their results and guide decision making.

One of the interesting things I see when gathering community leaders is that offering a sneak preview of new data on local entrepreneurs can bring together people who rarely attend the same community events. By convening a more diverse group of leaders, the act of sharing can encourage collaboration and enhance the development of common objectives among community members.

3. **Praise and Raise.** I regularly see hundreds of people attend presentations on local measurement projects. Mayors, national ministers, and even the founders of local "unicorn" companies clear their schedules to attend discussion groups on measurement findings. This can give leaders a valuable platform to engage with and elevate entrepreneurship.

The way that you share information will act as an important feedback loop to influence how people think and act in the ecosystem. Leaders should use this opportunity to praise the types of behavior they want more of and raise community members' expectations of what can and should be accomplished.

Promoting role models who embody the types of actions that lead to the goals you seek can be very effective. Whether they like to admit it or not, most community members are concerned about their status. (They are only human, after all.)

Raising the bar in terms of what people believe can be accomplished and how people should be acting locally can help to prevent stagnation and bring about more positive behavior change. In cities that have used network mapping to measure how active each community member is in terms of mentoring and supporting others, it isn't usual to see people start to compete over how many people they help instead of just how much money they have made.

4. **Refine and Repeat.** Last but not least, leaders need to incorporate measurement into their long-term planning for entrepreneurship community development. This requires both refinement and repetition.

There are two things that need to be refined: community strategy and the process for measurement. Communities change. Once your current objectives are accomplished, it's important to update your goals and plans. This usually requires realigning your measurement process to capture new data in order to assess your progress and provide feedback on how you can improve.

Repetition is also essential to success. Effective measurement is not a one-time event or a quick-fix solution. Leading organizations are now planning for annual or even semi-annual measurements of their entrepreneurship communities.

PART III

FROM THE BOULDER THESIS TO THE STARTUP COMMUNITY WAY

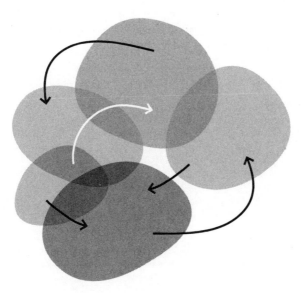

CHAPTER TWELVE

SIMPLIFYING COMPLEXITY

Startup Community Way Principle

The best startup communities are interconnected with other startup communities. Startup communities become stronger when they share ideas and resources with others. Continued exposure and engagement strengthen bonds forged across geographic boundaries.

The *Startup Community Way* differs from traditional entrepreneurial ecosystem thinking because it puts the startup community and entrepreneurs at the center of the ecosystem. We focus all of the activity on the entrepreneur. Enhancing relationships by taking a network-centric approach around cultural, social, and behavioral factors creates a startup community that is more supportive and collaborative.

Our limitations—as individuals and as a collective whole—become magnified within the broader social dynamic of the community.

Changing the ways we think, behave, collaborate, share, and support enables us to be much more effective, regardless of the existing resources at our disposal. This is difficult to do because it requires people to take accountability for their current situation and to change deeply ingrained thought and behavior patterns that hold a startup community back. However, startup communities anywhere have the power to improve their situations immediately, even if it's little by little.

Two existing cultural-behavioral startup community models inform how we approach this change. The first of these is the Boulder Thesis from *Startup Communities*. The other is *The Rainforest*, a powerful cultural-social-behavioral model put together by Victor Hwang and Greg Horowitt, two entrepreneurs, investors, and startup community builders.[1] Systems thinking is a set of tools, methodologies, concepts, and language that can further guide us to structure activities for maximum impact.

THE BOULDER THESIS

The central intellectual framework of *Startup Communities* is the Boulder Thesis, which explains why Boulder, Colorado, a small city of just over 100,000 people, consistently produces a very high rate of high-impact startups. While there are observable measurements like startup density, many exciting things are going on that result in the vibrancy of Boulder.[2]

Startup Communities broke new ground in 2012 when I observed that something about Boulder was different than other entrepreneurial ecosystems. Woven into the fabric of the Boulder startup community is a set of principles that gave fledgling companies a higher chance of success. I distilled this into the Boulder Thesis, which has four key components:

1. **Entrepreneurs must lead the startup community.** Although a range of participants—including government, universities, investors,

mentors, and service providers—are critical to a startup community, the entrepreneurs must lead organizing efforts. Entrepreneurs in this sense are people who have founded or co-founded a growth-oriented startup.

2. **The leaders must have a long-term commitment.** Entrepreneurs must be committed to building and maintaining a startup community over the long term. Leaders should take at least a 20-year view—a view that refreshes every year (the horizon is always 20 years out). For a startup community to be lasting it must be more consequential than the latest fad, or considered a response to an economic downturn.

3. **The startup community must be inclusive of anyone who wants to participate in it.** Startup communities should embrace a philosophy of extreme inclusion. Anyone who wants to get involved should be able to, whether they are new to town or new to startups, or whether they are company founders, employees, or simply want to help out. A startup community that embraces diversity and openness is a more flexible, adaptable, and resilient startup community.

4. **The startup community must have continual activities that engage the entire entrepreneurial stack.** Participants in a startup community must be continually engaging—not through passive events like cocktail parties or award ceremonies but through catalytic activities like hackathons, meetups, open coffee clubs, startup weekends, or mentor-driven accelerators. These are venues for tangible, focused engagement among members of the startup community.

Since 2012, entrepreneurs and startup community builders around the world have incorporated this simple yet powerful framework and adapted it for their local conditions. Practitioners embrace the Boulder Thesis because it is accessible and reflective of what startup communities are like in practice. While my approach was anecdotal in nature, a study by the

Kauffman Foundation found empirical support for the Boulder Thesis in Kansas City—establishing entrepreneurship as a local phenomenon, led by entrepreneurs, with a network-centric structure to promote peer-learning and relationship-building that requires a diverse set of entrepreneurial needs and interests.[3]

THE RAINFOREST

Around the same time that *Startup Communities* came out, Victor Hwang and Greg Horowitt, two entrepreneurs, investors, and startup community builders, published *The Rainforest: The Secret to Building the Next Silicon Valley*. Insights include:

1. Innovation occurs from the way that a diverse set of people inter-relate to combine and share ideas, skills, and capital.
2. People don't readily engage freely and openly because human beings distrust others, especially those who are different from them. Social barriers such as geography, language, culture, and social status get in the way of meaningful collaboration.
3. This issue around engagement creates a central challenge to high-impact entrepreneurship. It requires extreme openness to a diverse set of ideas and people, but the principal means of acquiring those resources requires going against our fundamental human instinct to distrust others.
4. Communities like Silicon Valley can overcome these barriers because of extra-rational cultural motivations and social norms such as implicit contracts of trust and positive-sum games.
5. Silicon Valley sustains a system built on diversity, trust, selfless motivations, and cultural norms through repeated practice, role modeling, face-to-face interaction, social feedback loops, networks of trust, and social contracts.

6. It's not just the existence of ideas, talent, and capital that matters, but also the velocity at which these resources flow through the system. Lowering social barriers is critical to accelerating their flow through the startup community.

7. Leaders play a central role in facilitating and promoting flow and the confluence of these factors, motivating and leading people to behave in a way that is best for the long-term sustainability of the entire system.

A healthy startup community creates and maintains a set of practices and norms that allow individuals with diverse views and talents to work together in a trusting and mutually supportive environment, enabling them to openly share and combine ideas, expertise, and capital. The underlying social contract that exists is reinforced and repeated many times over through personal interactions and by motivations that go beyond short-term self-interest. The nature of relationships distinguishes the health of the startup community.

As far as we know, the Boulder Thesis and *The Rainforest* are the only significant frameworks on the subject of entrepreneurial ecosystems that have been put forward by people who have experience both as entrepreneurs and as startup community builders. These two models also happen to be different from more traditional approaches to ecosystem development. We think this is because entrepreneurs have a fundamentally different way of seeing the world.

Values and Virtues: Practice Implicit Trust

Approach each new relationship from the perspective of implicit trust versus implicit suspicion. Assume that most people will act with honesty and integrity and aren't out to screw you over. This doesn't mean you should be naive; every system has bad actors or situations where good people act poorly. A healthy startup community, as an organism, will quickly filter out the bad actors. It will also quickly forgive the inevitable poor decisions made by good people. If you approach new people with implicit trust, intending to be inclusive of anyone who wants to engage, they are more likely to respond in kind. When they don't, their reputations quickly spread, and they will get explicit feedback. If they don't modify their behavior, the startup community will recalibrate around them.

One way to enforce an implicit trust code is to apply my two-strikes-and-you're-out rule. I enter every new relationship from the perspective of implied trust and allow this trust to be violated once. If that happens, it's my responsibility to address the violation. If there's a second violation of trust, I'm done with the relationship.

It's pretty simple.

This approach of implicit trust reduces friction in the network. Acting with integrity becomes reinforced as the vast majority of participants in a startup community act from this perspective.

APPLYING SYSTEMS THINKING

Another entrepreneur turned investor, Ben Horowitz, expressed related sentiments, but used in a different context, during a recent interview.[4] When asked what predicts exceptional managerial intelligence, he pointed to two skills: the ability to understand the deeper motivations and desires of one's colleagues, and, critically to this discussion, the ability to apply systems thinking.

While the complexity framework helps us understand the characteristics and behavior of startup communities and entrepreneurial ecosystems, how to deal with them is the domain of systems thinking, which guides us in effectively influencing complex systems.[5]

At the heart of systems thinking are a few key concepts. For example, systems thinkers:

- Approach problems simultaneously or holistically rather than in partial or siloed ways.
- Promote a mindset of constant learning, adaptation, and resilience instead of planning, execution, and rigidity.
- Rely on intuition and synthesis over rationalization and analysis.
- Take accountability for current conditions and know that both the problems and the solutions for a system come from within—they are not caused by nor solved by external forces.
- Understand that meaningful, lasting change requires addressing deep, structural problems over a sustained period—they know that surface-level quick fixes don't work.
- Know that a small number of high-leverage interventions to produce reinforcing feedback loops have a more significant impact than many smaller, more isolated ones.

In his book, *Systems Thinking for Social Change: A Practical Guide to Solving Complex Problems, Avoiding Unintended Consequences, and Achieving Lasting Results*, applied systems thinker David Peter Stroh compared elements of conventional thinking versus systems thinking.[6] We've modified his language a little and added a third column with our interpretation in the following table.

Conventional Thinking versus Systems Thinking

Conventional Thinking	Systems Thinking	Our Interpretation
The connection between problems and their causes is obvious and easy to trace.	The relationship between problems and their causes is indirect and not obvious.	Directly linking cause and effect is an illusion in complex systems.
Others, either within or outside our organization [or system], are to blame for our problems and must be the ones to change.	We unwittingly create our problems and have significant control or influence in solving them by changing our behavior.	Systems themselves are the cause of and the solution to their problems. The answer is "in here" not "out there."
A policy or program designed to achieve short-term success will also assure long-term success.	Most quick fixes have unintended consequences. They make no difference or make matters worse in the long run.	Simple solutions to complex problems are ineffective and often make things worse.
To optimize the whole, we must optimize the parts.	To optimize the whole, we must improve the relationships among the parts.	Systems improve by changing the connections, not the parts.
Aggressively tackle many independent initiatives simultaneously.	Only a few coordinated changes sustained over time will produce large systems change.	Prioritize a small number of sustained, high-impact interventions over more of everything

Source: Adapted from Stroh (2015), *Systems Thinking for Social Change.*

LOOKING DEEPLY

In 1990, Peter Senge, a systems scientist and a professor of management at MIT, published *The Fifth Discipline: The Art and Practice of the Learning Organization. The Fifth Discipline* became essential reading for those interested in systems thinking and management. A framework that came out of Senge's work is the iceberg model of systems thinking.

Iceberg Model of Systems Thinking

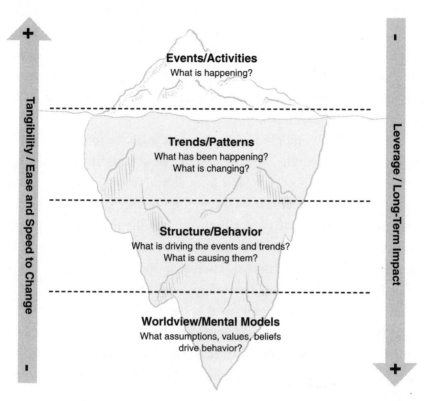

We tend to focus on the things happening around us because they are easy to observe. This causes us to fail to recognize the deeper structures shaping our world that exist below the surface. To deal effectively with complex systems, we must go more in-depth and examine the structures driving system behaviors. To understand the values, beliefs, and assumptions that drive those behaviors, we must go even deeper to explore the underlying mental models (abstractions of reality) of the people involved.

Let's use crime as an example.[7] At the surface, we see that a crime has been committed. We then see a recent spike in criminal activity. To go deeper, we ask why. Perhaps we discover that the crime wave coincides with the elimination of a social program. Suppose we also see that the new criminal offenders come from a marginalized group that has experienced a rise in poverty and declining economic mobility. By cutting a social program that was a fundamental source of support for this marginalized group, a sense of desperation and social unrest among the group increases, energizing a preexisting belief that the entire social, economic, and political apparatus is against them.

A surface-level response to a rise in crime might be to increase policing or incarceration rates. A systems-level view would take a different approach—alleviating poverty and inequality through increasing social and educational programs. It might even go further still to remove the institutional barriers that systematically repress the marginalized group. The first type of intervention is easy to implement, and it may feel useful to those in control—we fixed things! However, it won't do anything to change the underlying problem and likely will make things worse.

In many startup communities, the attention focuses on superficial things that are easy to observe and quantify. Consider the measurements around the number of startups created, venture capital dollars invested, or startup events held in a given time frame. These measurements are compared to other geographies, written about, and endlessly promoted. This discussion about what is happening cannot reveal what's driving things on a deeper level.

The next layer down, where trends and patterns are determined, can be partially seen through useful measurement. If the measures are discussed and diagnosed, rather than simply promoted, interesting patterns emerge. Questions about how and why things are changing can be instructive. The focus here is on changes in quantifiable metrics over time. These metrics reflect what has been happening in a community.

But current events and trends provide a limited view of what drives a startup community and why it evolves. They are the outputs and outcomes of the system. They are the symptoms, not the cause, of what is going on.

To understand what's driving system patterns, one has to look further below the surface at the behaviors, interactions, and network structures in the startup community. What is driving the events and trends? What is causing them? And why?

Shifting our focus to what's happening below the surface allows us to explore the mindset, culture, values, beliefs, and assumptions in the startup community. The focus should be on transforming human behavior and removing mental roadblocks that prevent meaningful and lasting change from taking shape. Efforts that stay atop or just below the surface are intervening in ways that won't produce lasting change or are far too inconsequential to have a significant impact. You are just "tinkering with a broken system" or "diddling with the details."[8] Rarely do these actions change behavior.[9]

To create change in your startup community, you have to work on the whole iceberg, not just the tip of it.

LEVERAGE POINTS

Jay Wright Forrester, the famed MIT professor who founded the field of system dynamics in the 1950s, defined "leverage points" as places where small actions—adopted widely and sustained over a period of time—can produce substantial and occasionally predictable changes throughout a complex system.[10] A classic example of a leverage point is a vaccine, where a brief medical procedure produces long-term changes in the human immune system. And, when repeated many times over to reach a critical threshold of the population, vaccines significantly impact broader long-term health conditions for an entire society. Or, when a central bank adjusts interest rates on overnight loans to banks— a seemingly mundane action—it affects the short-term performance of the entire economy.

In other words, one or a few well-placed interventions that seem quite small in relation to the scale of the system they are meant to change can actually shift the entire system dynamics and alter its behavior. They may feel small, but they stimulate change in a big way. They're called leverage points, and they are the key to influencing complex systems.

Leverage points are a powerful force to harness when dealing with startup communities, but they are rare and difficult to locate with precision. A continuous process of trial and error through experimentation, learning, and adjustment is needed to discover them.

Making it more challenging to work with leverage points, they often work counterintuitively. This means that, even when they are apparent, it is easy to apply them in the wrong direction. Forrester said:

> People know intuitively where leverage points are... Time after time I've done an analysis of a company, and I've figured out a leverage point—in inventory policy, maybe, or in the relationship between sales force and productive force, or in personnel policy. Then I've gone to the company and discovered that there's already a lot of attention to that point. Everyone is trying very hard to push it IN THE WRONG DIRECTION![11]

The infinite interdependencies, feedback loops, delayed effects, nonlinear behavior, and historical legacy often make leverage points work in unexpected ways. Well-intentioned initiatives that had destructive unintended consequences litter our history.

So how do we better understand the leverage points and the direction we want to apply force?

Donella Meadows, an environmental scientist at Dartmouth College and a former student of Jay Forrester's, provides some guidance. She developed a broad approach for identifying the leverage points in complex systems, which are outlined in her book, *Leverage Points: Places to Intervene in a System*.[12] In it, she details 12 leverage points in complex systems in ascending order of the impact they provide.

Meadows observed that many initiatives to influence complex systems are too small and limited in scope. She found that interventions to shape complex systems too often made surface-level adjustments. People would tinker with quantities or parameters, without going deeper into the root causes (or structures) and paradigms (or mental models) that give rise to the overall system behavior.

We've distilled Meadows's 12 leverage points down to four that can be used for levers in startup communities: physical, information, social, and conscious.[13] These four levers provide a compass for where to look for intervention points in startup communities to have maximum impact. It also demonstrates the inherent challenges in accessing them, as the most potent levers are the most difficult to see and change since they rely on humans to alter the way they think and behave.

The physical lever refers to the tangible assets in a startup community, such as office space, financial capital, infrastructure, employees, and organizations like corporations and universities. These are the areas where many startup community–building efforts are focused because they are the most straightforward levers to pull, with an immediate and tangible impact. But, changes in the physical lever have the least effect on the system over the long term. Efforts that focus here result in a feedback loop of doing things that feel good in the short-term but have limited impact on the long-term vibrancy of a startup community. And, initiatives that just add more stuff to a poorly functioning community will have limited impact and may even exacerbate a decline.

The information lever contains data flows, feedback loops, and connections between the system elements. Improvements here include linking together startup community participants, increasing physical density, democratizing information flows, maintaining an open, inclusive network, and collecting, analyzing, and disseminating better data on activities and programs. Enhancing and creating new pathways for feedback loops to

Leverage Points in a Startup Community or Entrepreneurial Ecosystem

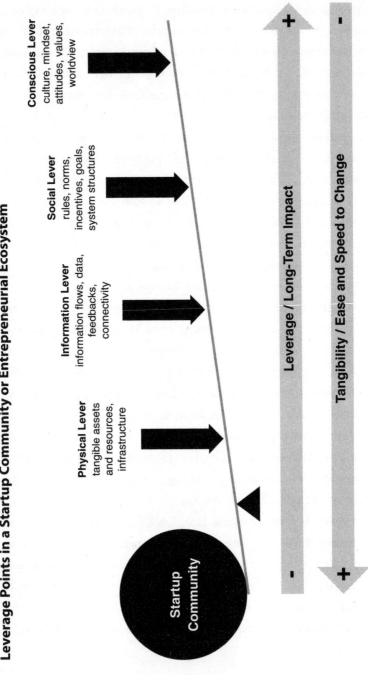

occur amplifies virtuous behavior and ideas, resulting in better knowledge about and a shared awareness of the situation. As startup community participants operate from a shared set of facts, assessment, learning, and adaptation can occur. However, unless the underlying behaviors and attitudes are transformed, connecting people, co-locating them, improving information flows, and collecting better data can only do so much. A well-integrated and well-informed startup community seeded with poor practices, norms, and ways of thinking won't be a vibrant one—it will just be a turbo-charged unhealthy community.

The social lever is where the development of rules, norms, behaviors, incentives, goals, structure, and organization occurs. As more people engage with the system, how they are engaged becomes more critical than if they participate. Collaborating across different groups in the system (*bridging*) becomes much more important than collaboration within them (*bonding*).[14] Ultimately, the system goals derive from behaviors, rules, norms, and incentives.[15] You can change the system through exceptional leadership and aligning a few, high-leverage goals.

The conscious lever represents the values, assumptions, mental models, thought patterns, belief systems, and worldviews that underlie the system. Examples include how people see the role of entrepreneurs in society, how they think about helping others, what leadership roles and styles are, who is responsible for conditions in their startup community, how trust works in the system, and how people view accountability and personal responsibility. Here, you transform the way you see the world and your role in it, focusing us on the value of collaboration, stewardship of place, and being a part of something that helps other people. Without personal transformation around collaboration, even the best system organizations, connectivity, and resources in the world won't be enough to produce a lasting startup community.

Finding, applying, and evolving these leverage points often isn't easy and can take a long time. As Meadows said:

> I have come up with no quick or easy formulas for finding leverage points in complex and dynamic systems. Give me a few months or years, and I'll figure it out. And I know from bitter experience that, because they are so counterintuitive, when I do discover a system's leverage points, hardly anybody will believe me.[16]

Startup communities have many people and organizations pursuing individual agendas simultaneously. These agendas are often in conflict with one another. A certain amount of this is natural, inevitable, and even healthy as the best ideas and strategies win out. But just as often, worthwhile goals are being pursued that work against one another and produce adverse outcomes. This dynamic typically occurs inadvertently because startup community participants, pursuing goals in isolation and unaware of others' activities, end up undermining each other and the community as a whole.

Sharing information and ideas and discussing common priorities as a community can go a long way toward improving coordination, mitigating unhelpful conflict, putting a critical mass of concentrated effort behind the essential areas, and reducing the prevalence of the "accidental adversaries" phenomenon, as described by Peter Senge.[17,18] This information sharing also creates transparency and trust, and enhances understanding within the startup community. In contrast, the absence of openness creates misunderstanding and conflict. When startup community participants can't see the whole system, they will fill in the blanks with what they think is going on or should be done, which may not be the best course of action or even reflective of what's really going on.

When dealing with a complex human social system like a startup community, there is no script to follow and no master algorithm to deploy. There will be continuous setbacks, disagreements, futile efforts, and endless points in time where it feels like progress has stalled. The path forward in a complex world is an inherently uncertain one. But it is the only choice as applying a linear-systems worldview onto a complex system simply won't work. The only alternative is a long-term path that requires perseverance and uncertainty, versus one that feels easy and comfortable but is doomed to inevitable failure.

Applying the Entrepreneurial Mindset to Cultivate University Entrepreneurship

Bill Aulet (Cambridge, Massachusetts)
Managing Director, Martin Trust Center for MIT Entrepreneurship
Professor of Practice, Sloan School of Management, MIT

I have had a great honor and fortune to teach entrepreneurship for over a decade at MIT, and it has been a journey of continuous learning and improvement. Here are 11 key lessons learned that I encourage universities everywhere to consider.

1. **Define your terms.** What do we mean by entrepreneurship? What is the difference between SMEs (small and medium enterprises) and IDEs (innovation-driven enterprises)?[19] What is innovation? What's the difference between entrepreneurship and innovation? These differences matter and too many people treat *entrepreneurship* as a catch-all term or as a single-minded focus on billion-dollar unicorn startups. At MIT, we believe entrepreneurship is about more than just startups.

2. **Understand your mission and don't get distracted.** Beyond the individuals driving entrepreneurship, three additional groups play a role. Each is important but has different objectives. Economic development organizations

(e.g., publicly funded regional initiatives) want to see a large number of companies produced. Investment organizations (e.g., venture capital, angel groups) want a stake in high-growth companies that provide an attractive return. Academic institutions (e.g., colleges, universities, educational centers) *should* focus on creating entrepreneurs by educating them on how to succeed. Blurring the lines between these three categories is very tempting and easy to do, but in the long term, it is incredibly destructive. When academic institutions take on the roles of creating or investing in companies, it makes entrepreneurship education much less effective by skewing incentives. The students know this. Do they look at us as educators focused on their personal development, or are we investors driving a particular outcome? Should they be open and honest with us, or should they try to impress us? What happens to those we do not invest in, what signal does that send? The moment we are something other than 100 percent educators is the day we lose our "honest broker" uniqueness. Vanity metrics like companies started, money raised, jobs created, awards won, and the like can distract universities from our unique mission—as educators first.

3. **Entrepreneurship can be learned.** Historically, there has been a widespread perception that entrepreneurship success is nature rather than nurture. But the data demonstrate something else: The more times a person engages in an entrepreneurial venture, the more likely they are to be successful.[20] Having been a serial entrepreneur, I know this to be true. I understood much more the second time around than the first, and even more the third time.

We get better over time in most things in life, so why should entrepreneurship be different? It isn't. The data do not lie. The question then becomes, can we teach it? I believe that we can.

4. **Entrepreneurship is a craft.** Part of the frustration many people have when thinking about entrepreneurship education is that they want the field to be a deterministic science; that is, if we do A and B and C, we will get outcome D. That is not at all how entrepreneurship works in reality. Entrepreneurship is also not an art that is abstract, with success being limited to only a gifted few. Instead, it is a craft, which means it is both accessible, and it produces different outputs.[21] Entrepreneurship is also learnable because there are fundamental concepts that increase your odds of success. Like a craft, teaching it using an apprenticeship model, where the theory (fundamental concepts) is applied through practical application, can convert knowledge into capability.

5. **Entrepreneurship is not a spectator sport.** Entrepreneurship education offerings should focus more on doing than listening and reflecting. Hands-on work and achieving results are tenets of an entrepreneur.

6. **Entrepreneurship is a team sport.** Research by numerous academics has shown that the odds of success are materially higher with founding teams versus single founders.[22] People focus too much on having a brilliant idea, but pay too little attention to the strength of their founding team.[23] That's why a big part of our teaching involves having students work in project teams. They must also learn how to make tough decisions to add and

remove team members. The team is the essential factor in the success of an entrepreneurship initiative, and that is something universities must emulate in their teaching.

7. **Entrepreneurship education is in its infancy.** Entrepreneurship education is relatively new compared to other business disciplines, such as finance, accounting, strategy, and organizational design. As a result, the collective knowledge base is still evolving. Demand far outstrips the supply of rigorous, high-quality entrepreneurship education. We must avoid filling the gap with less rigorous storytelling, which at times assumes that assembling successful entrepreneurs in front of students so that they can spout platitudes about working hard is sufficient preparation for the significant challenges ahead.[24] Storytelling has a role in fostering spirit within potential entrepreneurs but is not a substitute for teaching rigorous fundamentals.

8. **Systems thinking is essential.** I cringe when I hear simple solutions to entrepreneurship. Entrepreneurship is a complex, multifaceted challenge that requires a systems-thinking approach rather than a linear mindset. We have to continually look for connections and relationships between the different parts of the system. At the same time, we must realize that a time delay exists between an action and the effects of that action. Doing this is daunting when teaching because it makes it difficult to assess the success of any one program. However, systems thinking is the only way to create high-quality entrepreneurs we need for the future. You have to experiment, learn, adapt, and iterate, always thinking through the ripple effects of any action taken.

9. **An open system with a common language is the best way to scale.** The collective wisdom of the group is greater than that of an individual. Entrepreneurship knowledge does not come from a person, institution, or country. We all have to contribute if we want to foster a discipline that is respected by academics, practitioners, and students. We frame our educational approach using the metaphor of a toolbox, and we regularly incorporate tools from many sources if they are appropriate for our students. The new tools are curated and integrated with the existing ones. When new concepts are proven worthy, we can easily incorporate them without throwing out all of the previous good work we have done. Instead, we build off of what has come before, making continuous improvements, and then sharing what we've learned with the rest of the entrepreneurship community.

10. **Apply the 4 Hs.** At MIT, the 4 Hs are central to our teaching on entrepreneurship. The first of these is *heart*. Entrepreneurship requires not only a willingness to be different and to explore the unknown, but also an understanding of the arduous journey ahead, a belief that success is possible, and that the effort will all be worth it in the end. The next two Hs are the *head* and *hands*. We must teach our students the first principles and knowledge that will optimize their chances of success; this is the *head*. We then must create projects where students learn by doing, allowing them to translate their knowledge into capability— the *hands*. This combination of theory and practice is essential because it reinforces and deepens both. Finally, *home* is the ability to build and be a productive member

of vibrant and sustainable communities. Entrepreneurs lack many resources, so they have to be efficient and embrace decentralization. They need to have a core set of skills, but build community with other entrepreneurs and partners to ensure the success of their companies and the community as a whole.

11. **Have fun!** Failure is part of the entrepreneurship process, and if they take themselves too seriously, not only will they not survive, but their organization won't, either. As instructors, we teach by our actions at least as much as with our words. So, when teaching, let's not take ourselves too seriously, but let us take our responsibility of teaching very, very seriously. Enjoy the good times and teach our students how to celebrate them as a team. There are endless bumps in the road on the entrepreneurial journey, and we all need to keep our spirits up to survive and thrive.

CHAPTER THIRTEEN

LEADERSHIP IS KEY

Startup Community Way Principle

Entrepreneurs must lead the startup community. A startup community that is not led by entrepreneurs will not grow, thrive, or last.

The first principle of the Boulder Thesis is that entrepreneurs must lead the startup community. When I wrote that, I wasn't thinking about the idea of contagion in complex systems. As we worked through this book, we realized that contagion was an underlying reason for why entrepreneurs needed to lead the startup community.

When most people hear the word *contagion*, they have a negative response and think of the spread of something harmful, like disease or a financial crisis. As we send this book to the publisher for final revisions in April 2020, we and the rest of humanity are being painfully reminded of this reality as the COVID-19 coronavirus wreaks havoc on the world.

However, contagion can also be a powerful force to harness for good because it spreads positive behaviors and attitudes, too. In complex systems, ideas, behaviors, and information can spread quickly to a large number of people. This gets magnified in an era of connectivity. Healthy practices are adopted while harmful behaviors are reinforced. Individuals with stature or visibility magnify both good and bad behavior. Unfortunately, this works both ways. Sometimes it seems like bad ideas and behaviors can spread even more than helpful ones.

Increasing returns reinforces the useful elements of contagion. When something is working and going well, more people adopt the values, and the contagion spreads faster. Instead of a linear process of improvement, an exponentially increasing positive feedback loop occurs, which, over time, can produce a state change.

In contrast, when the spread of harmful ideas and behaviors occurs, the startup community leaders must aggressively avoid reinforcing it. Rather than metaphorically pouring fuel on a fire, starve it of oxygen instead. For example, when a bad actor abuses power or otherwise mistreats entrepreneurs, rather than continue to subject themselves to mistreatment, entrepreneurs should find other ways to do business without the bad actor. Or, when an existing feeder is operating in ways that are antithetical to a healthy startup community, don't reinforce their behavior by continuing to fully include them in the startup community. This works only if the startup community is cohesive and forms an alternative critical mass that works around the feeder, which is likely to be resource abundant.

Consider the case of a state-sponsored innovation center in a city with limited resources for entrepreneurs. When this innovation center exhibits a natural but unhealthy set of behaviors around trying to control what is going on in the startup community, it's easy to feel like everyone has to go along because it's the only game in town. However, if the local entrepreneurs operate openly and collaboratively and don't react positively to the innovation center's need for control, it deprives the innovation center of its ability to create a negative contagion on the startup community. When, instead, the entrepreneurs are inclusive of people who work for the innovation center, but only engage in healthy collaboration, the innovation center may change its approach. A shift like this would typically take place over a long period, so it relies on consistent behavior on the part of entrepreneurs.

Negative contagions exist everywhere. An example from *Startup Communities* is the *patriarch problem*, which occurs when people with power in a city (often known as "the city fathers") control and restrict rather than enable the next generation of leaders. In these situations, who you are and whom you know matters more than what you know or what you do. Entrepreneurs should play the long game and ignore the patriarchs while still being inclusive of anyone who wants to engage. The enlightened patriarchs will come out and play with the next generation while the rest will gradually fade into the background.

A particularly destructive example of negative contagion on the part of experienced entrepreneurs is the *bitter founder problem*, which occurs when a successful founder from a prior generation refuses to be helpful to today's upstart founders. These founders are often angry about the challenges they went through and rationalize that because they built their businesses in an underdeveloped startup community, others should struggle in the same ways.

This way of thinking is extremely short-sighted. Rather than helping the next generation of founders, the bitter founder hangs onto the idea that founders need to go through the same challenges and be denied the same resources before they succeed. Ultimately, high-value companies will be produced with some regularity, and the startup community will reach a critical mass of success. When this occurs, the bitter founder will be left by the wayside, ignored by the startup community, and become even more bitter against the backdrop of others' success. In the end, the bitter founder hurts himself while depriving the startup community of his involvement, resources, and experience. That's a loss for everyone involved.

We appeal to these bitter founders, and other bad actors who seek to control the startup community in a self-serving way, to follow the advice of His Holiness the Dalai Lama: "Our prime purpose in this life is to help others. And if you can't help them, at least don't hurt them."

BE A MENTOR

Entrepreneurship is fundamentally a learning process—about one's product, one's team, one's company, one's customers, and especially oneself. It has become widely understood and acknowledged that mentors significantly help founders navigate the challenges of high-growth entrepreneurship.[1]

Mentors are usually experienced entrepreneurs or others with deep expertise in business, industry, or technology, who also have the right personality and communication skills to bring empathy, support, and a growth mindset to relationships with company founders.[2] They combine relevant knowledge and temperament to help entrepreneurs navigate the many challenges of building and scaling a business. They must inspire, challenge, guide, question, be honest and direct, express an eagerness to learn, and above all, be personally vested in the outcome of mentees.[3] While much of the information about how to be an effective mentor is a function of tribal learning from other mentors, organizations like Techstars have begun codifying the approach through documents like the Techstars Mentor Manifesto and continuous proactive education of mentors.[4]

Mutual learning is an essential element of the mentor-mentee relationship over time. Still, to begin, mentors must place the needs of the mentee front and center. It cannot be weighed the same as many other priorities, such as a monetary benefit for self-reward.[5] From *Startup Communities*:

> Mentors are experienced entrepreneurs or investors who actively contribute time, energy, and wisdom to startups and can be part of a startup community.

Often the terms *advisor* and *mentor* are conflated. An advisor has an economic relationship with the company he is advising. In contrast, a mentor doesn't. The mentor is helping startups without a clear set of outcome goals or economic rewards.

Mentorship, shared learning, and support are at the heart of vibrant startup communities. Experienced entrepreneurs must give their time and knowledge to the next generation of founders. A good mentor has no expectations of what she will get out of the relationship. Instead, she should approach it with a #GiveFirst dynamic and a willingness to let the relationship evolve naturally.

Entrepreneurial leaders must embrace the mentorship role and build time for it into their regular activities. This mentorship occurs on three levels—mentoring other entrepreneurs, mentoring future startup community leaders, and mentoring each other. The ultimate mentor relationships become bidirectional, where the mentor and the mentee each learn from the other over a long period. Fundamentally, mentorship is an activity based around networks, not hierarchies, with peer-mentorship being incredibly powerful to startup communities.

ENTREPRENEURS AS ROLE MODELS

Entrepreneurs can serve a critical leadership function as role models.[6] The presence of entrepreneurs and entrepreneurial successes in a community can inform the next generation of founders by raising awareness about entrepreneurship as a viable career path.[7] These role models motivate would-be entrepreneurs to make the leap and inspire existing entrepreneurs to stick with things through all their ups and downs.

This living embodiment of what is possible is especially important in places where entrepreneurship is less prevalent. The local nature of those successes makes them more tangible. Being visible, telling stories, and elevating successful entrepreneurial leaders is critical. Aspiring entrepreneurs will be inspired and motivated by those who have done it before, similar to other high-performance endeavors and creative vocations, such as music, film, and sports.

Role models have the most impact when they lead by example through showing what works and what doesn't while also setting the tone for how people should conduct themselves. Mentorship, as discussed above, is a powerful example. From *Startup Communities*:

> The best leaders can be incredible mentors. They recognize that being a mentor is a key part of the role of a leader and allocate their energy accordingly.
>
> Most important is the "lead by example" role. In my case, I continually tell people why it's important to be a mentor, but I also show it by being a mentor.

By giving back to the next generation, helping others without expectation of something in return, carrying themselves with integrity, and being inclusive of anyone who wants to get involved, the odds increase that others will do the same. Feedback loops result in spreading this positive behavior throughout a startup community and are a powerful example of positive contagion.

Values and Virtues: Be a Leader

Be the change. Mentor the young and less experienced. Teach them the Startup Community Way. Give back. Lead by example. And have fun.

Nobody conveyed this principle better than Dr. Seuss, in his 1971 children's book, *The Lorax*, when he wrote:

Unless someone like you cares a whole awful lot,
nothing is going to get better.
It's not.[8]

KEY LEADERSHIP CHARACTERISTICS

There are many different leadership styles, and almost as many leadership frameworks describing different styles. For example, one framework includes the categories of: coach, visionary, servant, autocratic, laissez-faire, democratic, pacesetter, and transformational. Another framework has charismatic, transformational, laissez-faire, transactional, supportive, and democratic. Another could include structural, participative, servant-leader, freedom-thinking, and transformational. Individual leaders in a startup community can come in many different styles, and there is no specific leadership framework required, but there are several key characteristics of leaders in startup communities.

Fundamentally, leaders have to be people, not organizations. While the Boulder Thesis stated that "Entrepreneurs must lead the startup community," we've realized that members of feeders can also play leadership roles. Today, these participants are called startup community organizers, startup community leaders, or startup community builders—all of whom are instigators. These instigators are people, not organizations. The moment an organization tries to be the leader, things break down quickly. Instead, these organizations should be supporters of the entrepreneurs and the startup community.

These leaders should be change agents. In fact, being a change agent is the very essence of what it means to be an entrepreneur, and what it means to be a leader. In the work of building startup communities and entrepreneurial ecosystems, it's striking how much of the focus is on how the external environment shapes entrepreneurs, yet so little is focused on how the entrepreneurs shape the external environment around them.[9]

Rather than asking for permission and waiting for someone else to tell them what to do, leaders should just do stuff. While some things will work, and some things will fail, the continued experimentation by the leaders is a foundational part of the evolution of the startup community. This approach of being a change agent corresponds to any type of leadership style that takes action rather than asks for permission.

A central component of systems thinking is accepting that we are the cause of and the solution to our problems. Startup community participants must shift from a mindset of blaming others for failures to one of taking accountability. While no one wants to take responsibility for failures, it is necessary to take responsibility for your startup community. Systems thinker Peter David Stroh wrote the following in *Systems Thinking for Social Change*:[10]

> . . .another critical benefit of this methodology. . . is its emphasis on responsibility and empowerment. Every day, we can look around and see unintended consequences arising from what seemed at one time to be best-laid plans. Undoubtedly, whoever cast those plans had the best of intentions. . . .
>
> For any complex problem to be solved, the individual players all need to recognize how they unwittingly contribute to it. Once they understand their own responsibility for a problem, they can begin by changing the part of the system over which they have the greatest control: themselves.

Looking at external solutions to solve the problem is a related form of not being accountable and occurs when startup community participants convince themselves that the answer is "out there" rather than "in here."

More external resources will only work to exacerbate those problems. It's like the lottery-winner's curse, where ordinary people become incredibly wealthy overnight and, instead of leading to a life of happiness, it often leads to despair. It turns out that piling millions of dollars onto a shaky foundation only accelerates its imminent collapse, and all of the venture capitalists, incubators, and co-working spaces in the world won't save a weak and ineffective startup community.

Ultimately, when startup community participants, especially the leaders, blame other people for the problems they are facing, it creates a toxic environment that makes it hard for anyone to succeed. Taking responsibility for problems is necessary. Instead of asking for someone or something to save your startup community, take the initiative to lead the change. Being accountable and taking responsibility demonstrates real leadership, and it is liberating to know that you are in charge of your destiny.

Taking responsibility and accountability means more than not blaming others, it also means taking charge. The startup community's helpfulness can only be as strong as what its entrepreneurs put into it. Waiting for someone else to lead is a recipe for failure.

How an Entrepreneur-Led Funding Model Can Build Community and Help Founders

Jenny Fielding (New York, New York)
Managing Director, Techstars
Founder and Managing Partner, The Fund

New York City is one of the best places to build a startup. It's a city teeming with talent, corporations, and customers, not to mention a number of venture capital funds and investments second only to Silicon Valley. On the surface, everything looks terrific. However, when you look deeper, the funding options available for New York's early-stage companies is much more limited.

Although rarely spoken about, I've seen this issue firsthand leading Techstars programs in New York. Consistently, incredible founders building high-impact companies have struggled to secure their first checks locally and have had to go west to the Valley to raise capital. With all the money flowing through NYC, this funding gap is particularly puzzling.

To solve this critical challenge, a few experienced local startup founders and operators got together to look more closely at the dynamics within venture capital and angel investing. We wanted to find a way to ensure that early-stage capital would better flow to the startups that need it most.

Our assessment identified three problems. First, venture capital as an industry has scarcely evolved, particularly concerning output. VC doesn't scale well. The hours and elbow grease that a VC's limited staff provides determine its productivity.

Next, founders and operators in NYC see deals before most VCs do. Because NYC has an active startup community, the very same entrepreneurs who receive capital from venture funds become the first line of contact from emerging founders when seeking advice, mentoring, business model development, funding, and introductions to VCs. Yet, although operators have an advantage with deal flow, few are active angel investors. The reasons are obvious: they're already too busy building their own companies, and most don't have the liquidity to write a significant number of checks per year.

Finally, while successful Silicon Valley entrepreneurs have a long-standing tradition of reinvesting their wealth into the next generation of founders, this mentality is less prevalent in New York.

Founders tend to buy real estate or travel instead of becoming active angel investors in startup companies.

It's in response to this perfect storm of factors that we created The Fund—an investment vehicle designed to transcend the traditional limitations and constraints of venture capital firms by harnessing the collective power and resources of a community of founders and operators. We gathered 75 notable NYC-based individuals around the shared mission to unlock capital and share expertise with the next generation of founders building companies in New York. Together, we pooled our cash, networks, knowledge, and time to help grow NYC's tech ecosystem in a radically new way. It's an experiment, and we love it!

We focus solely on New York City, both in terms of our investors and portfolio because we believe that by doing so, we can source the best deals, effectively support our portfolio companies, and help build our community. Yes, we think there's a financial return, but just as important, it's about community development and creating momentum for a culture of entrepreneurship that can outlast any single fund. We are not an angel group or a scout program, and we don't replace traditional venture capital. Instead, we are building a new model focused on the earliest stages of a company's life cycle, when founders—especially inexperienced ones—need outside support the most.

We view investing as a community endeavor and have created fund dynamics to reflect this belief where we share the fund profits among the core group of operators. This structure provides a compelling financial incentive for some of the most experienced founders and operators in New York City to invest not just their capital into promising young startups, but more importantly, their time and expertise.

Everyone building The Fund is doing so part-time by design. We have a conviction that active community participation of our founding members is more potent than retaining a full-time staff. By focusing most of our working hours on our entrepreneurial endeavors, we stay in the thick of startup life and close to the most promising deal flow.

Our community has a thriving digital and physical presence. Deal sourcing, discussion, and diligence happen collectively online, where a spirited discussion helps inform investment decisions. Once a month, we come together in person to break bread, build relationships, and share experiences. Our firm includes founders who have built companies spanning healthcare, crypto, digital media, software as a service (SaaS), consumer, fintech, and hardware. This depth of knowledge allows us to invest across sectors and verticals. We also believe in, and support diversity as 50 percent of our investment committee is female and way more than 50 percent of our investments are into female founders or people of color.

The Fund is small by design, but our vision is big. We imagine a world where every city, region, and community has its very own version of The Fund. And to make this happen, we've assembled a playbook and put in place infrastructure to launch in additional locations. Now it is time for us to scale.

CHAPTER FOURTEEN

THINK IN GENERATIONS

Startup Community Way Principle

The leaders must have a long-term commitment. Leaders should make at least a 20-year commitment to the startup community and incorporate long-term thinking into strategies and decision making. They should reset the clock each year so the 20-year view into the future is permanent.

The second principle of the Boulder Thesis is that the leaders must have a long-term commitment. Initially, I defined this as a 20-year view, which roughly corresponded with the traditional definition of a generation.[1] My goal with this was to create some texture around what *long-term* meant, and, as I discussed this with people in various startup communities, I realized that I originally meant a continuous long-term view. I modified "a 20-year view" to "a 20-year view from today" and gave the example that, while I know I have lived in Boulder for 25 years, I don't have a minus-five-year view. Instead, I'm looking forward from year 25 to year 45.

This perspective corresponds nicely with how change occurs in complex systems. Rather than being consistent and constant, change is often either disproportionate (nonlinear) or can appear to be nearly instantaneous (phase transition).[2] Recent examples include the Arab Spring or the #MeToo and #TimesUp movements in the United States, where a few brave people sparked significant systemic changes. These shifts were the result of forces that were building over a long period, but the noticeable change suddenly occurred.

Tipping points are situations, processes, or systems where significant, unstoppable change occurs once a particular threshold is surpassed. As this book goes to press, many people around the world are facing this as the COVID-19 coronavirus is expanding in ways that are hard for the human mind to process. In startup communities, this can occur after a single high-profile entrepreneurial success or the adoption of a critical mass of virtuous behavior. Conversely, it can follow a series of high-profile failures, ethical lapses, or misdeeds. Tipping points can shift the balance toward the widespread adoption of either healthy or destructive behaviors and attitudes.

These tipping points result in phase transitions which undermine linear systems thinking and resource-based approaches. Rather than steadily increasing inputs to get the desired output, unexpected activities stimulate a tipping point. The tipping point doesn't correspond to the specific inputs or a well-defined output, but instead it suddenly and dramatically appears. It's like a dam breaking. Up until one moment, the dam holds all the water back. Then it doesn't, and things in the ecosystem change significantly, resulting in a transition to a new phase.

For over a decade, the external rap against the Boulder startup community was that it was awesome but too small and remote to support a public company. Then, in a short period between mid-2013 and the fall of 2014, two companies, each started in Boulder sometime in the preceding decade, went public at significant market caps, and a third was acquired for $1.2 billion.[3] Suddenly, in addition to having several very successful and wealthy founders in town, there were hundreds of employees who were overnight millionaires because of the value of their stock options. The Boulder startup community shifted dramatically.

PROGRESS IS UNEVEN AND OFTEN FEELS SLOW

Linear systems show steady and consistent progress, or at least progress that is predictable given the inputs and energy applied to them. Complex systems are the opposite—progress is unpredictable and inconsistent. There can be periods of significant advances, followed by periods of stagnation or decline. You can feel like you are making progress, only to realize that nothing has changed. This dynamic can be frustrating, especially when it feels like a lot of work is happening with no visible impact, or that things are going backward. This is especially true when exogenous factors, such as the Global Financial Crisis of 2007–2008 or the COVID-19 coronavirus pandemic in 2020, impact the macro dynamics of a system.

The interaction of the people in a startup community drives its performance. The individual participants have unique and shared life experiences, ingrained thought patterns, and behavioral traits. As new things happen in the startup community, exposing participants to new ideas and experiences, it takes a while for each person to absorb and embrace what has occurred. The new has to be integrated, and the old needs to be unlearned.

A wide variety of feedback loops occur. While some things work, many don't, and the problems and responses appear unevenly and with delays. These problems are often present long before we become aware of them, and improvements are made well in advance of our noticing their impact. However, when applying a set of healthy behaviors and attitudes to a complex system, they have staying power, creating strong inertial effects that are resilient and help move a startup community forward.

Many people don't realize that the seeds of Silicon Valley were planted over 100 years ago.[4] Fred Terman led the development of what is now Stanford Research Park in the early 1950s but had been encouraging his Stanford University students to start new high-tech businesses as early as the 1930s (and even investing in some of them).[5] One key catalyzing event (there were many of them but this was a big one), when the "Traitorous Eight" left Shockley Semiconductor to start Fairchild Semiconductor, occurred more than 60 years ago, in 1957. It's easy to point to today's successes without understanding what it took to get there. Silicon Valley has been a very long time in the making, and continues to evolve to this day.

As a startup community leader, you have to stick with it, trust the process, and be okay knowing that the outcome might be different from what you expect or hope for. The continuous 20-year view is essential, as there is no fixed destination to reach. It can feel like nothing changes for a long time, and then suddenly everything changes overnight as a result of all of the work you have been doing. And then more things happen, and it changes again.

Values and Virtues: Honor Commitments

Say what you mean and do what you say. It is vital that people can rely on your word and that you will follow-through with your commitments. Building trust and generating social capital is the glue that holds relationships, and therefore startup communities, together. Often people become overextended because they aren't realistic about what they can do or because they are timid about saying no. This behavior lacks transparency and honesty. When you realize you've committed to doing something that you can't follow through on, own it and communicate it. If you don't want to do something, just say no to it.

Whatever the cause, when people commit to doing something and then fail to meet their obligations, it undermines trust and sows the seeds of discontent in a startup community. Reputations are system-wide, and information travels quickly through a startup community. If you are known to be unreliable, people won't want to work with you. And worse yet, if you are a leader in the startup community, it will prompt others to adopt your behavior. The startup community is then infected with the idea that being unreliable is okay. It's not.

Reliability as a means of cohesion is an old yet well-tested idea. The German philosopher Max Weber wrote in 1905 that the foundation of Western capitalism was rooted in virtuous Puritan norms of honesty, reciprocity, and honoring commitments.[6] That model represents very little of what capitalism has evolved into today, as we now operate in a more formal, contract-based, and transactional world. But the early inspiration for capitalism is a model for startup communities to adopt.

Startup communities function better in environments that are more fluid, less formal, and less transactional. One means of achieving this is demonstrating your reliability, especially if you are a leader.

THE ENDLESS LONG-TERM GAME

When playing an endless long-term game, you have to transcend time. Doing this is hard in our current society, given economic cycles, political calendars, academic years, and the latest short-term trend. Corporations run on quarterly and annual rhythms. Academia runs on a cycle with a summer vacation that doesn't correspond with a calendar year. Political rhythms are either two or four years, with at least 25 percent of the time consumed by elections and transitions. The time frame of macroeconomic cycles is indeterminate and impacts different geographies and industries at what can feel like random intervals.

While this impacts a startup community, leaders have to operate with a completely different frame of reference. Startup communities must function on a generational cycle. While the participants who come from feeders have to function within the norms and context of their organizations, they should apply a long-term view to their interactions with the startup community, especially if they play leadership roles in the feeder organizations. The lack of long-term commitment by any leader inhibits the health and development of the startup community.

While Fred Terman may have generated a tipping point for Silicon Valley, there have been many others. Hewlett Packard started in 1939; Fairchild Semiconductor began in 1957; Stanford Research Institute connected to ARPANET in 1969; Xerox PARC opened in 1970; and industry giants Apple, Atari, Oracle, and others were founded in the 1970s. Even Google is now more than 20 years old; Facebook will be, too, before you know it. The linkages in Silicon Valley cross time and company boundaries.

Accepting that it takes a long time to build a vibrant and sustainable startup community is one of the biggest challenges currently facing startup communities. A philosophy of non-control—which is requisite for a sustainable startup community—is essential. There will be the temptation to force things or to focus on problems that are easier yet less impactful. It is important to resist those urges and let the complex system evolve.

As I wrote in *Startup Communities*:

> If you aspire to be a leader of your startup community, but you aren't willing to live where you are for the next 20 years and work hard at leading the startup community for that period of time, ask yourself what

your real motivation for being a leader is. Although you can have an impact for a shorter period of time, it'll take at least this level of commitment from some leaders to sustain a vibrant startup community.

While we are currently experiencing a high interest in entrepreneurship from cities around the world, the cycles, and exogenous factors that shift attention, always happen. When the inevitable setbacks occur, such as the COVID-19, the startup community leaders must continue to lead. The resilience of startup communities and their leaders are being tested in a major way right now in the spring of 2020.

How a Long-term View of Committed Leadership Helped Transform and Accelerate the Startup Community in Durham, North Carolina

Chris Heivly (Durham, North Carolina)
Senior Vice President, Techstars

Like many of the best startup communities, the formation of Durham, North Carolina's is the result of many pieces coming together in unexpected or counterintuitive ways, driven from the bottom-up by committed leadership. The story of Durham's transformation is one of generational commitment and evolution. But, to really understand Durham's nearly two-decade resurgence, you also have to grasp its entrepreneurial history.

Durham had a thriving tobacco and textile industry throughout the early-20th century. American Tobacco Company—the manufacturer of Lucky Strike cigarettes—was such a titan that in 1945, it grossed $5.4 billion (inflation adjusted). Not a small amount for a Southern city of less than 75,000 people at the time.

Like many Southern cities, Durham saw its key industries collapse. Tobacco and textiles, the second foundational industry of

Durham's economy, shuttered and moved offshore. By the 1990s the city was less known for tobacco and textiles, and more as the setting for the iconic movie *Bull Durham*. Housing vacancy rates in downtown Durham hovered in the 50 percent range by the late-1990s and the American Tobacco headquarters, a one-million-square-foot complex in the heart of Durham, was abandoned.

But that was all about to change, once an unlikely hero got involved.

Durham's renaissance began in many ways with a fourth generation, family-owned broadcast business called Capitol Broadcasting Company (CBC), based in the neighboring city of Raleigh. CBC has a long-standing history of community engagement, perhaps most notably with its purchase of the minor league baseball team the Durham Bulls and the subsequent development of a new downtown baseball stadium in partnership with the city of Durham. Across from the stadium sat a reminder of Durham's fabled yet abandoned tobacco factory called American Tobacco Campus (ATC). CBC attempted to convince several developers to take on the ATC redevelopment, but without success. So, despite not knowing much about commercial real estate, CBC took on the project in 1999 and redeveloped the campus over four years.

So, what do the Durham Bulls, an abandoned tobacco factory, a downtown with as many empty buildings as occupied ones, and a fourth-generation family led by late-in-career southerner Jim Goodmon have in common?

By 2009, a group of entrepreneurial enthusiasts in the area started looking for an inexpensive, creative space to gather. Chapel Hill had the University of North Carolina and a college-town vibe but was limited in terms of available workspace. Raleigh had plenty of real estate options but was almost too large and disjointed to create a meaningful critical mass. Durham had the grit (abandoned buildings, history) and a leader who heard the call (Jim Goodmon) and who was willing to invest his time and investment dollars into turning the city around.

Years later, ATC housed a handful of tech companies that began to create some buzz and became a destination of sorts. In 2009, a group of civic-minded entrepreneurs gathered with Jim and his son Michael to chart a plan to develop relatively inexpensive space to house entrepreneurial support programs. Both ATC and Durham had that buzz that was a natural destination for the creative class. Out of those discussions came a simple vision for a startup space now known as the American Underground. The vision, with help from successful entrepreneurs, became the creative hub of the Research Triangle region by prioritizing those who could contribute to a unique mix of tenants, rather than those who could pay the most rent.

The American Underground launched that year with 30,000 square feet in a basement at ATC. A key factor, the Goodmons learned, was to create a safe space for the local entrepreneurs. Using a handful of entrepreneurs as a sounding board, the space rented only to founders, their companies, and organizations specifically supporting entrepreneurs. They turned down 72 rental inquiries from established companies in that first year. That early long-term commitment to the startup community was essential.

In addition, there was a strategic mix of companies brought in to serve as anchor tenants. Two of the four were startup accelerators (Joystick Labs and Triangle Startup Factory), as well as CED (a mentoring organization) and NC IDEA (a statewide entrepreneurship foundation). Next up were a few successful founders who were building their next startup. In total, the American Underground began with roughly 35 companies, including those participating in the accelerator programs. Add-in free Internet, some free co-working tables, and great coffee, and the American Underground quickly became the destination for entrepreneurs in our community.

In 2012, CBC/AU hired a point person—Adam Klein—to build on the previous momentum and to represent Jim and Michael's vision of building a world-class startup space to serve a diverse set of local entrepreneurs. Around that time, a small but dedicated group of entrepreneurs and startup community leaders gathered over beers once a month. This wasn't a formal group. It did not have a name. No one set the agenda and the conversation was free form, but always centered on how to grow the startup community. Leaders like me and Dave Neal of the Startup Factory, as well as John Austin of Joystick Labs, Joan Siefert Rose of CED, and Casey Steinbacher of the Durham Chamber, were regulars. These conversations shaped a common vision for how Durham's startup community would grow and was comprised of the people who had the resources and zeal to make it happen.

In 2013, the American Underground expanded from ATC two blocks north to downtown Durham and nearly tripled the number of startups they supported to 100. An informal conversation between Adam Klein and me reinforced the concept of entrepreneurial density posited by Brad Feld.

Physical space was not the only investment in the startup community that was made by the Goodmon family. As needs were identified, new activities and opportunities emerged. Where some leaders might choose to control or dictate terms, the Goodmon family took a chance and invested in the passion projects of the entrepreneurial leaders. The Goodmons provided an example of how prominent families can spur bottom-up change, rather than dominating activity from the top-down.

The American Underground has expanded three more times in downtown Durham and downtown Raleigh, today occupying 135,000 square feet and hosting 275 startups. Durham has grown up and around the American Underground as companies expanded to find their own space.

In the Durham startup community, leaders take a collaborative, bottom-up approach. We have a group of thoughtful and broad-minded community leaders, with financial support from some key business leaders, who pay close attention to what the startups in our community need most. Through our focus on collaborative leadership and genuine support for each other, our startup community has become much more vibrant than if we'd spread out the action and operated independently from each other. Our networks are much tighter and stronger because of the attitudes exhibited by our leaders and density of our community. The end result is a true community of startups willing to leverage their networks for the benefit of others.

The lesson exhibited by Jim Goodmon and his family is that great communities are built with a consortium of diverse and passionate leaders who come from all different roles and personalities. Eschewing control, and taking a generational view, the Goodmons show that a vision of collaboration and support of others is the magic startup communities need to accelerate their growth.

CHAPTER FIFTEEN

DIVERSITY IS A FEATURE, NOT A BUG

Startup Community Way Principle

The startup community must be inclusive of anyone who wants to participate. Complex problems require a diverse set of perspectives. Radical acceptance of a broad range of ideas, identities, and experiences builds the trust that is necessary to unlock the creative potential of the entire community.

The third principle of the Boulder Thesis is that the startup community must be inclusive of anyone who wants to participate in it. Today, diversity and inclusion are front and center in many discussions around entrepreneurship and our society—a development that is long overdue. Gender and racial diversity are dominant themes, and phrases like "diversity of thought" are often used as political dog whistles or an effort to undermine gender and racial diversity. However, when I wrote *Startup Communities*, I was thinking about diversity both specifically (e.g., gender, race, ethnicity, and age) and generally (e.g., experience, education, socioeconomic, and perspective). To a degree, these are overlapping. Both are important to be mindful of and are vital to the performance of a startup community.

CULTIVATE DIVERSITY

Complex systems, such as starting and scaling an innovation-driven startup, are best handled through teamwork. Diverse teams are more innovative and resilient to constant and inevitable change than are less diverse ones. Strong complementarities and novel combinations drive innovation while resilience results from greater adaptability.[1]

In complex systems, diversity is much more than a nice to have—it's a necessity. Recall that synergies, which describe nonlinear behavior due to the interaction of parts, are a primary source of value in a complex system. If all of the system parts are identical, this reduces or negates valuable nonlinear behaviors resulting in the system becoming equal to the sum of the parts instead of greater than them.

Although we take a view of diversity beyond "identity diversity," which addresses differences in gender, race, ethnicity, religion, sexual orientation, age, socioeconomic background, and geographic origin, among others, we care deeply about identity diversity for reasons of morality and fairness. Our own country, the United States, has a deep history of discrimination against individuals based on these factors that is sadly still all too real today. We realize that, as white, well-educated, heterosexual, American males, we are in a privileged position. We are both strongly committed to diversity and inclusion, and we are self-aware of the resources and power dynamics that our privilege provides us. We are also self-aware that we will never fully understand what it's like to walk around without that privilege. Consequently, we learn from all others, listen carefully to those who are less privileged, try hard not to let our privilege constrain our thinking on this topic, and engage in this area with extreme humility and empathy. We encourage others to do the same.

We don't want to argue for identity equality purely based on morality and justice. It pains us to say this, but not everyone may be persuaded by that argument. In many countries, identity equality is an even bigger problem than in our native United States. Gendered roles have failed to modernize; racial, religious, and class divides seem insurmountable; and tribal or familial divisions go back centuries. We strongly support equality and diversity along the dimension of identity, but we'd also like to advocate for a broader type of diversity in startup communities.

When we describe the importance of diversity on the performance of systems like startup communities and entrepreneurship, we do so with the broad view of "cognitive diversity," defined as a diversity of opinions, ideas, experiences, expertise, education, and skills.[2] Startup communities need people who think differently, bring complementary skills, and see the world through unique lenses that have been shaped by their life experiences. Groupthink and monocultures are deadly for startups and startup communities. Our individual identity shapes and is shaped by our environment, our opportunities, our experiences, and ultimately, who we become. In this way, identity diversity partly drives cognitive diversity.

Diversity is necessary for a high-functioning environment where startups can thrive. Research by Scott Page of the University of Michigan reinforces this by showing that diversity outperforms raw ability.[3] In other words, diverse teams outperform teams made up of "the best" individuals.[4] In short, diversity produces better outcomes.

Diversity initiatives that focus narrowly on identity diversity without seeing the importance of cognitive diversity are self-limiting. Many startup communities have a long way to go on this front. The phrase "culture fit" is thrown around as code for "like us." That way of thinking is a mistake and a missed opportunity. Being "not like us" could be the very reason you *should* bring someone on board. Instead of searching for "culture fit," look for "culture add."[5] Doing so will produce value in novel and expected ways.

Values and Virtues: Have Porous Boundaries

Participants in the best startup communities know that it's beneficial to be inclusive of anyone who wants to engage. While all members of a startup community should endeavor to communicate with each other, leaders, in particular, should talk, sharing strategies, relationships, ideas, and resources. Participants who come and go, either because of priorities, commitments, or geographic relocation, should be embraced and welcomed back when they return.

One challenge is trust. In many situations, people haven't yet developed confidence in each other, and founders often feel the need to protect their ideas and keep them held closely. In entrepreneurship, while there is often intellectual property associated with innovation, the fundamental concepts around a new startup are rarely original. Instead, the value created is a function of execution, rather than the initial idea. And, collaboration and diverse viewpoints often generate better ideas.

The Netflix Prize, an open competition for teams to improve the company's user-rating prediction algorithm, is an excellent example of this. After several valiant efforts, not one team was able to meet the improvement benchmark on its own. It wasn't until several of the teams came together that a winner was crowned. The winning team—or rather, the winning combination of teams—came from different backgrounds and brought unique perspectives. This "diversity bonus," as Scott Page of the University of Michigan calls it, allowed them to produce a better rating algorithm for Netflix.[6]

EMBRACING DIVERSITY

Inclusivity is the mindset or the practice of promoting an environment where diverse groups feel welcome, respected, and able to participate fully. If diversity is an imperative—both for performance and ethical reasons— then an approach of radical inclusion is a set of actions that enables diversity to flourish.

Startup communities should embrace anyone who wants to engage, regardless of experience, background, education, gender, ethnicity, sexual orientation, citizenship, age, and perspective, among others. There should be a strong belief within the startup community that having more, and different, people participate is a good thing. Startup communities are not a zero-sum game where there are only winners and losers. The success of one member of the community is likely to have a positive impact on the community overall.

Startup community leaders set the tone and have a duty to ensure the door is open to anyone. As a common point of the first contact, leaders and instigators should introduce newcomers to high-impact, easy-to-access events, and a handful of key individuals. Leaders and instigators should make room for and nurture the next generation of leaders—handing off existing activities and taking on new responsibilities.

Startup communities that don't welcome all who want to get involved are unhealthy. Complex systems require openness and a lack of control;

they thrive best when they are exposed to diverse talents. Shunning outsiders or demanding that newbies earn their way in is ineffective and inhibits the development of a startup community. The impact of this behavior is even more apparent today as many cultures are beginning to come to grips with profoundly entrenched discrimination in so many domains across society.

Participants in healthy startup communities think as broadly as possible about how to be inclusive, which goes well beyond the characteristics we defined above. Take, for example, the time of day or the day of the week that events occur. If events only happen in the evening, does that make it less likely for some to attend? Some aspiring entrepreneurs may be single parents or have evening jobs that prevent them from attending events at this time of day. What about during daytime business hours? Maybe some people who are looking for on-ramps into entrepreneurship can't take time away from work to make it to an event held during the morning. The same is true of weekends or any other day and time of the week. There are many circumstances in which this might apply beyond day and time, such as when events require a significant financial commitment, among others. Always be looking for ways to make it easy for others to get involved. Now extend this idea to any number of ways that decisions in the startup community are systematically aligned against individuals or groups. Remove those barriers.

THINK BROADLY ABOUT ENTREPRENEURSHIP

Innovation and entrepreneurship are distinct activities. Often, entrepreneurial ventures commercialize innovation, but the entrepreneurial process is different from innovation overall. As a result, startup communities are broader than one sector or technology and apply to any company that seeks to grow a business around a novel idea.

Research that Ian and others have done demonstrates that although high-tech companies are disproportionately likely to achieve high-growth, the majority of high-growth companies are in industries outside of high-tech.[7] In a study done two years ago, Ian found that 30 percent of high-growth companies are high-tech companies, which is a remarkable share given that just 5 percent of companies overall are in high-tech. Even so, that leaves 70 percent of high-growth companies as being outside of the high-tech sector.

The proliferation of software and computing is blurring the lines between tech and non-tech. As a result, entrepreneurs in nontraditionally high-tech sectors can learn from high-tech entrepreneurs, and entrepreneurs in high-tech can learn from successful entrepreneurs in other industries. Do you remember what we said before about thinking broadly about diversity? This is a prime example.

Exposure to startups in adjacent or unrelated sectors yields fresh perspectives and unique insights that wouldn't have naturally become visible in your industry. While there are benefits from sharing industry-specific knowledge, many of the challenges of managing a high-growth young business in the presence of a network of local peers, advisors, mentors, and investors are common to all.

In *Startup Communities,* I described the parallel startup communities around different industries in Boulder at the time. Tech had a startup community, as did each of natural foods, biotech, cleantech, and LOHAS (lifestyles of health and sustainability). While the level of vibrancy varied, over the past six years there have been efforts, such as the Blackstone Entrepreneurs Network Colorado, to provide more cohesion between the various industries within a single startup community. [8]

Diversity Is Profitable

Miriam Rivera (Palo Alto, California)
Managing Director, Ulu Ventures

Talent is evenly distributed across genders and people of all races, but access to opportunity is not. Creating healthy ecosystems to include all races, backgrounds, and genders is essential to building strong entrepreneurial and investment communities. Although investors are key to supporting and nurturing those communities, the venture industry systematically overlooks entire categories of people. Not only is this a poor outcome for entrepreneurs, and society, it's a poor outcome for investors.

At Ulu Ventures, diversity is our investment thesis. We assert that not overlooking such categories leads to superior financial performance. Ulu applies objective criteria for every investment, and everyone gets evaluated against the same, not shifting criteria. Here are some practices and principles that have helped guide our firm that we think can be replicated elsewhere.

Mentoring

Venture capital is still predominantly a white-male–dominated culture with its language and nuance. This investor-speak is foreign for many entrepreneurs, particularly for women, immigrants, and people of color. At Ulu, we do a lot of mentoring, helping entrepreneurs navigate the startup world and translate their story into language VCs understand, thereby increasing their chances for success. We also try to help VCs understand how unconscious bias and inconsistently applied criteria lead to underinvestment in certain groups.

Storytelling

Ulu's use of decision analysis and market mapping guides entrepreneurs of all backgrounds to develop investor-speak skills, enabling them to tell compelling and quantitative market stories. Those stories help them better understand their own business from both an entrepreneur's and investor's perspective. Market mapping creates a visual picture of how entrepreneurs are going to pursue their market as well as a quantitative model of the opportunity in their business. It also gives them a glimpse into the kinds of problems that may crop up after gaining dominance in one market and what types of risks they'll encounter over the life cycle of their company. It enables entrepreneurs to articulate the journey of their business in a more effective way.

Collaboration

There's a design-thinking principle that says instead of tearing apart people's ideas, you should endeavor to make their ideas better. A lot of what we do in our mentoring conversations is collaboratively helping the entrepreneur identify better ways to conceive of or describe their business opportunity or business model. Or perhaps we can help them identify better entry points in their market by inputting the disparate knowledge and intuition gained from their immersive experience building a business into comparative, sensitivity-analyzed financial models.

Adding Value

As a team, Ulu can make these contributions because we want to be transparent with entrepreneurs about what constitutes a good investment. In a target-rich environment where we can only invest in about 1 percent of opportunities we see, we want to add value to entrepreneurs we won't meet or where we don't invest. Why? Entrepreneurs are one of our best sources of referrals, and we want to make a genuine contribution to the entrepreneurial ecosystem by sharing our knowledge and experience in a more scalable way than the number of meetings we can take or the number talks we offer every year. We've been entrepreneurs and understand the value of entrepreneurs' time; we want to reduce the time spent in unproductive, unhelpful, and even discouraging fundraising meetings.

Data Reduces Bias

The decision analysis process helps reduce bias, so our entrepreneurs are quite diverse by industry standards. As of October 31, 2019, Ulu's portfolio includes approximately 39 percent women co-founders, 37 percent minority co-founders, 37 percent immigrant co-founders, and 13 percent underrepresented minority (URM) co-founders. (Note, some founders are both women and URM or immigrant or minority, so the numbers do not add to 100 percent.) This level of diversity is significantly higher than the industry and more similar to the representation of such personnel in the tech sector.

Targeting Unseen Markets

We also advocate for diverse people to be heard; VCs need to increase their ability to understand, hear, and see diversity. Often one's own life experiences are insufficient to address markets that are targeted at diverse markets or different life experiences. Some of our companies are focused on financial inclusion in markets that are often characterized by financial exploitation of certain consumers. For example, there's a $70 billion U.S. industry around payday lending, rent to own, title loans, and other usurious practices, which disadvantage those with lower or less stable incomes. Unfortunately, there's often an intersection between race and income. While VCs are in the top 1 percent of earners, about half of Americans struggle with a very different economic reality and are not able to make purchases online because they lack access to a credit card. Yet many VCs aren't willing to invest in companies that are building white-hat brands in the financial inclusion space because they can't relate to such markets and don't have a gut sense of the opportunity. Quantification can help, as well as a positive frame on why a founder's awareness and/ or lived experience in such markets gives them the comparative advantage all VCs are looking for in developing access to given market opportunities. We want VCs to see what they're missing. Our quantified market maps, the high hurdle rate for making investments, a portfolio construction based on quantification of risk, and track record help us speak the language of VCs and limited partners while providing access to capital to more diverse entrepreneurs. We expect these strategies will lead to outlier successes. Diversity is aligned with our mission of driving superior economic returns for LPs.

Transparency Builds Trust

We commit to the entrepreneur, through the process, to share all the due diligence information generated by the collaborative market mapping exercise, whether or not Ulu decides to invest. We share all the data we've collected and the assumptions in the model regardless of whether they're the source or we are. We do the financial model in a way that they can re-run all the analyses using their numbers or assumptions. We offer a customized written report so they can understand how to use the tool as opposed to just having a one-time conversation, allowing them to ingest information privately and not when they're in the emotional throes of raising capital. These are some methods for us as investors to engage with entrepreneurs in ways that we hope will help them to succeed. Because we value relationships in our business and the world more generally, we believe if we're helpful to people, either through mentorship or through the decision analysis process, we build goodwill that may directly or indirectly help us and others we want to help.

Some ways in which this goodwill is demonstrated is the number of people in whom we haven't invested, who generate referrals to Ulu. In competitive situations, we nearly always get an allocation. The relationship an entrepreneur builds with an investor in diligence is a part of how they should pick their investors. For Ulu, the return on our give is long-term relationships with entrepreneurs who share similar values or who respect our approach, and that leads to many opportunities that may have nothing to do with the original investment conversations.

CHAPTER SIXTEEN

BE ACTIVE, NOT PASSIVE

Startup Community Way Principle

The startup community must have continual activities that meaningfully engage the entire entrepreneurial stack. Constant engagement develops relationships and builds trust across boundaries, creating opportunities for experimentation and learning. Including the whole community in the activity of entrepreneurship provides the basis for diversity to be embraced.

The fourth principle of the Boulder Thesis is that the startup community must have continual activities that engage the entire entrepreneurial stack. This means that infrequent or irregular contacts between startup community participants won't establish meaningful enough connections to drive real change, and that the nature of these events should be active (e.g. hackathons, competitions) rather than passive (e.g. cocktail parties, awards ceremonies). This also means that activities must offer opportunities to engage with the breadth of participants in the startup community.

SELF-SIMILARITY AND REPLICATION

Complex systems exhibit self-similarity by replicating smaller scale patterns into higher-order ones, which occurs when subsystems show similar patterns of behavior as those within a larger system. Consequently, a larger system is the product of an infinite number of more minor interactions that can be understood and influenced by examining and changing the patterns at a smaller scale.[1]

Efforts to improve behavior and mindset, even among small groups within a startup community, can have a profound impact on the overall system with time and persistence. You don't have to design a top-down plan and get everyone to agree to it. Instead, just start doing things. Economist David Colander and physicist Roland Kupers describe this nicely in their book on complexity and public policy:

> So what looks complex, and is impossibly complex when considered in the whole, can be relatively simply understood as the result of an almost infinite set of small changes, all following relatively simple rules. It is the simple replication of rules over time that leads to the complex pattern. Looking for simple rules that govern the evolution of a system. . . is the primary way in which complexity social science differs from standard social science.[2]

These are not rules in the traditional sense, but rather informal norms and activities that emphasize helpful behavior, a collaborative mindset, and active leadership. Small-scale interventions can catalyze meaningful change that impacts the entire system.

My experience in Boulder reflects this. In 1995, my wife Amy Batchelor and I randomly moved to Boulder.[3] We only knew one person in Boulder at the time, and he moved away within a year. I didn't expect to do any business in Boulder as I was on the road, continually traveling between cities on the East and West Coasts, where I had investments. But, after a few months, I decided to find some other entrepreneurs in town. I got introduced to a lawyer and a banker by a friend who used to live in Boulder and asked them for introductions to all the entrepreneurs they knew. I invited this extended group to a dinner in the fall of 1996, and the Boulder chapter (which quickly became the Colorado chapter) of the Young Entrepreneurs Organization was founded.[4]

As Internet companies started popping up in Boulder and Denver, I got a bunch of the founders together for dinner in Denver, and we ended up creating the Colorado Internet Keiretsu in 1997.[5] A few years later, there was a vibrant and well-connected group of entrepreneurs in Boulder. An underlying philosophy that came from involvement in each of these organizations was simply "help each other be successful." For me, it was an early and significant example of the power of peer-mentorship, which has become a foundational part of any startup community.[6]

DON'T WAIT OR ASK PERMISSION

In each of the cases above, I didn't wait for someone to invite me along to something or ask permission from others who had been around longer than me. I just co-founded YEO Colorado and co-founded the Colorado Internet Keiretsu. I didn't try to get any other stakeholders on board but was inclusive of anyone who was a founder and wanted to participate.

I was simply emulating what I had seen in other complex systems, specifically my experience in Boston and with the Young Entrepreneurs Organization around the world. I started doing things in Boulder on a small scale with a core group of highly committed people. Many people were attracted to these activities, and new patterns of involvement formed.

Almost 25 years later, this pattern and approach of an entrepreneur deciding to create a new activity, event, or organization are commonplace in Boulder.

This behavior is intensely liberating. Many startup community builders feel trapped and at the mercy of significant donors, nonprofits, universities, or local governments. While we acknowledge the importance of having financial resources in the system to pay for things, you can have an impact right away by just going out there and catalyzing meaningful connections. The answer doesn't have to be a new building, program, or organization. It can be simple. Find an excuse to get local entrepreneurs together in an environment that is fun and engaging and forge meaningful bonds with them.

PLAY A POSITIVE-SUM GAME

Many people approach personal and business relationships as a zero-sum game where there are winners and losers. In some situations, like a chess match or a baseball game, zero-sum thinking is the optimal strategy: for me to win, you have to lose. However, this type of thinking is very harmful to a startup community because it erodes trust and makes it impossible for people to collaborate and share information freely. Startup community participants must reject a scarcity mindset and instead embrace an abundance and growth mindset. In information-rich environments, accept that everyone gains more by contributing positively to the collective, which results in the collective growth.

Operating from a growth mindset is critical in the context of entrepreneurs, as they are essentially creating something new where nothing previously existed. This construct has been well-established by researchers who study evolutionary biology and game theory. Individuals, when faced with repeated interactions where cooperation is beneficial, are more likely to do so in the future. This cooperative behavior rewards them over time.[7] Such paths to cooperation include kinship (being in the same "family") and indirect reciprocity (paying it forward or receiving back from someone else in the community).

Elinor Ostrom, an American political economist, was awarded the Nobel Prize in Economics for demonstrating this empirically.[8] Her work on cooperation and collective governance showed that standard economic theory—people pursue a rational self-interest that leads to the depletion of shared resources—didn't match observations in the real world. She found that people with established bonds, such as social capital and repeated engagement, who also shared common resources, were highly likely to cooperate to increase the resources available for everyone in the system.

Startup communities are a type of shared resource. They are assets that no one person owns, but from which many benefit. Ostrom's research justifies why playing positive-sum games with others over a shared resource ensures strength, stability, and longevity of that precious resource over time. As a result, Ian decided to give Ostrom the Nobel Prize in Startup Communities.[9] He wrote:

> Elinor Ostrom, an American political economist, was awarded the 2009 Nobel Prize in Economic Sciences for her work on cooperation and collective action. She challenged the notion that in the absence of a central governing authority, shared resources will be underdeveloped and over-utilized. Conventional thinking at the time was that our selfish human nature prevented us from cooperating in a way that would ensure the sustainability of shared resources (like those in a startup community).
>
> But Ostrom overturned this thinking. Through the use of experimental techniques and the observation of societies that relied on shared (scarce) natural resources, she demonstrated that under the right conditions, people are willing to cooperate for the greater good and engage with a positive-sum mindset.

In her Nobel acceptance speech, she described her work in the following way:

"Carefully designed experimental studies in the lab have enabled us to test precise combinations of structural variables to find that isolated, anonymous individuals overharvest from common-pool resources. Simply allowing communication, or 'cheap talk,' enables participants to reduce overharvesting and increase joint payoffs, contrary to game-theoretical predictions."

Said differently, we tend to cooperate with people we know and trust. And, conversely, it's easier to defect or play a zero-sum game against people we don't.

The central thinking behind Startup Communities is to improve human relationships in a way that allows for collaboration, cooperation, and idea-sharing to become second nature. Social cohesiveness and trust are essential for the sorts of norms and informal rules that will enable collaboration to occur in a startup community. Frequent engagement allows that to develop.

In *Startup Communities*, I referred to this as "playing a non-zero-sum game."[10] Recalling the concept of positive contagion, we think a better label for this is to play a positive-sum game, which is also a nod to increasing returns and nonlinearity in complexity science. At any stage of development, startup communities are a tiny fraction of what they can ultimately become. As a result, there is a vast amount of untapped opportunity.

Begin by fully embracing the notion of increasing returns. The goal of everyone in the startup community should be to create something that lasts for a very long period of time. Although ups and downs with individual companies will always happen, view the startup community as a whole entity. If there is more startup activity, this will generate more attention to the startup community, which will create even more activity.

Next, view the percentage of your local economy that the startup community contributes as its market share. If the macro environment gets better, so will the overall dynamic of the startup community. The cycles are unpredictable, but these up-and-down swings will likely only have an impact on the global environment. During downturns, there are opportunities for the startup community to gain market share of the local economy.

We saw this aggressively play out in the financial crisis that started in 2007. While the downturn cast a dark cloud over world economies for a long time, startup communities in the United States and throughout the world grew significantly during this period. Eventually, attention turned to the power of entrepreneurship to revive the global economy.

Values and Virtues: Convene and Connect

A permissionless approach to connecting people is another attribute of vibrant startup communities. If you are a trusted person in the startup community and believe that two people should engage, don't ask for permission first, just make the introduction. This radical approach to connecting people reduces friction in the network, embraces the notion of implicit trust, and sets the example that no one is too busy or too important to be connected with another person.

Some busy people prefer opt-in introductions. Be respectful of that. If someone prefers this approach, ask them before you make the introduction. Usually, they will accept your request for an introduction to someone else. But, if not, you enhance your reputation with them through being respectful of what they prefer.

If you trust the person doing the connecting, you accept that there is a reason for the connection. If you are doing the connecting, you believe that the connected individuals will work out for themselves whether a relationship should take place. Sometimes a relationship will develop right away; other times, it will lead to something down the road, or it may even lead to a dead end. In our experience, some of the most meaningful conversations come from places we least expect.

An example of this is the creation of Techstars. David Cohen first met me on one of my "random days."[11] For about a decade, I set aside one day each month, where I spent 15 minutes with anyone who wanted to meet with me. These meetings were queued up over six hours so I could do around 20 random meetings in a day. I met David at one of these. He handed me an overview of this new thing he was thinking about called Techstars, said he was raising $200,000, and would personally put up $80,000 of it. After talking for about 10 minutes, I said, "As long as you aren't a flake or a crook, I'm in for $50,000." David then told me that David Brown (now CEO of Techstars), who had been his partner in their first company (Pinpoint Technologies), would likely invest $50,000 as well. After David left, I called Jared Polis, a good friend whom he had met a decade earlier via an introduction from my first business partner. I told Jared that I was investing $50,000 in a new thing called Techstars and would Jared like to hear more about it. Jared responded, "Sure, count me in for $50,000. What is it?" And, just like that, the first financing for Techstars was raised.

Ultimately, it is essential to convene founders and other startup community participants and create space to improve the odds of making connections. An excellent example of this is Silicon Flatirons, a program at the University of Colorado Law School, which, among many other activities, literally opened its doors to the Boulder startup community to use as a meeting place. Our friend, Brad Bernthal, a professor at the school, wrote about this dynamic in *Startup Communities*:

> Universities are great, natural conveners with often excellent and sometimes underutilized facilities. Leveraging this, we launched a series of public events that connect and celebrate the startup community, with the ambition to connect the CU campus and the software/telecom/geek portions of the entrepreneurial ecosystem.

CONTINUOUSLY AND ACTIVELY ENGAGE

Entrepreneurship is not a spectator sport. Neither is building a startup community. Passive events such as cocktail parties or award ceremonies highlighting successful entrepreneurs and companies are interesting but not sufficient. Instead, catalytic and continuous events such as hackathons, topical meetups, open coffee clubs, Startup Weekends, and mentor-driven accelerators are required. These are venues for tangible, focused engagement around the activity of entrepreneurship among members of the startup community.

You will have reached critical mass and another tipping point in your startup community when there is more than one startup community–related event each day. When you start having to choose between events, you are reaching a point of saturation that corresponds to a vibrant startup community. You want super-saturation—many more events in number and in scope than any individual could participate in. And, as an individual member in the startup community, instead of skimming the surface with a wide variety of different events that you don't engage in, go deep on a few events consistently over time.

Startup Community Programs: Pipeline Building for Underrepresened Founders

Jackie Ros (New York, New York)
Regional Director (Americas), Techstars
CEO and Co-Founder, Revolar

When I accepted the role of Regional Director of the Americas for Techstars community programs it felt karmic to now support the very same programs that made it possible for me, a Latinx with no prior tech or business experience, to launch a wearable safety company.

I co-founded Revolar because I was inspired by my little sister and family that I wanted to keep safe after having not felt safe for a very long time. The six-year journey that my co-founder and I went on with Revolar was incredible. We launched multiple products thanks to our awesome team, met incredible mentors and friends, wrote for *Forbes*, and learned some seriously painful lessons. At many moments in time, I wondered how we had become several of the first Latinas to raise millions from VCs.

While the journey had extreme highs and even deeper lows, our startup community kept us sane and was the only reason we existed in the first place. There were many community leaders who quietly orchestrated life-changing opportunities behind the scenes for us and whom I never knew to thank. There were also mentors who helped us learn how to build a team and grow our company. I encountered incredible support from the community in Boulder and Denver well before I even understood what it meant to be in a strong startup community. All I knew when choosing to move to Colorado was that my Dad had told me Colorado was where he was happiest in his life and I'd be able to go rock climbing as often as I wanted. I'm proof that the Boulder Thesis works, but I wondered if it was true for other startup communities in different geographies.

After two years of being involved in startup community programs, with a focus on diversity, throughout the Americas, I have an in-depth view of innovation and entrepreneurial ecosystems in many different places. It's clear to me that supporting startup community programs at a grassroots level is critical for supporting diverse founders and having more diversity in tech in general.

Underrepresented and underestimated founders regularly meet in a startup community program such as Techstars Startup Weekend or Week, Launchpad, Startup Grind, and 1 Million

Cups. Events like this allow the founders to get involved in the entrepreneurial ecosystem through well-developed events, which then result in their getting connected to the local networks. As they engage with key connectors, their networks overlap, and help expand and unify the various networks in the ecosystem. While attendees of these programs may branch into different aspects of entrepreneurship, they get their start and find their niche thanks to the power of startup community programs.

Truly inclusive startup communities are proactive about inviting people, not just welcoming them when someone happens to make it. After being invited to and participating in events, diverse founders will feel more comfortable connecting with others, finding their way into other programs, accelerators, or networks. They'll follow a path like I did, from Denver Startup Week, to Innosphere, a local incubator, to Techstars. Given the opportunity for these experiences, they are now in a position to #GiveFirst to the rest of their community.

The biggest misconception I see is that people think events have to be perfect and have lots of attendees to be impactful. Communities are at different stages and learn different lessons at different times. As long as the leaders bring energy and authentic enthusiasm to the table, diverse communities can develop within the ecosystem. Alongside, organizations such as Google for Startups, Kapor Center, HBCU.vc, Patriot Bootcamp, Deaf Entrepreneurs Network, and the Kauffman Foundation band together to create spaces for these networks to overlap. These events expose people in these communities to hope that they, too, can have access to a greater opportunity and be an entrepreneur.

My experience as Regional Director at Techstars has reminded me much of my time with Teach for America (TFA). The little tweaks we make in communities add up dramatically in the most wonderful and unexpected ways. But like my TFA experience, these programs are severely underfunded, and the teams are stretched trying to serve as many communities as they can. If you look at the ripple effects of community programs in countries where many community leaders feel unstable or unsafe, they find hope and inspiration in the tenets of transparency, service to community, and authentic leadership.

It takes my breath away to meet community leaders from across the globe and find hope and guidance from them on how to help their communities. Through the help of Elizabeth Becerril and Preta Emmeline, the Regional Managers of LATAM and Brazil respectively, I was able to rapidly learn about the ecosystems in which they live. My first language of Spanish at first felt clumsy as I navigated new business settings. My Portuguese was severely lacking, but the communities were always welcoming. Once, I saw one of Brad's quotes from *Startup Communities* on a t-shirt in Florianopolis, Brazil. It was about taking the long-term view on community, and it was in Portuguese. That really hit home how, despite the nuances and differences in our communities, certain tenets around startup communities resonate no matter what language you speak.

It was a heartbreaking moment for our team last year when the sanctions were put in place in Venezuela and we could no longer support the startup community leaders there the way we used to. Elizabeth had been coaching them for years. I thought of my best friends growing up in South Florida who were Venezuelan, Cuban, or Colombian like me. My worldview widened even further when

I learned more about the challenges for disabled entrepreneurs to access the same support, the challenges veteran families face in launching businesses, or even those founders who are held back by their own countries' policies that make entrepreneurship difficult to thrive, such as high barriers of entry to incorporating a business or filing for bankruptcy.

My understanding of diversity has grown through this experience and through experiencing the world through the eyes of my fellow global team members. It's truly incredible to see the impact diverse and underrepresented founders have on a global level as they build bridges between communities locally and around the world.

PART IV

CONCLUSION

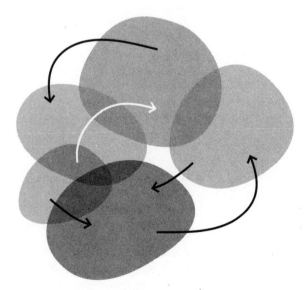

CHAPTER SEVENTEEN

CONCLUSION

REFLECTIONS

The Startup Community Way is a set of principles and practices that will improve the performance of startup communities and entrepreneurial ecosystems everywhere. We stress the principles point because every city is fundamentally different from the next. While there are common problems in many places, and these principles apply broadly, the specific details about what ends up working can only emerge through a process of discovery that will be unique to each time and place.

Our central message is that any startup community can be improved by enhancing collaboration, support, and knowledge-sharing, taking a #Give-First approach, and placing the entrepreneurs at the center of things. Since startup communities are human social systems, they evolve and improve when the relationships are underpinned by trust, reciprocity, and stewardship of place. In many cities, this will require a transformation of how people think and behave. That's not easy to do, especially when the incentive structures inside of many organizations work against this. It takes time and there are no shortcuts in this work. A commitment of a generation or more is required. Once a critical mass of dedicated individuals is reached, things become easier by involving more people who learn to adopt the established norms and behaviors of the community. Your job is to make sure the norms and behaviors are the right ones.

The entire point of startup communities is to help entrepreneurs succeed. This idea is simple, yet problems emerge when our analytical brains and our need for structure and certainty guide our actions. Startup communities and entrepreneurial ecosystems are complex adaptive systems that we never fully understand, nor are we able to predict or infer from history what exactly to do at a given place and time. (We are still arguing over what made Silicon Valley great!) Resist the urge to overcomplicate things. Instead, look for ways to improve the chances that entrepreneurs will succeed, by helping them in meaningful ways—big and small—on a consistent basis. Success will vary from community to community, but in our view, success is more about improvement over time and getting the most out of the resources *your* city currently has rather than about artificially increasing some type of output or meeting some allegedly objective definition of success set by another city.

This is not a playbook or a step-by-step guide for how to build a startup community. While we believe more work can be done in this area, it's important to remember that practical guidance has its limits because each place and time are different. The benefits of generalization are limited. For every city where something worked, there's a long list of others where that same thing didn't. Similarly, something that used to work in the past may no longer be effective because the underlying conditions have changed. Test empirically, through a trial-and-error discovery process. It's a hopeless exercise to attempt to turn this work into a boilerplate recipe or a formula to replicate in many places, but there is immense value in having a clear philosophy and process, which we've tried to explain. If the solutions were obvious, vibrant startup communities would exist everywhere.

SUMMARY OF THE BOOK

We thought it would be helpful to provide a recap of the book in one place. We begin with an overview of the individual components of a startup community. First, we describe the forces that explain why startup communities exist, including the role and basic function of entrepreneurs, the importance of the external environment to entrepreneurship, the organization of startup communities through networks of trust over hierarchies, the value that is produced by entrepreneurial density, and why quality of place matters in the modern economy. Building on this last point, Ben Weiner explains how the rise of the creative class and a spirit of rebellion helped revive the startup community in Jerusalem after a decade of decline.

Next, we detail the individual components within startup communities and entrepreneurial ecosystems. We describe the roles of individuals and organizations, which we call actors. Startup community leaders must be entrepreneurs. Instigators are non-entrepreneurs who still play critical leadership roles. Feeders are everyone else. The resources and conditions required for entrepreneurship to thrive are called factors. We organize them into the Seven Capitals: intellectual, human, financial, network, cultural, physical, and institutional. This framework has the dual purpose of acknowledging the qualities of the factors as value-producing assets that require the investment of time or resources and also encourages actors to think about the term "capital" as more than just financial resources. In this section, Arlan Hamilton describes how a #GiveFirst approach and setting the right intention allowed her to build a community for underestimated founders. Bobby Burch details *Startland News*, explaining how the power of story can unlock value in startup communities in unexpected ways.

We conclude the first section with a breakdown of the similarities and differences between startup communities and entrepreneurial ecosystems, with the former representing the beating heart of entrepreneurship in a city, and the latter wrapping key actors and factors around it. Startup communities are narrower and deeper where participants have a tighter alignment around identity, values, fellowship, and a fundamental commitment to helping entrepreneurs succeed. Entrepreneurial successes serve as an attractor for startup communities that engage and activate additional people, organizations, resources, and support from the ecosystem. We call this community/ecosystem fit. Scott Resnick describes how this sequencing of events helped propel the entrepreneurial ecosystem forward in Madison, Wisconsin.

The next section explains that startup communities and entrepreneurial ecosystems are complex adaptive systems. We begin by emphasizing the need to take the implications of systems seriously, starting with a whole-system view. We define three systems—simple, complicated, and complex—and why the differences, implications, and strategies for dealing with complex systems are vastly different from the other two. Complex systems are defined by having many interdependent actors who interact with and are adaptive to each other. This creates a series of feedback loops where individuals and the system perpetually coevolve. Brad Bernthal describes how a whole-system view taken by the New Venture Challenge improved entrepreneurship at the University of Colorado Boulder.

We then introduce the concept of emergence as a process of unpredictable creativity, which is what makes each complex system valuable and unique. Emergence, or valuable patterning, occurs because of the interactions between the parts. These synergies produce nonlinear behavior, where the emergent whole is much greater than and substantially different from the sum of the parts. Emergent behavior in complex systems is self-organized, meaning that it occurs naturally with no plan and no one in control. Complex systems, like startup communities, are valuable because of the interactions, not the parts themselves, and the process of value creation occurs naturally without a plan or a controlling authority. This requires a very different approach to building startup communities from the traditional command-and-control strategies applied in the industrial era that linger on still today. Rick Turoczy tells his story about the acceptance of failure and unpredictable creativity in the development of PIE in Portland, Oregon.

The first of three chapters on the implications of startup communities as complex systems begins with the myth of quantity, where we diagnose how the more-of-everything approach is inherently flawed. In complex systems, the focus should be on the outliers, not the averages or quantities, because a small number of high-impact entrepreneurial successes drive the overall system value. One phenomenon is entrepreneurial recycling, where founders, investors, and employees from a successful startup invest their time, wealth, knowledge, and networks back into the next generation of entrepreneurs or their own next startup. Startup communities where the most influential network nodes are successful entrepreneurs or organizations led by them have better outcomes than communities where the influential actors lack this experience. Scott Dorsey—who led the development of the startup community in Indianapolis, Indiana, while growing ExactTarget to an eventual $2.5 billion acquisition and has continued his leadership with his new company High Alpha—explains how this is done.

Startup communities and entrepreneurial ecosystems cannot be controlled—only guided and influenced. Participants succumb to the illusion of control because of our deep-seated human instincts to avoid uncertainty, a desire for a full understanding of the world around us, and to be the masters of our destiny. We convince ourselves that all of this is true, but it's not. Constant feedback loops (information flows and adaptive behavior) make it impossible for us to fully understand what's happening because they produce nonlinearities—including substantial delays, phased transitions (where major system shifts occur that redefine the system), and contagion (both good and bad), where ideas and behaviors spread and are quickly adopted. The human mind can't process these dynamics effectively and responds by attempting to control things. In order to be successful in complex systems, we have to let go of the illusion that we are in control because we are not, and efforts to control only end up doing damage. Troy D'Ambrosio explains how the University of Utah did what few universities do when given a mandate to build an entrepreneurship center, by ceding top-down control and including student entrepreneurs in the process, leading to a great outcome.

Many researchers, consultants, and community builders search for a blueprint to become the next Silicon Valley. The allure of a formulaic approach to startup communities stems from the narrative fallacy, where our brains fill gaps in understanding with a simplified version of events. Such ideas are flawed because each startup community is unique and deeply influenced by local history and culture. Small differences in the past can produce large differences in the future in complex systems. As perpetual evolution occurs, startup communities are propelled toward one of many semi-stable states, where healthy or unhealthy patterns become ingrained and difficult to counteract. Given the absence of a blueprint, the only path forward is a process of trial and error, learning from failures, and building on a city's unique strengths. Cultivating a deep love of place (called topophilia) helps startup community participants endure the inevitable ups and downs. Rebecca Lovell describes how the City of Seattle took a bottom-up approach to respond to the needs of the startup community, rather than dictating what should be done from the top-down.

The measurement trap occurs when startup communities let the desire for data and "proof" that things are working drive poor strategies. In complex systems, the least important factors are the easiest to measure, so strategies get shaped around these factors instead of the factors that actually matter. It is a major problem in startup communities that what is easily measured get prioritized. This gets magnified when standardized metrics are built into rankings, which oversimplify ecosystems and position cities against each other. It's essential to remember that the most important qualities of a startup community are not the parts but the interactions (which are harder to see and measure). In addition, the most useful comparisons are those done within the same city at different points in time. To measure these, one must look to connectivity and system structure (network models) and the underlying behaviors and attitudes of the people involved (cultural-social models). A pragmatic approach draws from a number of other methods, including categorical, comparative, dynamic, logic models, and agent-based models, which provide a more complete picture of an entrepreneurial ecosystem and reinforce that there is no single correct answer. Rhett Morris shares his last decade measuring ecosystems and explains how themes of clarity and alignment, sharing and discussion, community engagement, and an ongoing process of repetition, are critical.

In the final section, we attempt to simplify complexity and make it actionable. While complexity describes system characteristics, systems thinking is the set of tools and methodologies for effectively working with a complex system. We describe "leverage points" in complex systems, which are places to intervene with maximum impact. The most effective leverage points are improving network connectivity and structure along with the underlying norms, thought patterns, and values of the participants. The next most impactful is increasing information flow and feedback channels. The least impactful is adjusting input quantities. Unfortunately, this last group is where a large amount of energy is applied in startup communities because they are the most tangible and easiest to change. Two existing frameworks that support our prioritization for lasting change are the Rainforest and the Boulder Thesis from *Startup Communities*. The latter of these is the most actionable, and therefore, we spend the next four chapters going deeper on it while using the lens of complexity to support it. The chapter closes with an essay from Bill Aulet, who describes how applying an entrepreneurial mindset and systems thinking makes MIT among the best universities globally for student entrepreneurship.

The first principle of the Boulder Thesis is that entrepreneurs must lead. This is not to say that others, whom we call instigators, cannot play leadership roles, but a startup community without a sufficient number of entrepreneurial leaders is not a lasting one. Successful and serial entrepreneurs hold a special role of importance among other entrepreneurs. Having been through the entrepreneurial process, these leaders can be the best role models and mentors in a startup community. They have the best ability to instill virtuous ideas and behaviors in the community while dampening the bad. But inspired leadership is not automatic, as experienced entrepreneurs in many communities demonstrate poor behavioral traits. These bad actors can be marginalized if a critical mass of entrepreneurs—even less influential ones—collaborate to form an alternative center of gravity. Jenny Fielding describes how a founder-first approach led to the creation of a new community-driven investment model in New York City.

The Boulder Thesis also states the leaders must have a long-term view— a perpetual 20-year commitment. The complex systems properties of phase transitions, tipping points, time delays, feedback loops, and nonlinearities are supportive of this view. It takes a long time for people to change behavior and thought patterns in a way that is conducive for entrepreneurship to thrive. Even Silicon Valley's success is more than one hundred years in the making. Chris Heivly discusses the long-term view of the startup community in Durham, North Carolina, along with the willingness of civic and philanthropic leaders to embrace the principles of noncontrol and letting entrepreneurs lead, allowing the solutions to emerge from the bottom up.

The third principle of the Boulder Thesis is that startup communities must be inclusive of anyone who wants to participate. Complex systems rely and thrive on diversity. Where hierarchical, top-down approaches seek tight control and therefore uniformity (a lack of diversity), startup communities benefit from the opposite. Current discussions of diversity tend to focus on identity diversity (e.g., gender, race, and sexual orientation), however, we advocate a more expansive view of cognitive diversity—one that includes identity diversity (which is a subset of cognitive diversity since identity influences thought) but adds in other types of diversity, such as experience, background, and perspective. Taking an inclusive approach also means thinking broadly about entrepreneurship—not just high-tech, venture-backed startups, but all founders and people with a growth mindset. For diversity to take hold, we must practice radical inclusion, which welcomes everyone. Miriam Rivera describes how Ulu Ventures improves its performance by embracing diversity and building tools to remove bias from the investment decision-making.

The final principle of the Boulder Thesis is that communities can only be sustained with continual and meaningful engagement. One empowering thing about community building is that you don't need permission or a budget to get started—you just need a small number of energetic people who are committed to making things better for entrepreneurs. This approach is supported by a related concept from complexity science known as self-similarity. In complex systems, change can take place at any scale, and these patterns—for example, a small group of founders who are committed to changing a toxic environment—can then be replicated or extended throughout the entire system. If something good is happening, even with a lot of bad around it, eventually the good can spread and become the new norm. Bringing a positive-sum mindset, an active practice of catalytic engagement (not just cocktail parties and awards banquets), and a radical embrace of convening and connecting, is essential. We close with a story from Jackie Ros, whose journey as a startup founder was made possible by her discovery of many top-of-funnel activities available in her community in Colorado.

FINAL THOUGHTS

The book you just read is very different from what either of us envisioned at the beginning of our journey. We started with the simple ambition to expand and modernize *Startup Communities*. As our initial thoughts came together, and we talked to more people, we realized that we were on a different mission. We knew that what was needed most was a book that convincingly made the case for why we should view and engage with startup communities differently. Much of the *what*, *who*, and *how* was already established in *Startup Communities*. This book has been additive in those areas, but our hope is that we've advanced the *why* in significant ways.

Complexity was not even on our radar at the start, and yet it became the centerpiece of the book. The development process of this book is pleasantly recursive and typifies the essence of a complex, emergent process. By combining our diversity of talents, and applying them with patience, persistence, curiosity, and a willingness to take things where they needed to go, even if uncomfortable at times, we produced something that is much better and substantially different than if we had plowed our way through in a linear, controlled process, following our initial goal, outline, and timeline.

We stress this point because complex, emergent processes are everywhere in our lives. The more we can normalize complexity, the easier it will be to embrace it in the work of making startup communities more helpful to entrepreneurs. The normalization and bridge-building around complexity should become a central focus of startup community participants moving forward. Complexity has been increasing exponentially in recent years, as the world becomes more integrated both digitally and physically. This trend will continue for the foreseeable future. Realize you are dealing with complexity in any situation that involves the interaction or coordination of people in a context where objective definitions of success and procedures are unclear, and control is elusive.

So, that's what the book covered, what did we miss?

The first thing is that *The Startup Community Way* is less practice-based than we originally planned. Notice we didn't say *practical* but *practice-based*. Although deeply supported by theory and evidence, the book is targeted primarily at practitioners. We hope our work is educational and useful to those people, by providing a framework and language for them to explain to feeders why top-down control doesn't work, and why bottom-up experimentation is the only effective way. However, this book isn't practice-based in the sense of having a central focus of outlining a laundry list of key problems and mapping them to tangible solutions.

By using this book to firmly establish the linkage between startup communities and complex systems, we provided space for more practice-based work to follow. However, it's important to understand that any practice-based approach will still need to be customized for every startup community and entrepreneurial ecosystem. Each situation is different, and the solution can only emerge through trial and error. It's next to impossible to imagine and describe the endless number of scenarios that could play out. A "how-to" manual of solving X problem with Y solution is an oversimplification, but we believe a larger volume of structured storytelling can illuminate pathways and the imagination.

As we iterated on the book and decided to organize it around complexity, we threw away the second half, which was the more practice-based portion. That leads to a second limitation of our book: fewer stories from a broader group of people than we would have liked. We intended to have many guest essays included in the book. The second half of the book was loaded with them and was organized around key areas of practice, including startup support organizations (accelerators, incubators, studios), community-building organizations, universities, government, large corporations, service providers, rural startup communities, and startup communities in challenging places. As the content around complexity took shape, we realized those belonged in a separate publication. We believe strongly in the power of a story, which is why we've included at least one in each chapter. However, we simply could not accommodate the breadth of those while staying with our core mission, which emerged during our journey. A book that included it all would have been unwieldy and disjointed, but fortunately, there are other vehicles for the stories we couldn't include here.

Additionally, we are fully aware that the guest essays in this book lack the diversity we had hoped for—particularly with regard to geography (in the global sense). Part of this was due to bad luck. We solicited submissions more than two years before the publication, and so the topics and key themes of the book shifted around. The essays we included fit the final book structure best. It happened to be that many of the submissions from geographies outside of the United States aligned with the areas of the book that got cut. That's unfortunate and we will look for ways to highlight this work—and to bring in more of it—in future publications, especially online.

Finally, we believe the behaviors, attitudes, norms, and values espoused in this book have useful applications in many domains spanning professional, personal, and civic life. Any situation that involves the collaboration of human beings to solve complex problems that lack clear definitions of success or roadmaps to achieving an outcome can benefit from adopting principles from *The Startup Community Way*. In that regard, we hope this is a jumping-off point for people working to improve company culture, personal relationships, or any number of interpersonal interactions that are important. The complexity lens has illuminated the path for us in better understanding and engaging with startup communities. It also was the underlying force that produced unpredictable creativity in the writing of this book. What will it do for you?

ABOUT
THE AUTHORS

B rad Feld has been an early stage investor and entrepreneur since 1987. Prior to co-founding Foundry Group, he co-founded Mobius Venture Capital and, prior to that, founded Intensity Ventures. He is also a co-founder of Techstars.

Brad is a writer and speaker on the topics of venture capital investing and entrepreneurship. He's written a number of books, including Venture Deals, Do More Faster, Startup Boards, Startup Life, and Startup Opportunities.

Brad holds Bachelor of Science and Master of Science degrees in Management Science from the Massachusetts Institute of Technology. He is also an art collector and long-distance runner, having completed 25 marathons as part of his mission to finish a marathon in each of the 50 states.

Brad lives in Boulder, Colorado with his wife Amy Batchelor and two golden retrievers named Brooks and Cooper.

Read more on Brad's blog at www.feld.com or follow him on Twitter @bfeld.

Ian Hathaway is an analyst, strategic advisor, writer, and entrepreneur. He has been a consultant to leaders in the technology, media, and finance sectors on a range of innovation, strategy, and public policy engagements. He advises and invests in software, media, and consumer startups in the United States and Europe.

Ian is also an experienced researcher, author, and speaker on the subjects of entrepreneurship, innovation, and the economy. His work has been published with prominent research institutions and is regularly featured in leading press outlets, such as *The New York Times, The Economist, Financial Times,* and *The Wall Street Journal,* among others.

Ian earned a master's degree from the University of Chicago in economics and political economy, and a bachelor's degree in history and government from the University of Dayton. He is an amateur chef and a loyal fan of the band Phish, having attended more than 100 shows since 1997.

Ian lives in Santa Barbara, California with his wife Suzy, their two sons Teddy and Charlie, and Frankie, a King Charles Cavalier Spaniel. They previously lived in London and San Francisco.

Read more of Ian's work on his blog at www.ianhathaway.org or follow him on Twitter @IanHathaway.

ACKNOWLEDGMENTS

We couldn't have completed this book without the help of many people.

First and foremost, we'd like to thank our families.

Brad thanks Amy for her support of his writing. It is something we both love and will do together for the rest of our lives.

Ian thanks Suzy for her love and support throughout this process and all things in life. I couldn't have done it without you. To Teddy and Charlie, thank you for choosing me as your dad. I hope you can be proud of the work that I do. Frankie, you are a loyal friend who loves me no matter what. Mom and Dad, thank you for instilling in me the value of hard work.

Brad's partners at Foundry Group—Lindel Eakman, Seth Levine, Jason Mendelson, Ryan McIntyre, and Chris Moody—have been supporters of both the book as well as practitioners of all the activity around building startup communities throughout the world. Brad's assistant, Annie Heissenbuttel, has been an extraordinary help, putting up with endless requests for all kinds of random things from both of us. We also appreciate all the efforts from Brad's prior assistant, Mary Weingartner, who retired about a year after we started collaborating.

Ian is grateful to the countless people who have influenced this work through their writing, discussions, or encouragement. There are too many to name, but he extends a special thanks to several key collaborators. Chris

Heivly, I will never forget our weekly chats as we were both finding our way through the wilderness. I am grateful. Thanks to Nicolas Colin, Rhett Morris, and Scott Resnick for sharpening and expanding my thinking. John Dearie, you were there to coach me through the ups and downs of book writing.

The team at Wiley, including Bill Falloon and Purvi Patel, continue to be excellent partners. Near the end of the process, Rachel Meier, the director of Techstars Press, also jumped in to help us get everything completed. Thanks also to Phanat Nen for assistance with the graphics contained in this book and Christina Verigan for help editing the text.

A number of friends and colleagues provided comments on earlier drafts of this book. They include Brad Bernthal, David Brown, David Cohen, Richard Florida, Chris Heivly, Bob Litan, Jason Mendelson, Rhett Morris, Marc Nager, Zach Nies, Scott Resnick, and Phil Weiser. Thank you for taking the time out of your busy schedules to improve this work.

The entire team at Techstars, which now numbers over 300 people, has been a very important part of this book. Without Techstars, it's unlikely that many of the things we learned about would exist, or at least our exposure to them would be limited.

We benefited immensely from many people who submitted essays for this book. While in the end, we couldn't publish them all (some will be included in the second edition of *Startup Communities*), we are grateful for each one of these contributors. Thanks to all of you: Bill Aulet, John Beadle, Brad Bernthal, Bobby Burch, Jennifer Cabala, David Cohen, Kim Coupounas, Troy D'Ambrosio, Oko Davaasuren, Scott Dorsey, Jenny Fielding, Cameron Ford, Greg Gottesman, Andrew Greer, Arlan Hamilton, Chris Heivly, Matt Helt, Vikram Jandhyala, Rebecca Lovell, Jason Lynch, Brian McPeek, Monisha Merchant, Ben Milne, Lesa Mitchell, Chris Moody, Marc Nager, Saed Nashef, Tom Nastas, Akintunde Oyebode, Scott Resnick, Miriam Rivera, Greg Rogers, Chris Schroeder, Geoffrey See, Zachary Shulman, Jeremy Shure, Dianna Somerville, Pule Taukobong, Rick Turoczy, and Ben Wiener.

Eric Ries's books, *The Lean Startup* and *The Startup Way*, inspired our writing, thinking, and even our title. Eric graciously said *yes* when we asked if we could model our title after his, and he extra-graciously agreed to write the foreword for this book.

Finally, there are thousands of entrepreneurs we have worked with and many more people who we have encountered along the way as we spread the message of entrepreneurship and startup communities wherever we go. Thank you for the opportunity to know you, work with you, and learn from you.

NOTES

PREFACE

1. Casnocha (2008), "Start-up Town," *The American*, American Enterprise Institute, October 10, available at: https://www.aei.org/articles/start-up-town/.
2. The Kauffman Foundation (2012), Kauffmann Sketchbook 12, "StartupVille," October 8, Available at: https://www.youtube.com/watch?v=zXD5vt0xhyI.
3. You can watch that interview on YouTube at: https://www.youtube.com/watch?v=C7mV_Xk2gw0.
4. Brown and Mason (2017), "Looking inside the spiky bits: A critical review and conceptualization of entrepreneurial ecosystem," *Small Business Economics*, Volume 49, pages 11–30.
5. Allen (2016), "Complicated or complex–knowing the difference is important," *Learning for Sustainability*, February 3, available at: https://learningforsustainability.net/post/complicated-complex/.

CHAPTER 1

1. See Hathaway (2018), "America's Rising Startup Cities," *Center for American Entrepreneurship*; Florida and Hathaway (2018), "Rise of the Global Startup City: The New Map of Entrepreneurship and Venture Capital," *Center for American Entrepreneurship*.

2. Gross (1982), *An Elephant Is Soft and Mushy*, Avon Books.

3. This especially applies to Ian, although I read most of what Ian sends my way. I also send Ian anything I find that contradicts topics we are concluding. This ensures we bash through any confirmation bias that insidiously finds its way into our brains.

4. World Bank (2020), available at: https://data.worldbank.org/indicator/SI.POV.DDAY.

5. Freedom House (2019), *Freedom in the World: Democracy in Retreat*, available at: https://freedomhouse.org/report/freedom-world/freedom-world-2019/democracy-in-retreat.

6. International Labour Organization (2019), *Unemployment and Underemployment Statistics*; Global Entrepreneurship Monitor (2020), *Global Report 2019/2020*.

7. For evidence on this, see Audretsch, Falck, Feldman, and Heblich (2012), "Local Entrepreneurship in Context," *Regional Studies* 46:3 (2012), 379–389; Figueiredo, Guimaraes, and Woodward (2007), "Home-Field Advantage: Location Decisions of Portuguese Entrepreneurs," *Journal of Urban Economics* 52:2 (2002), 341–361; and Michelacci and Silva (2007), "Why So Many Local Entrepreneurs?," *Review of Economics and Statistics* 89:4 (2007), 615–633.

8. Jolly (2015), *Systems Thinking for Business: Capitalize on Structures Hidden in Plain Sight*, Systems Solutions Press.

9. McKelvey (2004), "Toward a Complexity Science of Entrepreneurship," *Journal of Business Venturing*, 19, 313–341; and Hwang and Horowitt (2012), *The Rainforest: The Secret to Building the Next Silicon Valley*, Regenwald.

10. *The Irish Times* (2015), "Harvard MBAs Give Up on Wall Street," August 6, available at: https://www.irishtimes.com/business/work/harvard-mbas-give--up-on-wall-street-1.2308774.

11. For a general discussion on how interest rates affect the supply of venture capital, see Gompers and Lerner (1998), "What Drives Venture Capital Fundraising?" *Brookings Papers on Economic Activity: Microeconomics*. For a discussion of the low-interest-rate environment, its impact on the venture capital industry, and its historical context, see Janeway (2018), *Doing Capitalism in the Innovation Economy: Reconfiguring the Three-Player Game between Markets, Speculators and the State*, Cambridge University Press.

12. Stanford and Le (2019), "Nontraditional Investors in VC Are Here to Stay," *PitchBook Analyst Note*.

13. Hathaway (2019), "The Rise of Global Startup Investors," *Ian Hathaway Blog*, January 14, http://www.ianhathaway.org/blog/2019/1/14/the-rise-of-global-startup-investors.

14. Hathaway (2018), "Startup Communities Revisited," *Ian Hathaway Blog*, August 30, http://www.ianhathaway.org/blog/2018/8/30/startup-communities-revisited.

15. See Hathaway (2018), "America's Rising Startup Cities," *Center for American Entrepreneurship*; Florida and Hathaway (2018), "Rise of the Global Startup City: The New Map of Entrepreneurship and Venture Capital," *Center for American Entrepreneurship*.

16. Hathaway (2018), "America's Rising Startup Communities," *Center for American Entrepreneurship*; Hathaway (2018), "High-Growth Firms and Cities in the US: An Analysis of the Inc. 5000," *Brookings Institution*; and Hathaway (2016), "Accelerating Growth: Startup Accelerator Programs in the United States," *Brookings Institution*.

17. Florida and Hathaway (2018), "Rise of the Global Startup City: The New Map of Entrepreneurship and Venture Capital," *Center for American Entrepreneurship*.

18. Taylor (1911), *The Principles of Scientific Management*, Harper & Brothers; Burrows, Gilbert, and Pollert (1992), *Fordism and Flexibility: Divisions and Change*, St. Martin's Press.

19. For a great primer on complexity theory and complex adaptive systems, read: Melanie Mitchell (2009), *Complexity: A Guided Tour*, Oxford University Press.

20. Ries (2011), *The Lean Startup: How Constant Innovation Creates Radically Successful Businesses*, Portfolio Penguin.

CHAPTER 2

1. Center for American Entrepreneurship, "What Is Entrepreneurship?" available at: http://www.startupsusa.org/what-is-entrepreneurship/.

2. Blank (2010), "What's a Startup? First Principles," *Steve Blank*, January 25, available at https://steveblank.com/2010/01/25/whats-a-startup-first-principles/.

3. In fact, about three-quarters of nascent entrepreneurs in the United States set out with no intention to grow. Instead, they focus on non-pecuniary reasons to start a business, such as flexibility and the desire to be one's boss. See, Hurst and Pugsley (2011), "What Do Small Businesses Do?" *Brookings Papers on Economic Activity*.

4. Wise and Feld (2017), *Startup Opportunities: Know When to Quit Your Day Job* (second edition), Wiley.

5. Romer (1986), "Increasing Returns and Long Run Growth," *Journal of Political Economy*, 94, 1002–37; Lucas (1988), "On the Mechanics of Economic Development," *Journal of Monetary Economics*, 22, 3–42; Romer (1990), "Endogenous Technological Change," *Journal of Monetary Economics*, 98, S71–S102.

6. Audretsch, Keilbach and Lehmann (2006), *Entrepreneurship and Economic Growth*, Oxford University Press; Acs, Braunerhjelm, Audretsch and Carlsson (2009), "The Knowledge Spillover Theory of Entrepreneurship," *Small Business Economics*, 32(1), 15–30; and Audretsch and Keilbach (2007), "The Theory of Knowledge Spillover Entrepreneurship," *Journal of Management Studies*, 44 (7), 1242–1254.

7. For a summary of evidence, see Audretsch (2012), "Determinants of High-Growth Entrepreneurship," *Organisation for Economic Cooperation and Development*; Haltiwanger, Jarmin, Kulick, and Miranda (2016), "High Growth Young Firms: Contribution to Job, Output and Productivity Growth," *U.S. Census Bureau, Center for Economic Studies*.

8. See, Hathaway (2018), "High-Growth Firms and Cities in the US: An Analysis of the Inc. 5000," *Brookings Institution*; Motoyama (2015), "The State-Level Geographic Analysis of High-Growth Companies," *Journal of Small Business & Entrepreneurship*, 27(2), 213 227; Li, Goetza, Partridge, and Fleming (2015), "Location Determinants of High-Growth Firms," *Entrepreneurship & Regional Development*; and Haltiwanger, Jarmin, Kulick, and Miranda (2017), "High Growth Young Firms: Contribution to Job, Output, and Productivity Growth," *Measuring Entrepreneurial Businesses: Current Knowledge and Challenges*, NBER.

9. Teece, Pisano, and Shuen (1997), "Dynamic Capabilities and Strategic Management," *Strategic Management Journal*, 18(7), 509–533.

10. Teece (1992), "Organizational Arrangements for Regimes of Rapid Technological Progress," *Journal of Economic Behavior and Organization*, 18, 1–25.

11. The seminal work on this subject is Pfeffer and Salancik (1978), *The External Control of Organizations: A Resource Dependence Perspective*, Harper & Row. For a summary, see Hillman, Withers, and Collins (2009), "Resource Dependence Theory: A Review," *Journal of Management*, 35(6) 1404–1427.

12. See, for example, McChrystal, Silverman, Collins, and Fussel (2015), *Team of Teams: New Rules of Engagement for a Complex World*, Portfolio Penguin; Hathaway (2018), "The New York Yankees and Startup Communities," *Ian Hathaway blog*.

13. Hwang and Horowitt (2012), *The Rainforest: The Secret to Building the Next Silicon Valley*, Regenwald.
14. Fukuyama (1997), *Social Capital*, The Tanner Lectures on Human Values, Oxford University.
15. Baker (1990), "Market Networks and Corporate Behavior," *American Journal of Sociology*, 96, pp. 589–625; Jacobs (1965), *The Death and Life of Great American Cities*, Penguin Books; Putnam (1993), "The Prosperous Community: Social Capital and Public Life," *American Prospect*, 13, pp. 35–42; Putnam (1995), "Bowling Alone: America's Declining Social Capital," *Journal of Democracy*, 6: 65–78; and Fukuyama (1995), *Trust: Social Virtues and the Creation of Prosperity*, Hamish Hamilton.
16. Hwang and Horowitt (2012), *The Rainforest: The Secret to Building the Next Silicon Valley*, Regenwald.
17. For a discussion of agglomeration economies, see Brueckner (2011), *Lectures in Urban Economics*, The MIT Press, and O'Sullivan (2011), *Urban Economics*, McGraw-Hill Education.
18. For more on this, see Carlino and Kerr (2014), "Agglomeration and Innovation," *National Bureau of Economic Research*.
19. Feld (2010), "Entrepreneurial Density," *Feld Thoughts blog*, August 23; Feld (2011), "Entrepreneurial Density Revisited," *Feld Thoughts blog*, October 11.
20. Cometto and Piol (2013), *Tech and the City: The Making of New York's Startup Community*, Mirandola Press.
21. Rosenthal and Strange (2013), "Geography, Industrial Organization, and Agglomeration," *Review of Economics and Statistics*, 85:2, pp. 377–393.
22. Arzaghi and Henderson (2008), "Networking off Madison Avenue," *Review of Economic Studies*, 75, pp. 1011–1038.
23. Feldman (2014), "The Character of Innovative Places: Entrepreneurial Strategy, Economic Development, and Prosperity," *Small Business Economics*, 43, pp. 9–20.
24. Catmull and Wallace (2014), *Creativity, Inc.: Overcoming the Unseen Forces That Stand in the Way of True Inspiration*, Bantam Press; McChrystal, Silverman, Collins, and Fussel (2015), *Team of Teams: New Rules of Engagement for a Complex World*, Portfolio Penguin.
25. Endeavor Insight (2014), *What Do the Best Entrepreneurs Want in a City? Lessons from the Founders of America's Fastest-Growing Companies*; Florida (2002), *The Rise of the Creative Class: And How It's Transforming Work, Leisure, Community and Everyday Life*, Basic Books.

26. Hathaway (2017), "The Amazon Bounce Back," *Ian Hathaway blog*, October 22; Feld (2018), "What Denver Should Do When Amazon Doesn't Choose It For HQ2," *Feld Thoughts blog*, February 1.
27. Chatterji, Glaeser, and Kerr (2013), "Clusters of Entrepreneurship and Innovation," *National Bureau of Economic Research*.
28. Hathaway (2018), "High-Growth Firms and Cities in the US: An Analysis of the Inc. 5000," *Brookings Institution*.
29. Lee, Florida, and Acs (2004), "Creativity and Entrepreneurship: A Regional Analysis of New Firm Formation," 38(8), 879–891; Boschma and Fritsch (2009), "Creative Class and Regional Growth in Europe: Empirical Evidence from Seven European Countries," 85(4), 391–423; Florida, Mellander, and Stolarick (2008), "Inside the Black Box of Regional Development," *Journal of Economic Geography* 8(5), 615–649.
30. Endeavor Insight (2014), *What Do the Best Entrepreneurs Want In A City? Lessons from the Founders of America's Fastest-Growing Companies*.
31. For evidence, see Figueiredo, Guimaraes, and Woodward (2007), "Home-Field Advantage: Location Decisions of Portuguese Entrepreneurs," *Journal of Urban Economics* 52:2 (2002), 341–361; and Michelacci and Silva (2007), "Why So Many Local Entrepreneurs?", *Review of Economics and Statistics* 89:4 (2007), 615–633.
32. Baird (2017), *The Innovation Blind Spot: Why We Back the Wrong Ideas—and What to Do About It*, BenBella Books.
33 Hickenlooper's final State of the State speech is available from *The Denver Post* at: https://www.denverpost.com/2018/01/11/john-hickenlooper-colorado-state-of-state-text/.

CHAPTER 3

1. See, Renando (2019), "Roles and Functions in Innovation Ecosystems," *LinkedIn*; Renando (2019), "Network Analysis of an Entrepreneur Ecosystem—Ph.D. in progress," *LinkedIn*.
2. We credit Chris Heivly and Matt Helt with originating the term *instigator*.
3. Morris and Török (2018), "Fostering Productive Entrepreneurship Communities: Key Lessons on Generating Jobs, Economic Growth, and Innovation," *Endeavor*; Goodwin (2014), "The Power of Entrepreneur Networks: How New York City Became the Role Model for Other Urban Tech Hubs," *Endeavor*.

4. Motoyama, Konczal, Bell-Masterson, and Morelix (2014), "Think Locally, Act Locally: Building a Robust Entrepreneurial Ecosystem," *Kauffman Foundation.*

5. I am currently working on a book titled *#GiveFirst: A New Philosophy for Business in The Era of Entrepreneurship.*

6. Feld (2012), *Startup Communities: Building an Entrepreneurial Ecosystem in Your City,* John Wiley & Sons, pp. 147–148.

7. Bernthal (2017), "Who Needs Contracts? Generalized Exchange Within Investment Accelerators," *Marquette Law Review,* 100: 997.

8. One of the iconic coaches of the Silicon Valley era is Bill Campbell, who is extensively described in the 2019 book, *Trillion Dollar Coach: The Leadership Handbook of Silicon Valley's Bill Campbell,* written by Eric Schmidt, Jonathan Rosenberg, and Alan Eagle. https://www.trilliondollarcoach.com/.

9. Reboot (https://www.reboot.io/) was founded by Jerry Colonna, a longtime friend of mine who was a successful venture capitalist at Flatiron Partners (with Fred Wilson) in the 1990s. Also see Jerry's excellent book, *Reboot: Leadership and the Art of Growing Up,* Harper Business (2019).

10. Calacanis (2017), *Angel: How to Invest in Technology Startups: Timeless Advice from an Angel Investor Who Turned $100,000 into $100,000,000,* Harper Business.

11. Hathaway (2017), "The Amazon Bounce Back," *Ian Hathaway blog,* October 22; Feld (2018), "What Denver Should Do When Amazon Doesn't Choose It For HQ2," *Feld Thoughts blog.*

12. Lach (2019), "Wisconsin's Foxconn Debacle Keeps Getting Worse," *The New Yorker,* January 30, available at: https://www.newyorker.com/news/current/wisconsins-foxconn-debacle-keeps-getting-worse.

13. Kanter (2018), "Apple Threw Shade on Amazon with New Campus in Austin, Texas," *Business Insider,* December 16, available at: https://www.businessinsider.com/apple-threw-shade-on-amazon-with-new-campus-in-austin-texas-2018-12?r=US&IR=T.

14. Auerswald (2015), "Enabling Entrepreneurial Ecosystems: Insights from Ecology to Inform Effective Entrepreneurship Policy," *Kauffman Foundation.*

15. Lerner (2012), *Boulevard of Broken Dreams: Why Public Efforts to Boost Entrepreneurship and Venture Capital Have Failed—and What to Do about It,* The Kauffman Foundation Series on Innovation and Entrepreneurship.

CHAPTER 4

1. Kim and Kleinbaum (2016), "Teams and Networks," *State of the Field*; Ruef (2010), *The Entrepreneurial Group: Social Identities, Relations, and Collective Action*, Princeton University Press.
2. Stangler and Bell-Masterson (2015), "Measuring an Entrepreneurial Ecosystem," *Kauffman Foundation*
3. Motoyama (2014), "Do's and Don'ts of Supporting Entrepreneurship," *Kauffman Foundation*.

CHAPTER 5

1. Pennings (1982), "The Urban Quality of Life and Entrepreneurship," *Academy of Management Journal*, 25, 63–79.
2. See, for example, Dubini (1989), "The Influence of Motivations and Environment on Business Start-Ups: Some Hints for Public Policies," *Journal of Business Venturing*, 4, 11–26; Van de Ven (1993), "The Development of an Infrastructure for Entrepreneurship," *Journal of Business Venturing*, 8, 211–230.
3. See, Aldrich (1990), "Using an Ecological Perspective to Study Organizational Founding Rates," *Entrepreneurship: Theory and Practice*; Moore (1993), "Predators and Prey: A New Ecology of Competition," *Harvard Business Review*, May–June, 75–86.
4. See, for example, Spilling (1996), "The Entrepreneurial System: On Entrepreneurship in the Context of a Mega-Event," *Journal of Business Research*, 36(1), 91–103; Neck et al. (2004), "An Entrepreneurial System View of New Venture Creation," *Journal of Small Business Management*, 42(2), 190–208; Isenberg (2010), "The Big Idea: How to Start an Entrepreneurial Revolution," *Harvard Business Review*, June; Isenberg (2011), "The Entrepreneurship Ecosystem Strategy as a New Paradigm for Economic Policy: Principles for Cultivating Entrepreneurship," *The Babson Entrepreneurship Ecosystem Project*.
5. These definitions were derived by a combination of Google search (https://www.google.com/search?q=define%3A+community/0), Merriam-Webster Dictionary online (https://www.merriam-webster.com/dictionary/community), and our adaptations.

6. For previous writing on a founders-first approach, see: Hathaway (2017), "#FoundersFirst," *Startup Revolution Blog*, available at: https://www.startuprev.com/foundersfirst/; Birkby (2017), "What it means to put founders first," *Startup Stories Blog*, available at: https://medium.com/startup-foundation-stories/what-it-means-to-put-founders-first-fa6f19921f61.

7. Meadows (2008), *Thinking in Systems: A Primer*, Chelsea Green Publishing.

8. Hathaway (2017), "#FoundersFirst," *Startup Revolution*, available at: https://www.startuprev.com/foundersfirst/.

9. Meadows (2008), *Thinking in Systems: A Primer*, Chelsea Green Publishing.

10. Griffin (2107), "12 Things about Product-Market Fit," *a16z blog*, February 18, available at: https://a16z.com/2017/02/18/12-things-about-product-market-fit/.

11. Florida and Hathaway (2018), "Rise of the Global Startup City: The New Map of Entrepreneurship and Venture Capital," *Center for American Entrepreneurship*.

CHAPTER 6

1. There are many resources on systems, but for an accessible introductory guide, see Carter and Gómez (2019), *Introduction to Systems Thinking*, Carnegie Mellon University.

2. Christaskis (2009), *Connected: The Surprising Power of Our Social Networks and How They Shape Our Lives: How Your Friends' Friends' Friends Affect Everything You Feel, Think, and Do*, Little, Brown Spark.

3. See Motoyama and Watkins (2017), "Examining the Connections within the Entrepreneurial ecosystem: A Case Study of St. Louis," *Entrepreneurship Research Journal* 7(1): 1–32.

4. Nason (2017), *It's Not Complicated: The Art and Science of Complexity in Business*, Rotman-UTP Publishing.

5 Nason (2017), *It's Not Complicated: The Art and Science of Complexity in Business*, Rotman-UTP Publishing.

6. See, for example, Kahneman (2012), *Thinking, Fast and Slow*, Penguin.

7. Horowitz (2019), *What You Do Is Who You Are: How to Create Your Business Culture*, Harper Business.

CHAPTER 7

1. This chapter stands on the shoulders of many pioneers in the complexity science field, and their work has influenced our work in immeasurable ways. That includes Waldrop (1992), *Complexity: The Emerging Science at the Edge of Order and Chaos*, Simon & Schuster; Miller and Page (2007), *Complex Adaptive Systems: An Introduction to Computational Models of Social Life*, Princeton University Press; Mitchell (2009), *Complexity: A Guided Tour*, Oxford University Press; Page (2010), *Diversity and Complexity*, Princeton University Press; Holland (2012), *Signals and Boundaries: Building Blocks for Complex Adaptive Systems*, MIT Press; Holland (2014), *Complexity: A Very Short Introduction*, Oxford University Press; Colander and Kupers (2014), *Complexity and the Art of Public Policy: Solving Society's Problems from the Bottom Up*, Princeton University Press; West (2017), *Scale: The Universal Laws of Growth, Innovation, Sustainability, and the Pace of Life in Organisms, Cities, Economies, and Companies*, Penguin Press.

2. Weaver (1948), "Science and Complexity," *American Scientist*, 36: 536.

3. Santa Fe Institute (n.d.), "History," Santa Fe Institute website, available at https://www.santafe.edu/about/history.

4. Meadows (2008), *Thinking in Systems: A Primer*, Chelsea Green Publishing.

5. Ibid.

6. https://www.vocabulary.com/dictionary/emerge.

7. Miller and Page (2007), *Complex Adaptive Systems: An Introduction to Computational Models of Social Life*, Princeton University Press.

8. Johnson (2001), *Emergence: The Connected Lives of Ants, Brains, Cities, and Software*, Scribner.

9. Complexity Labs (2017), *Complex Adaptive Systems*, Systems Innovation.

10. I got kicked out of the PhD program in 1990. I was a much better entrepreneur than I was a PhD student.

11. Von Hippel (1978), "A Customer-Active Paradigm for Industrial Product Idea Generation," *Research Policy*, 1978, vol. 7, issue 3, 240–266.

12. For more on Lean startup, see Blank (2005), *The Four Steps to the Epiphany: Successful Strategies for Products That Win*, K & S Ranch; and Ries (2011), *The Lean Startup: How Constant Innovation Creates Radically Successful Businesses*, Portfolio Penguin.

13. Seward (2013), "The First-Ever Hashtag, @-reply, and Retweet, as Twitter Users Invented Them," *Quartz*, October 13, available at: https://qz.com/135149/the-first-ever-hashtag-reply-and-retweet-as-twitter-users-invented-them/.
14. For more on this, see https://systemsinnovation.io/.
15. For more on power laws, see Clauset, Shalizi, and Newman (2009), "Power-Law Distributions in Empirical Data," *Society for Industrial and Applied Mathematics Review* 51(4): 661–703.
16. Bonabeau, Dorigo, and Theraulaz (1999), *Swarm Intelligence: From Natural to Artificial Systems*, Oxford University Press.
17. Jolly (2015), *Systems Thinking for Business: Capitalize on Structures Hidden in Plain Sight*, Systems Solutions Press.
18. Ibid.
19. Jolly (2015), *Systems Thinking for Business: Capitalize on Structures Hidden in Plain Sight*, Systems Solutions Press.
20. Ibid.
21. Forrester (1989), "The Beginning of System Dynamics," *Sloan School of Management, MIT*, Banquet Talk at the international meeting of the System Dynamics Society, Stuttgart, Germany, July 13, available at: https://web.mit.edu/sysdyn/sd-intro/D-4165-1.pdf.
22. Jolly (2015), *Systems Thinking for Business: Capitalize on Structures Hidden in Plain Sight*, Systems Solutions Press.
23. Emery and Clayton (2004), "The Mentality of Crows: Convergent Evolution of Intelligence in Corvids and Apes," *Science*, 306(5703): 1903–7.
24. See, for example, Kahneman (2012), *Thinking, Fast and Slow*, Penguin.
25. Winslow (1996), *The Making of Silicon Valley: A One Hundred Year Renaissance*, Santa Clara Valley Historical Association.
26. Feld (2018), "Binary Star Startup Communities," *Brad Feld Blog*, July 18, available at: https://feld.com/archives/2018/07/binary-star-startup-communities.html.
27 Jolly (2015), *Systems Thinking for Business: Capitalize on Structures Hidden in Plain Sight*, Systems Solutions Press.
28. Ibid.
29. Lerner (2012), *Boulevard of Broken Dreams: Why Public Efforts to Boost Entrepreneurship and Venture Capital Have Failed—and What to Do about It*, The Kauffman Foundation Series on Innovation and Entrepreneurship.

CHAPTER 8

1. Azoulay, Jones, Kim, and Miranda (2018), "Age and High-Growth Entrepreneurship," *NBER Working Paper*.
2. Motoyama (2014), "The State-Level Geographic Analysis of High-Growth Companies," *Journal of Small Business & Entrepreneurship* 27: 2; Hathaway (2018), "High-Growth Firms and Cities in the US: An Analysis of the Inc. 5000," *Brookings Institution*; Qian and Yao (2017), "The Role of Research Universities in U.S. College-Town Entrepreneurial Ecosystems," *SSRN Working Paper*; Hathaway (2016), "Accelerating Growth: Startup Accelerator Programs in the United States," *Brookings Institution*; Motoyama and Bell-Masterson (2014), "Beyond Metropolitan Startup Rates: Regional Factors Associated with Startup Growth," *Kauffman Foundation*.
3. Feldman and Zoller (2012), "Dealmakers in Place: Social Capital Connections in Regional Entrepreneurial Economies," *Regional Studies* 46.1: 23–37.
4. Chatterji, Glaeser, Kerr (2013), "Clusters of Entrepreneurship and Innovation," *NBER Working Paper*.
5. Saxenian (1994), *Regional Advantage: Culture and Competition in Silicon Valley and Route 128*, Harvard University Press; O'Mara (2019), *The Code: Silicon Valley and the Remaking of America*, Penguin Press.
6. Hwang and Horowitt (2012), *The Rainforest: The Secret to Building the Next Silicon Valley*, Regenwald.
7. Schroeder (2013), *Startup Rising: The Entrepreneurial Revolution Remaking the Middle East*, St. Martin's Press.
8. Schroeder (2017), "A Different Story from the Middle East: Entrepreneurs Building an Arab Tech Economy," *MIT Technology Review*, August 3. https://www.technologyreview.com/s/608468/a-different-story-from-the-middle-east-entrepreneurs-building-an-arab-tech-economy/.
9. For a review of this literature, see relevant sections and findings of the following papers: Shaw and Sorensen (2017), "The Productivity Advantage of Serial Entrepreneurs," *National Bureau of Economic Research*. See also Eesley and Roberts (2012), "Are You Experienced or Are You Talented?: When Does Innate Talent versus Experience Explain Entrepreneurial Performance?" *Strategic Entrepreneurship Journal*, 6(3): 207–219; and Parker (2013), "Do Serial Entrepreneurs Run Successively Better-Performing Businesses?" *Journal of Business Venturing*, 28(5): 652–666. See also relevant literature on the positive relationship between founder age and the probability of achieving high

growth: Azoulay, Jones, Kim, and Miranda (2018), "Age and High-Growth Entrepreneurship," *National Bureau of Economic Research.*

10. Feldman and Zoller (2012), "Dealmakers in Place: Social Capital Connections in Regional Entrepreneurial Economies," *Regional Studies*, Vol 46.1: 23–37.

11. Kemeny, Feldman, Ethridge, and Zoller (2016), "The Economic Value of Local Social Networks," *Journal of Economic Geography*, 16, 1101–1122.

12. Feldman and Zoller (2012), "Dealmakers in Place: Social Capital Connections in Regional Entrepreneurial Economies," *Regional Studies* 46.1: 23–37; Kemeny, Feldman, Ethridge, and Zoller (2016), "The Economic Value of Local Social Networks," *Journal of Economic Geography* 16(5), 1101–1122.

13. See, Mulas, Minges, and Applebaum (2016), "Boosting Tech Innovation Ecosystems in Cities: A Framework for Growth and Sustainability of Urban Tech Innovation Ecosystems," *Innovations.*

14. Morris and Török (2018), "Fostering Productive Entrepreneurship Communities: Key Lessons on Generating Jobs, Economic Growth, and Innovation," *Endeavor*; Goodwin (2014), "The Power of Entrepreneur Networks: How New York City Became the Role Model for Other Urban Tech Hubs," *Endeavor.*

15. Mulas and Gastelu-Iturri (2016), "New York City: Transforming a City into a Tech Innovation Leader," *World Bank*; Mulas, Qian, and Henry (2017), "Tech Start-up Ecosystem in Dar es Salaam: Findings and Recommendations," *World Bank*; Mulas, Qian, and Henry (2017), "Tech Start-up Ecosystem in Beirut: Findings and Recommendations," *World Bank*; Mulas, Qian, Garza, and Henry (2018), "Tech Startup Ecosystem in West Bank and Gaza: Findings and Recommendations," *World Bank.*

CHAPTER 9

1. Taylor (1911), *The Principles of Scientific Management*, Harper & Brothers; Burrows, Gilbert, and Pollert (1992), *Fordism and Flexibility: Divisions and Change*, St. Martin's Press.

2. See, Wolfe (1987), *Bonfire of the Vanities*, Farrar, Straus, and Giroux; and Nason (2017), *It's Not Complicated: The Art and Science of Complexity in Business*, Rotman-UTP Publishing.

3. Colander and Kupers (2014), *Complexity and the Art of Public Policy: Solving Society's Problems from the Bottom Up*, Princeton University Press.

4. Page (2017), *The Diversity Bonus: How Great Teams Pay Off in the Knowledge Economy*, Princeton University Press.

5. Hathaway (2019), "The J-Curve of Startup Community Transition," *Ian Hathaway blog*, January 15, available at: http://www.ianhathaway.org/blog/2019/1/15/the-j-curve-of-startup-community-transition. It was inspired by: Bremmer (2006), *The J Curve: A New Way to Understand Why Nations Rise and Fall*, Simon & Schuster.

6. Taleb (2012), *Antifragile: Things That Gain from Disorder*, Random House.

7. Ibid.

8. Nason (2017), *It's Not Complicated: The Art and Science of Complexity in Business*, Rotman-UTP Publishing.

CHAPTER 10

1. See, Motoyama and Bell-Masterson (2013), "Beyond Metropolitan Startup Rates: Regional Factors Associated with Startup Growth," *Kauffman Foundation*; Chatterji, Glaeser, and Kerr (2013), "Clusters of Entrepreneurship and Innovation," *National Bureau of Economic Research*; Qian and Yao (2017), "The Role of Research Universities in U.S. College-Town Entrepreneurial Ecosystems," *working paper*; Motoyama and Mayer (2017), "Revisiting the Roles of University in Regional Economic Development," *Growth and Change*, 48(4): 787–804.

2. See, for example, Motoyama and Watkins (2017), "Examining the Connections within the Entrepreneurial ecosystem: A Case Study of St. Louis," *Entrepreneurship Research Journal*, 7(1): 1–32; Motoyama, Fetsch, Jackson, and Wiens (2016), "Little Town, Layered Ecosystem: A Case Study of Chattanooga," *Kauffman Foundation*; Motoyama, Henderson, Gladen, Fetsch, and Davis (2017), "A New Frontier: Entrepreneurship Ecosystems in Bozeman and Missoula, Montana."

3. Lorenz (1972), "Does the Flap of a Butterfly's Wings in Brazil Set Off a Tornado in Texas?", presented before the American Association for the Advancement of Science, December 29; Lorenz (1993), *The Essence of Chaos*, University of Washington Press.

4. Thomas C Schelling (1969), "Models of Segregation," *American Economic Review*, 59(2): 488–493.

5. Colander and Kupers (2014), *Complexity and the Art of Public Policy: Solving Society's Problems from the Bottom Up*, Princeton University Press.

6. McLaughlin, Weimers, and Winslow (2008), *Silicon Valley: 110 Year Renaissance*. Santa Clara Valley Historical Association.

7. Vogelstein (2003), "Mighty Amazon Jeff Bezos has been hailed as a visionary and put down as a goofball. He's proved critics wrong by forging a winning management strategy built on brains, guts, and above all, numbers," *Fortune* magazine, May 26.

8. Hathaway (2018), "Startup Communities Revisited," *Ian Hathaway Blog*, August 30.

9. Kahneman (2011), *Thinking, Fast and Slow*, Farrar, Straus, and Giroux

10. Ariely, (2009), *Predictably Irrational: The Hidden Forces That Shape Our Decisions*, Harper.

11. Hume (1739), *A Treatise of Human Nature*.

12. Jolly (2015), *Systems Thinking for Business: Capitalize on Structures Hidden in Plain Sight*, Systems Solutions Press.

13. Nassim Nicholas Taleb (2007), *The Black Swan: The Impact of the Highly Improbable*, Random House.

14. See Janeway (2018), *Doing Capitalism in the Innovation Economy: Reconfiguring the Three-Player Game between Markets, Speculators and the State*, Cambridge University Press.

15. Hickenlooper (2018), State of the State speech, January 11, available at: https://www.denverpost.com/2018/01/11/john-hickenlooper-colorado-state-of-state-text/.

16 Feldman, Francis, and Bercovitz (2005), "Creating a Cluster While Building a Firm: Entrepreneurs and the Formation of Industrial Clusters," *Regional Studies* 39(1).

17. Feldman (2001), "The Entrepreneurial Event Revisited: Firm Formation in a Regional Context," *Industrial and Corporate Change* 10(4): 861–891.

CHAPTER 11

1. See Zak (2013), "Measurement Myopia," Drucker Institute website, July 4, available at: https://www.drucker.institute/thedx/measurement-myopia/. Credit to Danny Buerkli of BCG's Centre for Public Impact for inspiring the framing of this section: Buerkli (2019), "'What Gets Measured Gets Managed—It's Wrong and Drucker Never Said It," Medium, April 8, available at: https://medium.com/centre-for-public-impact/what-gets-measured-gets-managed-its-wrong-and-drucker-never-said-it-fe95886d3df6.

2. Zak (2013).
3. Caulkin (2008), "The Rule is Simple: Be Careful What You Measure," *The Guardian*, February 10, available at: https://www.theguardian.com/business/2008/feb/10/businesscomment1.
4. Principally among these is Isenberg (2011), "The Entrepreneurship Ecosystem Strategy as a New Paradigm for Economic Policy: Principles for Cultivating Entrepreneurship," *The Babson Entrepreneurship Ecosystem Project*. See also: Aspen Network of Development Entrepreneurs (ANDE) (2013), "Entrepreneurial Ecosystem Diagnostic Toolkit," *The Aspen Institute*; Global Entrepreneurship Network and Global Entrepreneurship Development Institute (2019), *Global Entrepreneurship Index*; Organisation for Economic Co-operation and Development (2008), *OECD Entrepreneurship Measurement Framework*; World Economic Forum, *Entrepreneurship Ecosystem*; and Stangler and Bell-Masterson (2015), "Measuring an Entrepreneurial Ecosystem," Kauffman Foundation.
5. Renando (2017, 2018, 2019), LinkedIn, available at: https://www.linkedin.com/in/chadrenando/detail/recent-activity/posts/.
6. Startup Status (n.d.), www.startupstatus.co.
7. Global Entrepreneurship Network and Global Entrepreneurship Development Institute (2019), Global Entrepreneurship Index; and Startup Genome (2019), *Global Startup Ecosystem Report*. In addition to these, see Aspen Network of Development Entrepreneurs (ANDE) (2013), "Entrepreneurial Ecosystem Diagnostic Toolkit," *The Aspen Institute*; World Economic Forum (2013), *Entrepreneurship Ecosystem*; Organisation for Economic Co-operation and Development (2008), *OECD Entrepreneurship Measurement Framework*; and Szerb, Acs, Komlosi, and Ortega-Argilés (2015), "Measuring Entrepreneurial Ecosystems: The Regional Entrepreneurship and Development Index (REDI)," *Henley Centre for Entrepreneurship, University of Reading*.
8. Other models aimed at modern, tech- and venture-backable startups include StartupBlink (https://www.startupblink.com/) and Startup Meter (http://startup-meter.org).
9. Feldman and Zoller (2012), "Dealmakers in Place: Social Capital Connections in Regional Entrepreneurial Economies," *Regional Studies*, Vol 46.1, pp 23-37; Kemeny, Feldman, Ethridge, and Zoller (2016), "The Economic Value of Local Social Networks Role: ProductionEditor," *Journal of Economic Geography*, 16(5), 1101–1122.
10. Morris and Török (2018), "Fostering Productive Entrepreneurship Communities: Key Lessons on Generating Jobs, Economic Growth, and Innovation," *Endeavor*; Goodwin (2014), "The Power of Entrepreneur Networks:

How New York City Became the Role Model for Other Urban Tech Hubs," *Endeavor*; Mulas and Gastelu-Iturri (2016), "New York City: Transforming a City into a Tech Innovation Leader," *World Bank*; Mulas, Qian, and Henry (2017), "Tech Start-up Ecosystem in Dar es Salaam: Findings and Recommendations," *World Bank*; Mulas, Qian, and Henry (2017), "Tech Start-up Ecosystem in Beirut: Findings and Recommendations," *World Bank*; Mulas, Qian, Garza, and Henry (2018), "Tech Startup Ecosystem in West Bank and Gaza: Findings and Recommendations," *World Bank*.

11. Endeavor Insight (2013), *The New York City Tech Map*, http://nyctechmap.com/.
12. Mack and Mayer (2016), "The Evolutionary Dynamics of Entrepreneurial Ecosystems," *Urban Studies*, 53(10): 2118–2133.
13. See, for example, Braunerhjelm and Feldman (eds.) (2006), *Cluster Genesis: Technology-Based Industrial Development*, Oxford University Press.
14. See also Mack and Mayer (2016), "The Evolutionary Dynamics of Entrepreneurial Ecosystems," *Urban Studies*, 53(10): 2118–2133; and Brown and Mason (2017), "Looking Inside the Spiky Bits: A Critical Review and Conceptualization of Entrepreneurial Ecosystems," *Small Business Economics*.
15. Lamoreaux, Levenstein, and Sokoloff, (2004). "Financing Invention During the Second Industrial Revolution: Cleveland, Ohio, 1870–1920," *National Bureau of Economic Research*.
16. Saxenian (1996), *Regional Advantage: Culture and Competition in Silicon Valley and Route 128*, Harvard University Press.
17. Pool and Van Itallie (2013), "Learning from Boston: Implications for Baltimore from Comparing the Entrepreneurial Ecosystems of Baltimore and Boston," Canterbury Road Partners; Stam (2015), "Entrepreneurial Ecosystems and Regional Policy: A Sympathetic Critique," *European Planning Studies*, 23(9); Spigel (2017), "The Relational Organization of Entrepreneurial Ecosystems," *Entrepreneurship Theory and Practice*, 41(1): 49–72; Stam and Spigel (2017), "Entrepreneurial Ecosystems," in Blackburn, et al. (Eds.), *The Sage Handbook of Small Business and Entrepreneurship*, forthcoming.
18. See for example, Carayannis, Provance, Grigoroudis (2016), "Entrepreneurship Ecosystems: An Agent-Based Simulation Approach," *The Journal of Technology Transfer* 41(3): 631–653.
19. Anderson (2010), "The Community Builder's Approach to Theory of Change: A Practical Guide to Theory Development," *The Aspen Institute Roundtable on Community Change*; Innovation Network, Inc. (2010), *Logic Model Workbook*.

20. Wilensky and Rand (2015), *An Introduction to Agent-Based Modeling: Modeling Natural, Social, and Engineered Complex Systems with NetLogo*, The MIT Press.
21. For more, see Santa Fe Institute, Introduction to Agent-Based Modeling, available at: https://www.complexityexplorer.org/courses/101-introduction-to-agent-based-modeling.
22. Schelling (1969), "Models of Segregation," *American Economic Review*, 59(2):488–493.
23. McKelvey (2004), "Toward a Complexity Science of Entrepreneurship," *Journal of Business Venturing*, 19(3): 313-341; Carayannis, Provance, and Grigoroudis (2016), "Entrepreneurship Ecosystems: An Agent-Based Simulation Approach," *The Journal of Technology Transfer*, 41: 631–653; Carayannis and Provance (2018), "Towards 'Skarse' Entrepreneurial Ecosystems: Using Agent-Based Simulation of Entrepreneurship to Reveal What Makes Regions Tick *Entrepreneurial Ecosystems and the Diffusion of Startups, Carayannis, Dagnino, Alvarez, and Faraci (eds.)*, Edward Elgar.
24. Roundy, Bradshaw, Brockman (2018), "The Emergence of Entrepreneurial Ecosystems: A Complex Adaptive Systems Approach," *Journal of Business Research*, 86: 1–10.

CHAPTER 12

1. Hwang and Horowitt (2012), *The Rainforest: The Secret to Building the Next Silicon Valley*, Regenwald.
2. Hathaway (2017), "Colorado and the Importance of Startup Density," *Startup Revolution*, available at: https://www.startuprev.com/colorado-and-the-importance-of-startup-density/.
3. Motoyama, Konczal, Bell-Masterson, and Morelix (2014), "Think Locally, Act Locally: Building a Robust Entrepreneurial Ecosystem," *Kauffman Foundation*.
4. Andreessen, Horowitz, and Cowen (2018), "Talent, Tech Trends, and Culture," *a16z* podcast, December 29, available at: https://a16z.com/2018/12/29/talent-tech-trends-culture-ben-marc-tyler-cowen-summit-2018/.
5. Stroh (2015), *Systems Thinking for Social Change: A Practical Guide to Solving Complex Problems, Avoiding Unintended Consequences, and Achieving Lasting Results*, Chelsea Green Publishing Co.
6. Stroh (2015), *Systems Thinking for Social Change: A Practical Guide to Solving Complex Problems, Avoiding Unintended Consequences, and Achieving Lasting Results*, Chelsea Green Publishing Co.

7. Meadows (2008), Stroh (2015).
8. da Costa (2013), "Exploring Pathways to Systems Change," *Sustainability Leaders Network*; and Meadows (1999), "Leverage Points: Places to Intervene in a System," *Sustainability Institute.*
9. Meadows (1999), "Leverage Points: Places to Intervene in a System," *Sustainability Institute.*
10. Meadows (1999).
11. Ibid.
12. Meadows (1999).
13. With guidance from da Costa (2013), "Exploring Pathways to Systems Change," *Sustainability Leaders Network,* which distills these 12 leverage points into four for environmental systems.
14. Putnam (2000), *Bowling Alone: The Collapse and Revival of American Community,* Simon & Schuster.
15. Meadows (1999).
16. Meadows (2008).
17. Stroh (2015).
18. Senge (1990), *The Fifth Discipline: The Art & Practice of The Learning Organization,* Random House.
19. Aulet and Murray (2013), "A Tale of Two Entrepreneurs: Understanding Differences in the Types of Entrepreneurship in the Economy," *Kauffman Foundation.*
20. Eesley and Roberts (2017), "Cutting Your Teeth: Learning from Entrepreneurial Experiences," *Academy of Management.*
21. Aulet (2017), "Entrepreneurship Is a Craft and Here's Why That's Important," *Sloan Management Review,* July 12, available at: https://sloanreview.mit.edu/article/entrepreneurship-is-a-craft-heres-why-thats-important/.
22. Wasserman (2013), *The Founder's Dilemmas: Anticipating and Avoiding the Pitfalls That Can Sink a Startup,* Princeton University Press.
23. Aulet (2015), "The Most Overrated Things in Entrepreneurship," *The Sloan Experts Blog,* December 17, available at: http://mitsloanexperts.mit.edu/the-most-overrated-thing-in-entrepreneurship/.
24. Aulet (2013), "Teaching Entrepreneurship Is in the Startup Phase: Students Are Clamoring for Instruction, but It's Hard. There Are No Algorithms for Success," *The Wall Street Journal,* September 11, https://www.wsj.com/articles/teaching-entrepreneurship-is-in-the-startup-phase-1378942182.

CHAPTER 13

1. Though the academic literature is nascent, robust studies include: Sanchez-Burks, Brophy, Jensen, and Milovac (2017), "Mentoring in Entrepreneurial Ecosystems: A Multi-Institution Empirical Analysis from the Perspectives of Mentees, Mentors and University and Accelerator Program Administrators," *Ross School of Business Paper*, No. 1376; and Hallen, Cohen, and Bingham (2016), "Do Accelerators Accelerate? If So, How? The Impact of Intensive Learning from Others on New Venture Development," *SSRN*. Program surveys include MicroMentor (2016) *Impact Report*.
2. Sanchez-Burks, Brophy, Jensen, and Milovac (2017).
3. Sanchez-Burks, Brophy, Jensen, and Milovac (2017).
4. Techstars (n.d.), "Mentoring at Techstars," available at: https://www.techstars .com/mentoringattechstars/.
5. Memon, Rozan, Ismail, Uddin, and Daud (2015), "Mentoring an Entrepreneur: Guide for a Mentor," *SAGE Open*, 5(1).
6. Bosma, Hessels, Schutjens, Van Praag, and Verheul (2012), "Entrepreneurship and Role Models", *Journal of Economic Psychology*, 33, pp. 410–424.
7. Easley and Wang (2014), "The Effects of Mentoring in Entrepreneurial Career Choice," *University of California, Berkeley working paper*; Easley and Wang (2017), "The Effects of Mentoring in Entrepreneurial Career Choice," *Research Policy*, 46(3): 636–650.
8. Dr. Seuss (1971), *The Lorax*, Random House. Ian thanks Jack Greco for bringing this idea to startup communities.
9. Feldman (2014), "The Character of Innovative Places: Entrepreneurial Strategy, Economic Development, and Prosperity," *Small Business Economics*, 43: 9–20; Feldman, Francis, and Bercovitz (2005), "Creating a Cluster While Building a Firm: Entrepreneurs and the Formation of Industrial Clusters," *Regional Studies*, 39(1): 129–141.
10. Stroh (2015), *Systems Thinking for Social Change: A Practical Guide to Solving Complex Problems, Avoiding Unintended Consequences, and Achieving Lasting Results*, Chelsea Green Publishing Co.

CHAPTER 14

1. The various generations of Americans are called Boomers, Gen X, Millennials, and Gen Z. Each ranges from 15 to 20 years, but it's much more nuanced

than that. See Kasasa (2019), "Boomers, Gen X, Gen Y, and Gen Z Explained," Kasasa.com, July 29, available at: https://www.kasasa.com/articles/generations/gen-x-gen-y-gen-z.

2. Colander and Kupers (2014), *Complexity and the Art of Public Policy: Solving Society's Problems from the Bottom Up*, Princeton University Press.

3. These three companies are Zayo (IPO, now in the process of going private), Rally Software (IPO, acquired by CA), and Datalogix (acquired by Oracle.) These three were the ones that created the tipping point, but other Boulder companies, such as SendGrid (IPO, acquired by Twilio), have had significant exits.

4. Winslow (1996), *The Making Of Silicon Valley: A One Hundred Year Renaissance*, Santa Clara Valley Historical Association.

5. Leslie and Kargon (1996), "Selling Silicon Valley: Frederick Terman's Model for Regional Advantage," *The Business History Review*, 70:04.

6. Weber (1905), *The Protestant Ethic and the Spirit of Capitalism*, Charles Scribner's Sons.

CHAPTER 15

1. Jacobs (1961), *The Death and Life of Great American Cities*, Random House; Jacobs (1984), *Cities and the Wealth of Nations*, Random House; Glaeser, Kallal, Scheinkman, and Shleifer (1992), "Growth in Cities," *Journal of Political Economy*, 100(6), 1126–1152; Quigley (1998), "Urban Diversity and Economic Growth," *Journal of Economic Perspectives*, 12(2): 127–138; and Page (2008), *The Difference: How the Power of Diversity Creates Better Groups, Firms, Schools, and Societies*, Princeton University Press.

2. Reynolds and Lewis (2017), "Teams Solve Problems Faster When They're More Cognitively Diverse," *Harvard Business Review*, March 30, available at: https://hbr.org/2017/03/teams-solve-problems-faster-when-theyre-more-cognitively-diverse.

3. Hong and Page (2004), "Groups of Diverse Problem Solvers can Outperform Groups of High-Ability Problem Solvers," *Proceedings of the National Academy of Sciences*; Page (2008), *The Difference: How the Power of Diversity Creates Better Groups, Firms, Schools, and Societies*, Princeton University Press; and Page (2017), *The Diversity Bonus: How Great Teams Pay Off in the Knowledge Economy*, Princeton University Press.

4. For an example from sports, see Hathaway (2018), "The New York Yankees and Startup Communities," *Ian Hathaway Blog*.
5. Feld (2017), "Go for Culture Add, Not Culture Fit," Feld Thoughts blog, June 12, available at: https://feld.com/archives/2017/06/go-culture-add-not-culture-fit.html.
6. Page (2017), *The Diversity Bonus: How Great Teams Pay Off in the Knowledge Economy*, Princeton University Press.
7. Hathaway (2018), "High-Growth Firms and Cities in the US: An Analysis of the Inc. 5000," *Brookings Institution*; Haltiwanger, Jarmin, Kulick, and Miranda (2017), "High Growth Young Firms: Contribution to Job, Output, and Productivity Growth," *National Bureau of Economic Research*; and Audretsch (2012), "Determinants of High-Growth Entrepreneurship," *Organisation for Economic Cooperation and Development*.
8. You can learn more about the Blackstone Entrepreneurs Network at https://www.bencolorado.org/.

CHAPTER 16

1. For more on scale properties in complex systems, see West (2017), *Scale: The Universal Laws of Growth, Innovation, Sustainability, and the Pace of Life in Organisms, Cities, Economies, and Companies*, Penguin Press.
2. Colander and Kupers (2014), *Complexity and the Art of Public Policy: Solving Society's Problems from the Bottom Up*, Princeton University Press.
3. We discuss this in more detail in our book *Startup Life: Surviving and Thriving in a Relationship with an Entrepreneur*, but the short version is that a few months before I turned 30, Amy said, "I am moving, and you are welcome to come with me if you want." We had been married for a while, so it was an easy decision for me.
4. Now called Entrepreneurs Organization (https://www.eonetwork.org/). I started the Boston chapter of YEO in early 1994 for a very similar reason, to get to know more entrepreneurs.
5. BizWest (1999), "Keiretsu: A Who's Who of Local Net Experts," May 9, available at: https://bizwest.com/1999/05/01/keiretsu-a-whos-who-of-local-net-experts/.
6. Feld (2000), "The Power of Peers," *Inc.*, July, available at: https://www.inc.com/articles/2000/07/19767.html.

7. For an introduction to game theory, see Binmore (2007), *Game Theory: A Very Short Introduction*, Oxford University Press. For works on evolutionary game theory, see Smith (1982), *Evolution and the Theory of Games*, Cambridge University Press.

8. For a summary of her work, see Ostrom (2000), "Collective Action and the Evolution of Social Norms," *Journal of Economic Perspectives*, 14(3), 137-158; and Ostrom (2009), "Beyond Markets and States: Polycentric Governance of Complex Economic Systems," *Nobel Prize Presentation*.

9. Hathaway (2018), "The Nobel Prize in Startup Communities," *Ian Hathaway blog*, March 12.

10. Feld (2012), *Startup Communities: Building an Entrepreneurial Ecosystem in Your City*, John Wiley & Sons: 49–50.

11. Feld (2016), "#GivingThanks: David Cohen and the Techstars Foundation," *Feld Thoughts blog*, November 25, available at: https://feld.com/archives/2016/11/givingthanks-david-cohen-techstars-foundation.html.

INDEX